The Upper Room
Disciplines
2001

The Upper Room
Disciplines
2001

UPPER
ROOM BOOKS®
NASHVILLE

The Upper Room Web site: http://www.upperroom.org

Cover photo: © Bill Terry / Picturesque 2000
Cover design: Jim Bateman
First Printing: 2000

ISBN: 0-8358-0878-5
Printed in the United States of America

Contents

CONTENTS

CONTENTS

Foreword

Welcome. Consider this the front door to a year of living with the word of God through daily scripture reading and reflection. *Disciplines 2001* is designed to help you live in the house of faith by praying with the Bible using the readings appointed in the Revised Common Lectionary, a table of readings for use in Christian worship. Each week you will be welcomed into another room in the house by a respected practitioner who will lead you in exploring the weekly readings.

During the last century a major shift took place in the way Christians understand and appreciate worship. The shift was from worship as a passive spectator endeavor to worship where all fully, actively, and consciously participate in proclaiming and responding to God's word. Using *Disciplines 2001* helps you more fully, actively, and consciously "present your bodies as a living sacrifice, holy and acceptable to God, which is your spiritual worship" (Rom. 12:1).

Disciplines enables your spiritual worship by encouraging the practice of the presence of God in daily life. When daily you read the scripture readings and prayerfully reflect upon them in light of your own life as a disciple, you live with the Word in ways that connect Christ and your opportunities for service to God and neighbor. Taking a word, phrase, or image from the selected reading into the day becomes a lens through which to see the love and power of God at work where you are; you become a sign of the risen Lord in those places. In you the Holy Spirit creates a meeting place for the Word and the world.

Daily reading of scripture and *Disciplines* prepares you to participate in corporate worship with body, mind, and spirit. The choir or musicians practice, and the pastor prepares for worship. By using *Disciplines*, you, as one of "Christ's royal priesthood," bring your week of reading, reflecting, and living the scriptures to the worship gathering. Along with the preacher, you have stories to tell and insights to bring to the proclamation of the Word.

You too bring fresh awareness and imaginative offerings to the shared feast of the good news.

The creation of a global community rooted in the word of God also enhances your spiritual worship. Nearly seventy percent of Presbyterian, United Methodist, United Church of Christ, United Church of Canada, Disciples of Christ, and other denominations, along with Anglican/Episcopal, Lutheran, and Roman Catholic congregations share in reading the same Bible lessons each week throughout the year. Think of the millions of Christians in North America, Europe, Africa, Latin America, Asia, and the Pacific who read and live in the Word using the same scripture readings. What is the cumulative impact of so many attending to God by reading and hearing common stories, images, poetry, and hope? Across borders, language barriers, and cultural differences, Christian disciples participate in common praise to the triune God and live the apostolic hope in daily life. It is a kind of Pentecost!

Imagine millions of Christians reflecting on the story of the Prodigal Son during the week leading up to worship on the Fourth Sunday in Lent. Imagine Canadians and South Africans and Filipinos struggling to find a balance between their inward journey and their outward journey in light of Jesus' dinner at the home of Mary and Martha (the week of July 16–22). Your daily use of *Disciplines* reminds you that you are not alone in the house of faith. You live in the company of others who together are the body of Christ offering full, active, and conscious worship to the God of our Lord, Jesus Christ.

—Daniel Benedict
Secretary, The Consultation on Common Texts*

*The Consultation on Common Texts (CCT) published *The Revised Common Lectionary* (Abingdon Press, 1992). Its predecessor was the Common Lectionary (1983) and a number of other church lectionaries including the Lectionary for the Mass (1970). CCT is made up of denominational leaders from the USA and Canada.

The Time of Your Life

January 1–7, 2001 • Larry R. Kalajainen*

MONDAY, JANUARY 1 • **Read Ecclesiastes 3:1-13**

Time. What an incredibly complex and ambivalent relationship we have with time! We were born "once upon a time." We grow up having "the time of our lives." We pass time, waste time, mark time, keep time, save time, lose time, gain time. We invent clocks and calendars to measure time. And when the end of someone's life comes, we say, "Well, I guess it was her time."

New Year's Day makes us especially aware of our relationship to time. We assign a very different meaning to December 31 than we do to January 1. On the last day of the year, time presses heavily on us; time has run out. We take inventory; we remember "those things we have done which we ought not to have done and the things we have not done that we ought to have done," as the old prayer of confession puts it. But on New Year's Day new opportunities open up before us. Time stretches out ahead full of promise and hope.

The sage of Ecclesiastes acknowledged our relationship to time. His litany in 3:1-8 celebrates the times of our lives, tuning our awareness of life's rhythms. His timeless wisdom strikes a balance between human ambition and humility. God has "made everything suitable for its time." We alone of God's creatures have a sense of past and future, yet we cannot see the end from the beginning as God does. So the writer of Ecclesiastes counsels us to accept time as a gift, living it fully with enjoyment.

SUGGESTION FOR MEDITATION: **In what ways can you see the time of this new year as a gift to enjoy rather than as a commodity to manage or an adversary to fear?**

---

*Ordained United Methodist, serves as the Senior Pastor of the American Church in Paris, having previously served congregations in Sarawak, East Malaysia, and New Jersey.

TUESDAY, JANUARY 2 • **Read Psalm 29**

For many of us a day at the seaside, swimming in the surf or walking on the beach or sailing before the wind, is paradise—or close to it. For the ancient Israelites, whose origins were in the arid deserts of the Middle East, paradise may have been an oasis with a good well, but it certainly was not an ocean. The ocean—vast, deep, and frightening—harbored unknown monsters. It symbolized the watery chaos out of which God's creative word brought life, light, and dry land (Gen. 1:1). In the vision of the new heaven and the new earth with which the the Book of Revelation concludes, the writer added, "And the sea was no more" (Rev. 21:1). If water was necessary to life, too much water was destructive to life. Only God could master the raging sea.

> *The voice of the Lord is over the waters;*
> *the God of glory thunders,*
> *the Lord, over mighty waters.*

Anyone who's ever been in a thunderstorm at sea can appreciate both the beauty and the awesome power those lines evoke.

Perhaps it's not so strange then that the rite of initiation into the Christian faith, baptism, would be the rite of passing through the waters. The waters of baptism figure prominently in our reflections for this week in which we celebrate the Feast of the Baptism of Christ. Though we have domesticated the waters by containing them within the baptismal font, we should not lose sight of the fact that they represent the power of wind and waves to threaten fragile human life. They also signify to us God's mastery of the death-dealing waters of the deep. The very waters that can drown us become a sign of God's saving power.

SUGGESTION FOR MEDITATION: **How are you living out your identity as one who has been drowned and brought to life again?**

WEDNESDAY, JANUARY 3 • Read Isaiah 43:1-7

For months before the birth of their new baby, the expectant mom and dad play the naming game. "If it's a girl, maybe we can call her Sarah after your mother." "If it's a boy, what do you think of giving him Eric as a first name after your grandfather and Robert as a middle name after my great-grandfather?" The possibilities are multitudinous. The decision making can be fun, but it is a serious process. After all, the name will become an essential part of the newborn's identity. He or she will no longer be an "it" but a real person with a name. Often the names chosen locate the child in a particular family—we honor our family's ongoing existence by naming new children after beloved parents or grandparents, aunts and uncles.

God apparently thinks names are important too.

Do not fear, for I have redeemed you;
I have called you by name, you are mine.
When you pass through the waters, I will be with you;
and through the rivers, they shall not overwhelm you.

When God names us, God claims us as beloved children. We belong to God's family. That is one of the meanings of our baptisms. We "pass through the waters" and receive assurance that we are not alone. We are not strangers or aliens. We are known. We are somebody. We are named. We are claimed. We belong. This fact gives our life its meaning; we can realize or fail to realize the meaning of our life by our subsequent actions, but the meaning itself is a given. It is God who gives our lives their meaning, and our baptisms signify that divine naming.

SUGGESTION FOR MEDITATION: **How have you allowed (or failed to allow) God's naming of you as God's own child to be realized in your life?**

THURSDAY, JANUARY 4 • Read Acts 8:14-17

Today's reading presents a rather strange story. Why must Peter and John lay hands on the heads of previously baptized new believers in order for them to receive the Holy Spirit? The practice of laying on hands at baptism or at confirmation probably stems from this account.

Given Luke's concern in the Book of Acts to establish the apostles as the authoritative guarantors of the gospel message, this story probably reflects that concern. It also reflects Luke's understanding of the church as a community of those empowered by the Holy Spirit. Peter's exchange with Simon Magus in the verses that follow demonstrates that the Holy Spirit is not for individual aggrandizement or manipulation. The Spirit is given to animate, equip, and empower the community of believers, who collectively are the body of Christ. Without the Spirit, the body has no life. In the power of the Spirit, the community of Christians actually is Christ to the world.

But if this story presents a concern for community order, empowerment, and apostolic authority, it also understands the gospel as something that human beings cannot confine. These new believers who receive the Holy Spirit through the laying on of the hands of Jewish apostles are alien Samaritans. God's word, Luke tells us, had been accepted by Samaria, and God's word creates community where none could otherwise exist. The gospel is for the world and, when received, has the power to effect radical social transformation.

SUGGESTION FOR REFLECTION: In what ways do you demonstrate that you are part of the body of Christ? How does your participation in that body, empowered by the Spirit, change the way you look at others and the world around you?

FRIDAY, JANUARY 5 • Read Luke 3:15-17

Baptism is not a Christian invention. Converts to Judaism were given a symbolic washing of the spiritual defilement that accompanied persons outside Israel's covenant community. However, John's baptism was a radical innovation because he did not call Gentiles to become Jews but asked his fellow Jews to undergo this ritual washing as a sign of their repentance for having broken covenant with God.

Luke tells us that crowds came out to be baptized by John and that "the people were filled with expectation." His message contained both good news and bad news. The good news was this: "I baptize you with water; but one who is more powerful than I is coming....He will baptize you with the Holy Spirit and fire." John emphasized that he was not the fulfillment of the expectation, the longing for a return to covenant relationship with their God that filled the hearts of the people. Rather, the coming one would fulfill their expectations. By accepting John's baptism, they prepared for an even greater baptism.

The bad news, however, was that this greater baptism of the Holy Spirit and fire would be a two-edged sword. It would separate wheat from chaff, bringing both grace and judgment. It would empower and destroy, gather up and cast away. Our baptisms signify the same double-faceted truth. By passing through the waters, we identify with God's judgment on human sin; we "die to sin" and are raised to "walk in newness of life."

SUGGESTION FOR REFLECTION: **Where do you see evidence or need in your life both of the empowering Holy Spirit and the purifying fire that your baptism signifies?**

SATURDAY, JANUARY 6 • Read Isaiah 60:1-6

EPIPHANY OF THE LORD

E*xile* is a word that strikes fear into most human hearts. To be exiled is to be cut off from one's roots, one's community, from all that grounds our sense of who we are. Even voluntary exiles who go abroad to follow a job opportunity or a marriage partner know something of the loneliness and the feeling of being out of place that true exiles feel.

But more painful than the loneliness of a long exile—whether voluntary or involuntary—is the homecoming when the exile is ended. Exiles come "home" to a strange land. Their experiences have changed them; former friends have found new friendships. The exiles discover they are "out of sync" with their own culture.

This is the situation to which our text for this Epiphany day speaks. The exiled leaders of Judea have returned to Jerusalem from their exile in Babylon, only to discover that they are as much strangers in their own land as they had been in the land of their conquerors. New leaders have arisen in the meantime; the people who remained behind have gotten on with their lives, rebuilding them in new and different ways.

To the returned exiles, aliens in their own land, the prophet's welcome word must have struck a deep chord. What a reassuring word that even in the midst of their personal darkness, the glory of God's saving presence and abundant generosity will be revealed; and all that makes life rich will be restored to them. To see the glory in the midst of the darkness—that is Epiphany.

SUGGESTION FOR REFLECTION: **In your own less than satisfactory homecomings, where might the glory of God be revealed?**

SUNDAY, JANUARY 7 • Read Luke 3:21-22

THE FEAST OF THE BAPTISM OF CHRIST

(some denominations will celebrate this feast day on January 14)

Unlike Mark and Matthew, Luke does not actually narrate Jesus' baptism but mentions it almost as an afterthought: "Now when all the people had been baptized, and when Jesus also had been baptized and was praying, the heaven was opened, and the Holy Spirit descended upon him." In Luke's Gospel and in the Book of Acts, the Holy Spirit plays a prominent role. Luke is not much interested in baptism as a symbolic washing from sin or as a death and resurrection; his interest is in baptism as the sign of empowerment by the Holy Spirit.

Jesus can do what he does, in Luke's mind, because he is filled with the Holy Spirit. His works of healing, his power over evil spirits, his courage in the face of opposition, his outspoken demand for justice for the poor—all these things are the fruits of empowerment or anointing by the Spirit. Baptism both commissions and equips us for our vocation. It is like the fuel that powers our cars; the most beautiful automobile with the most powerful engine can go nowhere without the gasoline that provides the controlled explosions inside the cylinders.

All Christians share in the ministry of the baptized. Ministry is not the preserve of the ordained clergy. Theirs is a specialized ministry that differs functionally but not materially from the ministry of all God's people. Each of us is equipped at our baptism to exercise the ministry of Christ in the world. Each of us at baptism gets a full tank of gas. The power of the Spirit is available. All we have to do is turn on the ignition and press the accelerator.

SUGGESTION FOR REFLECTION: Are you exercising the ministry God has equipped you for, or are you "idling"?

Good News!

January 8–14, 2001 • Marjorie L. Kimbrough*

MONDAY, JANUARY 8 • Read Isaiah 62:1-5

Isaiah's writing of the salvation and vindication of Zion reminds me of the Negro spiritual, "Ain-a Dat Good News." The spiritual tells of the crown, harp, robe, and wonderful new home that await with the Savior in the kingdom once the freed slaves lay down this world, take up their cross, and go home to Jesus. Ain-a dat good news!

Isaiah, like the preachers to the slaves who will come many years later, will not hold his peace. He vows to preach continuously; he will not and cannot keep silent for Zion's sake; he will not and cannot rest for Jerusalem's sake. God has instilled in him that godly, loving-parent quality that compels him to continue to preach, expressing love and concern for the child who has gone astray. Parents do not love and instruct for their own sake but for the child's sake. The child responds to the preaching, and God answers prayers. Ain-a dat good news!

Yes, good news awaits those of us who seek to build a new society, a new Zion, a new Jerusalem, by setting aside the sin so rampant in our society. We too will receive vindication. We will no longer be God's forsaken; we will be God's delight, God's bride. Oh, how we, like the bride, await that new status, that new happiness. We will have a new name, new dignity, and a wonderful new home once we lay down this world, take up our cross, and follow Jesus. Ain-a dat good news!

PRAYER: All-forgiving God, I thank you for the promise of a new name in my new home. Help me be worthy. Amen.

---

*Pastor's wife, Bible teacher, United Methodist Women member, public speaker, retreat leader, hospital volunteer, women's prison Bible teacher; living in Atlanta, Georgia.

TUESDAY, JANUARY 9 • Read Psalm 36:5-10

The goodness of God overwhelms the psalmist, and he uses God's own creation to describe that goodness worthily. What a beautiful picture the psalm paints: God's love extending to the heavens and God's faithfulness extending to the clouds. God's righteousness is like the mighty mountains; God's judgments are like the great oceans. From the heights to the depths, from the heavens to the great deeps, God's love is universal. What good news!

Life is a gift that we receive and that God nurtures. This great love, which extends to the heavens, is available to all. It offers refuge and provides for all our needs: food, drink, and shelter. Life in all its beauty flows from God's great fountain. The psalmist states, "For with you is the fountain of life; in your light we see light." This image calls to mind Jesus' words that will come many later. This fountain of life contains the living water that Jesus will describe, and we are enlightened by God's great light—Jesus, the light of the world. What good news!

Jesus, the light, has come into the world, and the darkness has not overcome it. The psalmist makes this same affirmation when he prays for God's continued support to those who know God and are upright in heart. God's presence is everywhere, offering power despite circumstances. God has provided the example of faithfulness. God has denied us nothing. No matter what, God's love and salvation are available. What good news!

PRAYER: Thank you, Father, for the beauty of the earth and for your great faithfulness. Teach me to be faithful to you. Amen.

WEDNESDAY, JANUARY 10 • Read 1 Corinthians 12:1-3

Paul wants the church at Corinth to know and understand the true manifestation of the Holy Spirit. The Corinthians have not been Christians for long; they have a pagan background. They need to be fully aware that not every experience or every encounter comes from the Holy Spirit. Even today people pursue false prophets and idol worship, and many of us have not been Christians for very long. Our background too is pagan. How then does one discern the workings of the Holy Spirit?

In the first century, idol worship and Greek philosophies competed with Jewish law. Paul reminds the Corinthians that idols are lifeless, helpless human creations. Therefore, humans, being more powerful than idols, certainly do not need them. In the first and in the twenty-first centuries, people need their creator, God.

In the past when the Corinthians did not know God, any impulse moved them. An ungodly impulse could cause one to curse the man Jesus who died on the cross like a common criminal. Paul may be recalling his own former life in Judaism, when he persecuted the church. Paul had forced Christians to denounce Jesus and had himself denied his lordship. The converted Paul knows that no one can deny Jesus and claim that the Holy Spirit has caused that denial. The Holy Spirit just does not work that way.

"Jesus is Lord" is the only proclamation the Holy Spirit influences, and that lordship is revealed to the believer by the grace of God. Anyone who utters that confession enters the sphere of the Holy Spirit's power. That is good news!

PRAYER: Lord, thank you for the revelation of the Holy Spirit. It is such good news! Amen.

Thursday, January 11 • Read 1 Corinthians 12:4-11

It appears that the church in Corinth has had some disagreement about the value of various spiritual gifts. Some members of the church, especially those who have the gift of speaking in and interpreting tongues, consider themselves more blessed than others. (Paul addresses this particular issue in 1 Corinthians 14.) This ability, or gift of tongues, still contributes to misunderstanding within the church.

Paul stresses that all gifts are bestowed for the common good, not for the individual. And as Paul indicates, all these gifts have the same source: Spirit, Lord, and God. God can best judge the serving of God's purposes through the various gifts of those within the community. The church, like any healthy organization, needs every entity to function according to its gifts for the good of the whole. When all members use their God-given gifts, the whole organization lives to God's glory. And that is good news!

Paul's use of the word *varieties* three times seems to emphasize his valuing of the body's diversity. He stresses the blessing of each gift, for he wants us to realize that unity is not uniformity. We have individual differences that we can understand and appreciate. As we acknowledge our differences, we come to realize God's greatness. And that is good news!

All gifts come from God and are given for use in God's service. Although we may know this intellectually, it is our faith that converts our knowledge into deeds. And that is good news!

PRAYER: Father, thank you for the varieties of spiritual gifts. Help me recognize my gifts and use them in your service. Amen.

FRIDAY, JANUARY 12 • Read John 2:1-5

A wedding is usually good news. Everyone is excited and happy. Well wishes and prayers for happiness and blessings abound. It is not surprising that Jesus, some of his disciples, and his mother all attend the wedding in Cana of Galilee. Weddings were festive occasions in which the whole community participated.

Wine, symbolizing joy, was a major part of the Cana wedding refreshments; the bride and groom would have been disgraced to run out of wine. Having been a part of the planning of a family wedding, I know that it would be most embarrassing to run out of refreshments. So Mary, who may have been one of the wedding planners or consultants, tells her son that the bridal couple have run out of wine. Mary knows her son can save the couple from disgrace. She knows where to go for help, and that is good news!

Although Jesus appears to respond only casually to his mother, she proceeds to tell the servants to do whatever he tells them. Perhaps Mary understands his response and his hesitancy to begin the stream of miracles that will follow, for this wedding represents the arrival of the Messiah. And that is good news! In this situation, responding obediently to the mother and following the direction of the master brings good news.

When we do whatever God tells us, the Messiah has arrived in our lives; we can expect miracles. And that is good news!

PRAYER: Thank you, Father, for the miracles of Jesus and for the mother who knew that his time had come. Amen.

SATURDAY, JANUARY 13 • Read John 2:6-11

Jesus directs the servants to fill the six jars with water. Each jar holds between twenty and thirty gallons, totaling between 120 and 180 gallons of water. The water, normally used for purification of the body, the ritual cleansing of the hands and feet, is now put to a new use. Everything Jesus touches has a new purpose. The water will be used for a miracle; the old will pass away; Jesus will make all things new. That is good news!

The abundance of wine produced is fascinating; the normal procedure was to dilute the wine with water to stretch it a little further. Once the better wine had been served liberally, the poorer wine was used. The wine that Jesus makes is better than the first, and the hosts have more than the guests can ever consume. Jesus offers abundant living; there is never a shortfall where he is concerned. That is good news!

The ministry of Jesus began with the water of his baptism, and his first miracle involved the use of water. Both instances involved conversion. Jesus was no longer the carpenter, the son of Mary and Joseph; he was recognized as the Son of God. The water in the six jars was no longer water; it became fine wine. The Messiah had come to bring about conversion, water to wine, old to new, sinners to saints. That is good news!

William Barclay, in his commentary on the Gospel of John, states that the six water jars represented an unfinished, imperfect number. We must add Jesus to reach the perfect number seven. He writes, "Jesus...turned the imperfection of the law into the perfection of grace." That is good news!

PRAYER: Thank you, God, for Jesus and the miraculous signs of his divinity. Amen.

SUNDAY, JANUARY 14 • Read Isaiah 62:1-5

The good news of Isaiah's promise not to keep silent for Jerusalem is like the good news of a marriage. This "everlasting covenant" (Isa. 61:8) between God and the people implies obedience to and trust in God, just as marriage partners enter into a relationship of mutual obedience and trust. When this happens there is good news!

Isaiah reminds the people of the blessings that are yet in store. The people of Israel can be restored to their virgin state, the state in which they first made covenant with God. Through prayer and praise the covenant can and will be restored. That is good news!

God longs to see Jerusalem blessed and made a blessing. She will no longer be the land that God forgot but the land in which God delights. She will become his new bride, and she will have a new name. Good news!

We, like Jerusalem, must renew our covenant with God. God does not wish to disown and abandon us; God wants to delight in us and receive with pride our praise and obedience. We must follow Isaiah's example and pray without ceasing for the salvation of all of God's Zions. The strength of prayer is good news!

PRAYER: Restore us, O God, to the joy of your salvation. Amen.

Hearing the Word of God

January 15–21, 2001 • Betsey Heavner*

MONDAY, JANUARY 15 • Read Nehemiah 8:1-3, 5-6

Our earliest written human records, fragments of words, and drawings reveal that people have always yearned to understand the meaning of human life and individual lives. Today's reading indicates that the Hebrew people had this yearning. After their return from Babylon, they resettle in Israel and then turn to the priest Ezra to teach them. The initiative for a public reading comes from the people themselves. The congregation gathers outside the Temple in a secular area, an area that allowed full participation by laypeople as well as clergy. This passage explicitly states that the congregation by the Water Gate includes women and some children—a presence unusual enough to mention! Notice also that the reading and teaching holds the people's attention for about six hours.

Two weeks ago we celebrated Epiphany, both the event of the arrival of the Wise Ones to Jesus' side and also those moments in our own lives when we are especially aware of Jesus' presence. The rhythm of the church year invites us now to examine how we live in "ordinary time."

These verses call us as laypeople and as clergy to seek God. In this new calendar year, you have committed (or recommitted) to daily reading with this guide. The words from Nehemiah encourage all of us—lay and clergy—to be "attentive to the book of law." As you follow your discipline of daily reading, listen for the word of God to you. What will God invite you to this week?

PRAYER: Holy God, make this ordinary day a holy day as I become aware of your presence with me. Amen.

---

*Director of FaithQuest, the General Board of Discipleship of The United Methodist Church; Christian educator, Northwest Texas Annual Conference member; living in Nashville, Tennessee.

TUESDAY, JANUARY 16 • **Read Nehemiah 8:8-10**

Nehemiah tells the weeping, grieving Israelites to rejoice, for the "joy of the Lord is your strength!" Carl is a man who has taught me about the strength that comes from joy in the Lord.

Several years ago Carl came into the church office looking disheveled and wild-eyed. He smelled bad, and listening to him took a lot of concentration. We fed him, and in a few days Carl was back to use the phone and bathroom. We tolerated Carl for months that stretched into years. As the church staff helped Carl through several crises, we began to realize that Carl had adopted us. Our church had become his home and we his family.

One day a new staff person invited Carl to a worship service. As the rest of us listened, we realized that we had been relating to Carl as an object of pity. We felt ashamed, then guilty, and then concerned about how Carl would act in worship. And he still didn't smell very good. Carl came to worship the next Sunday. He sat on the front row, and he loudly questioned the pastor several times about the proceedings. Carl returned the next Sunday. As he got comfortable, he took on the role of official greeter. Carl's joy on Sunday mornings was like that of a puppy who welcomes people home. He glowed with delight when someone called him by name and asked about his week.

On Christmas Eve, Carl was asked to be the Christ candle bearer. He knew it was important to carry the light into the darkened sanctuary at midnight. He practiced and worried for a week. We were all nervous, but the most anxious one was Carl.

The service included scripture, sermon, and music. Then the lights were extinguished, and the silence grew as we anticipated the coming of Jesus' light into the world. Carl processed with the large candle held high, reflecting the glow of God's love on his face and his own radiant joy. We knew Christ had come for all. The joy of the Lord is our strength.

PRAYER: Loving Father, help me see others as brothers and sisters. May I rejoice in your goodness. Amen.

WEDNESDAY, JANUARY 17 • Read 1 Corinthians 12:12-21

The Corinthians wrote to Paul asking questions similar to the ones we ask. Oh, we mask our questions in sophisticated ways and couch our words to justify our positions. The Corinthians asked Paul to tell them what (and who) is most important in the church. Is preaching the greatest gift? Is teaching most important? Surely mission outreach is highly valued! Evangelism is the greatest ministry! The many voices in the Corinthian church wanted Paul to affirm their position or gift as most important.

Today many groups argue for the superiority of their interpretation of scripture or their worship style or their prayer discipline. Just like the Corinthians, many voices today cry out for affirmation and validation. Recently one congregation bought a full-page advertisement in the daily newspaper to explain why their members would not participate with other city churches in an evangelistic crusade. The ad declared that the well-known and greatly respected evangelist was not "true to scripture."

Paul tells the Corinthians and us to look at the issues another way! We are the body of Christ, and all the parts together form the body. Paul declares this unity of the Christian body based on the oneness of the Spirit. We are baptized into one body. God has so arranged the body that there may be no dissension within the body, but the members may have the same care for one another.

What does it mean to be the body of Christ? We need to remember that Jesus' body literally was crucified in obedience to God's will and raised by the power of God. To be the body of Christ is to live a life of obedience to God and to remember that we do not wield power; power is God's alone. God gives us our place in the body, and to live obediently—no matter what our part in the body—is our ultimate call.

PRAYER: Loving God, help me accept myself and others as you created us. Help me be obedient today. Amen.

THURSDAY, JANUARY 18 • Read 1 Corinthians 12:22-31*a*

The modern study of chaos theory is revolutionizing the way we understand and think about the world. Young scientists and mathematicians in the 1960s first started to question the Newtonian clockwork machine view of the world. Events in the past that seemed chaotic are now understood in new ways. These ideas increasingly influence the way we think about our organizations, human relationships, the past, and the future.

A starting point for exploring chaos theory is what is called the butterfly effect—the notion that a butterfly's wings stirring the air on one side of the world can transform the weather pattern a month later on the other side of the world. The butterfly effect affirms that tiny differences can greatly influence a system's outcome. A small action can make a big (and often unpredictable) difference in a system—a weather system, a family system, an organizational system.

Paul tells us that the butterfly effect is operational in God's economy. The body of Christ has many parts. Any one part, however insignificant, can strongly influence God's purpose in the world.

In January 1989, one small youth group decided to collect dollar bills in soup pots on the last Sunday of January. The youth members made a pun of the term *Super Bowl* and told their congregation how a "soup bowl" of pocket change could make a difference for hungry people in their community. Last January, youth in 12,500 congregations across the United States collected $3,036,000 in soup pots. The money was donated to programs for feeding hungry people in the United States.

God gives spiritual gifts to every individual and to every congregation in the body of Christ. A small action by an individual or a congregation can make a big difference over time. How do we hear God's call to obedience in January 2001?

PRAYER: Loving God, show me today a small action I can take to make a big difference for you. Amen.

FRIDAY, JANUARY 19 • Read Psalm 19

Late in the afternoon, I finally left. It had been a difficult day. I had packed the car, wandered through the rooms of the house I had lived in for seventeen years; now I was finally leaving. I drove north. Through watery eyes, I worked to focus on the driving, dimly aware that the quality of light was changing as the setting sun moved toward the horizon on my left.

Suddenly the air in front of me had a rosy glow; the brown dirt and shrub mesquite in my peripheral vision were pink. I glanced out the left side window of the car and gasped. The sun, seemingly just a few inches above the horizon, had turned the line of puffy clouds to the ruby glow of campfire embers on a dark night. I pulled the car off onto the shoulder of the road.

I pushed open the car door and walked to the passenger side of the car where I would be protected from traffic and where I could lean my elbows on the car roof as I stared toward the west. I vaguely noticed the other cars on the road that had already pulled over.

The land of the Texas panhandle is flat and vast; a couple of oil derricks and farmhouses in the distance looked tiny. My whole attention turned to the sky. The deep crimson sun, a ball of fire with streaking flames, lighted the undersides of the huge billowing clouds. As I watched, the whole sky and even the land became red.

Truly, "the heavens declare the glory of God" were the words that came to my consciousness. I could feel my tense muscles relax as I stood there. Heaviness lifted from my heart, and in a moment I knew that my decision to leave was the right decision. I knew with certainty that God would be beside me, whatever happened in the days ahead.

PRAYER: Creator God, creating still, open my eyes today to your constant presence. Amen.

SATURDAY, JANUARY 20 • Read Luke 4:14-21

Last fall seventeen-year-old Kate preached in our sanctuary. She had come home from a month-long seminary youth institute. She said she had started to learn what it means to live with God every minute. Sometimes she met God in the new ideas in the classroom; sometimes she met God in the food line where she worked at the homeless shelter; sometimes she met God in the other teenagers from other parts of the world. As she described her new understandings and shared her life-giving experiences, our hearts swelled with pride at the insights one of our own young people was describing so articulately from the pulpit.

And then Kate challenged us. She said, "I have more to learn, but I know that God has called me to bring good news to everyone I meet and to declare with my life that I am part of the body of Christ. I know that God claims each one of us, and each of us must respond to our Creator with our lives."

A few of us actually squirmed in the pew. Someone said out loud, "Now you've gone to meddling." We laughed and the tension of our discomfort dissolved.

When Jesus came back to Nazareth, where he had been brought up, the home folks welcomed him. He was invited to preach, and they were proud that he was articulate and able. Then he said, "Today this scripture has been fulfilled in your hearing." In the verses beyond our assigned reading, the hometown folk were puzzled, then derisive, then "filled with rage" (vs. 28).

We are proud of our young people when they come back home. We are pleased until they challenge us to see the world in new ways. We react strongly when youth become prophets, calling us to new commitment.

PRAYER: Lord Jesus, open my ears to hear the words you speak through youth. Amen.

Sunday, January 21 • Read Luke 4:14-21

Some Bibles have section headings at the beginning of various passages. One Bible heads the verses for today's reading "The Beginning of the Galilean Ministry." I wonder, *If someone today were assigning a section heading to the story of my life, what would the title be?*

January is often a time of new beginnings. The New Year holidays in many cultures call us to reflect on our lives, assess, and dream of a new future. We make resolutions and set goals for more effective living. Perhaps we commit to new devotional practices or new service activities.

Many congregations do the same thing. New people fill church positions and responsibilities. Newly convened planning groups have retreats and set goals. The congregation plans a calendar of activities.

Dorothy C. Bass in her book *Receiving the Day* asks us to imagine how our daily experience might change if we could learn to receive time as a gift from God. She reminds us that our calendars, schedules, and time-management efforts can lead us to the false theology that somehow we, and not God, are the masters of time. We worry about "using" time well and feel guilty when we "waste" time. We think we need more time, when in fact what we need is time of a different quality. We need to recall that with light and dark, God creates each day. We need to remember God's intention for Sabbath rest as well as work.

At this time of new beginnings, let us shift our attention from our watches and calendars toward the vision Jesus lifts for us. In these verses Jesus announces the beginning of his ministry. Jesus' announcement follows time apart with God, a time of retreat and prayer in which Jesus came to understand his role in God's plan. Let us begin the year with God, and in God's good time we will clarify and announce our ministry.

Prayer: New every morning is your love, great God of light. Morning by morning new mercies I see. Amen.

God Calls and Enables

January 22–28, 2001 • *Jennifer Grove Bryan**

MONDAY, JANUARY 22 • **Read Jeremiah 1:4-5**

Known, consecrated, and appointed—before birth! Jeremiah testifies that even before being born, the Creator Lord who gives life clearly sees, thoroughly understands, and fully perceives him. This boggles the mind. God reveals to Jeremiah an intention, a divine plan for his life. And it is Jeremiah's trust in God that converts intent into reality. Receptive to God's word, the prophet dedicates himself to what he perceives as a "call" by the One who formed him in the womb.

Jeremiah is then driven by a clear conviction that compels him to live out what he has spiritually discerned. For more than forty years Jeremiah preaches the word of the Lord, despite the fact that in his career the messages are rejected, get him branded a traitor, and even provoke a murder attempt upon him. Doom. Violence. Destruction. That's what Jeremiah was given to speak! Who would want to be the harassed harbinger of such news? We have difficulty comprehending such single-minded determination. We have so few role models in our own age.

Jeremiah, on the other hand, understands the spiritual reality of our earthly existence: Nothing about us escapes God's notice—or God's governing omniscience. Therefore, what God makes known drives Jeremiah's obedience and fuels his faithfulness to embrace a life no sane person could possibly desire. For Jeremiah there's no turning back. Trusting God, he preaches as a "prophet to the nations."

PRAYER: Eternal God, strengthen my ability to discern your will for my life. Help me trust your purposes and commit to your desires for me. Amen.

---

*Laywoman engaged in several adult discipleship ministries of Lenexa United Methodist Church, Lenexa, Kansas.

TUESDAY, JANUARY 23 • Read Jeremiah 1:6-10

Jeremiah's conviction isn't instantaneously grasped or immediately exercised. We see from the text that it is acquired. Jeremiah is equipped to live out God's expectation through a process of hearing, trusting, and obeying—each experience lending credence and courage for the next.

Jeremiah's appointed assignment is daunting, and his initial, common sense response isn't some lame excuse or false humility. In fear, he speaks with sincerity: I don't know how to deliver unwanted news to the powerfully elite! Destroying and overthrowing nations and kingdoms—what do I know about such grandiose schemes?

Much like Moses at the burning bush, young Jeremiah shrinks at first from the frightening role revealed to him. However, what dispels the distrust of both begins with the same, simple prompting. Each receives God's assurance: I will be with you.

We want more, don't we? Driven by our culture to succeed in every attempt, abhorring the possibility of failure, we resist most struggle as sheer anathema in our vain attempts to stand out and win approval. Instead, we want material evidence of profitable payoffs or social enhancements before we will invest ourselves in projects—or people. We find it hard to risk.

Fears of frustration, being misunderstood, appearing ridiculous, losing status—such are the superficial, worldly concerns that all too often paralyze us. Unfortunately, we encumber our lives with these very real but unworthy claims.

God says to Jeremiah, don't be afraid for I am with you to deliver you. When Jeremiah trusts this truth, he eventually finds the wherewithal to transcend an impoverished existence of refusal to risk embarrassment for God.

PRAYER: O Lord, help me recognize my reluctance to risk myself for you. Dispel my doubts and distrust as I cling to your assurance, "Don't be afraid. I am with you." Amen.

WEDNESDAY, JANUARY 24 • **Read Luke 4:21-22**

Jesus arrives in Nazareth clearly convinced of God's call and willing to risk living out his destiny. Handed a scroll from the prophet Isaiah, Jesus stands and reads aloud in his hometown synagogue, then sits to teach, as was the custom of his day. To those gathered 'round him, Jesus calmly announces that Isaiah's long-ago prophecy is now satisfied, brought to completion (literally) "in your ears."

Isaiah's poetic phrases pointed to a glorious restoration of God's people, and those in Nazareth still yearned for that fulfillment. Yet they had preconceived ideas about the packaging of that promise. For now, when this native son personalizes Isaiah's phrases, making himself the one who ushers in that "year of the Lord's favor" (Isa. 61:2)—they find it perplexing and too marvelous.

Hadn't they known Jesus from childhood? What could they make of such a preposterous claim? Seemingly nothing has changed. Romans still control Galilee. Palestine is oppressed. Startled, they experienced this Sabbath gathering as something altogether different than what they'd expected. Wonder grips them but does not meet with responsive faith. What cannot be explained is hard to believe.

Jesus' listeners cannot receive reconciliation and spiritual transformation. Like those in Nazareth, we so often want the tangible, while God asks us to trust. How are our expectations shortchanging what God longs to realize in our lives? When we refuse to relinquish what blinds us to God's possibilities, we reject the wonder God wants to unfold.

PRAYER: Eternal Lord, when truth surprises me and startles my sensibilities, help me hear and trust nonetheless. When others disdain what has been revealed, send me forward in your Spirit, though even I am amazed. Amen.

THURSDAY, JANUARY 25 • Read Luke 4:23-30

People in Capernaum accepted what Jesus gave them. There, less than twenty miles from Nazareth, they began bringing to him "all who were sick," and Jesus healed them (Mark 1:32). Mark reports that "At once [Jesus'] fame began to spread throughout the surrounding region of Galilee" (Mark 1:28).

But members of his hometown have difficulty accepting what Jesus offers them. Perhaps their desire to witness more of the miraculous prevents them from receiving. Perhaps Jesus just seems too ordinary. Anointed One, indeed! To those familiar with Jesus' humble human heritage, the idea is too preposterous. Isn't it easier to reject outright what cannot be understood than to struggle with the wonder of its divine possibility?

What we cannot explain, we impatiently cast aside. That God would appoint Jesus as the long-awaited messiah is resoundingly rejected. It is too strange, too outrageous to accept. Surely the man is deranged. While the people of Capernaum know Jesus has healed elsewhere, to them the physician himself needs a cure! The hometown decisively discards the opportunity to embrace truth.

Therefore, Jesus recalls Elijah and Elisha, both of whom God sent elsewhere when God's word through them met with deafness and refusal to participate in divine purposes. Smiles quickly fade, fury now rages, and the mob moves to render death to Jesus outside the city. Nazareth disregards the message and disdains the messenger.

Luke's Gospel uses this incident to relay the word that the world's savior went first to his own people but was not accepted. Now Jesus will take God's good news to those outside the covenant community.

PRAYER: Physician Lord, heal my deafness and keep me receptive to your truth, no matter who voices it. Protect me from rejecting outright what I don't understand. Amen.

FRIDAY, JANUARY 26 • Read 1 Corinthians 13:1-3

Love is central to the Christian life, as Paul's lyrical argument emphatically states. Without love our spiritual gifts have no meaning. Without love, our witness to God is left wanting.

Paul poses three suppositions to support the superiority of love. While all of these spiritual gifts are marvelous, we don't need such extraordinary "credentials" for others to see God reflected in our lives. To the contrary, what is essential, what is necessary to distinguish us as disciples of Christ is love that motivates our actions and prompts us to bless others.

Without love we operate out of self-centered, self-obsessed, and self-destructive motives—in fact, godlessly. Isn't that why God tells us to love? In loving we submit to God's transforming spirit, allowing our relationship with Jesus Christ to change us!

I cannot love without God. I cannot love singularly, for love is relational. When I pour myself out for another's benefit, I allow God's spirit to sanctify me, energize me, and "employ" me in the eternal, redemptive, divine plan for this world.

The author of First John writes, "My dear friends, let us love one another, because the source of love is God. Everyone who loves is a child of God and knows God, but the unloving know nothing of God, for God is love. This is how he showed his love among us: he sent his only Son into the world that we might have life through him" (4:7-9, REB).

When we love, we extend Jesus' grace to others, becoming the essence of who God means us to be. Love is the litmus test for those created in the image of God.

PRAYER: Loving God, who is love and who calls us to love, renew your love in me. Let me serve others rather than insisting upon being served. Amen.

SATURDAY, JANUARY 27 • **Read 1 Corinthians 13:4-13**

Faith, hope, and love constitute life in God's spirit. All three motivate our spiritual gifts, but love's importance resides in the fact that when the kingdom of God arrives in completion, the need for the others won't exist. Our tremendously valued spiritual gifts eventually will be warranted useless, for the New Testament promises that in time we will come face to face with love itself, God. We come from love and return to love.

Therefore, we must let love have its way with us, relying upon God's spirit if we strive to love as flawlessly as the biblical text dictates. The New Testament assures us that as we "grow up" in faith, such love becomes possible in an increasing measure. As we submit to the spirit of Christ, Christ transforms our lives, degree by degree. Such pure love must be our aim.

The increasing measure of love is what Paul emphasizes to the Corinthians. Yet persons often remove Paul's exaltation of love, one of the most beautiful and familiar of all passages, from its biblical context. It is actually part of an instructional aim about "a still more excellent way" (1 Cor. 12:31) we are to live. Some of the Corinthians are flaunting their spiritual gifts with selfish aims rather than building up the Christian community. Hence Paul writes, insisting that love is the way we please God and help others, especially when exercising our gifts. Without *agape*—that selfless love demonstrated by Christ and generated only by God—no one is benefited, our gifts are meaningless, and we are nothing.

PRAYER: As I submit to your spirit, O Christ, use my gifts and transform me to love as you do. Amen.

Sunday, January 28 • Read Psalm 71:1-6

The psalmist echoes Jeremiah's understanding of God's intimacy with us when he declares, "From birth I have relied on you; / you brought me forth from my mother's womb. / I will ever praise you" (Ps. 71:6, NIV). Security for both these saints comes from their certainty that God can be trusted with our welfare. The same can be said for Jesus and for the Apostle Paul, as we've seen this week.

The psalmist knows that God is righteousness, and God alone sustains and provides for those who recognize and rely upon that divine goodness. To whom do you turn when faced with difficulties? As days deliver tough choices and harsh realities, on what do you depend?

May you declare, as Eugene Peterson paraphrases verse 1 of the text, "I run for dear life to God, I'll never live to regret it" (Ps. 71:1, *The Message*). Like the psalmist, once convinced of God's gracious character and merciful nature, we relish the grace to find refuge there!

In Christ we see how far God will go to convince us that the spirit of Truth is completely trustworthy. In the life of Christ we witness God's desire for all humanity. We see salvation.

God, who is steadfast love, desires that we trust in the one who knows us best and loves us most. Where does your confidence come from? In what times and situations have you looked in wrong places or to wrong persons as you made your way in the world? Those who turn to God for deliverance—no matter the circumstances—need never fear. God is with us!

PRAYER: Reliable, redeeming God, in you I take refuge. Help me to hear, trust, and obey your gracious Spirit. Amen.

Responding to God's Call

January 29–February 4, 2001 • *Steven J. Christopher**

MONDAY, JANUARY 29 • **Read Isaiah 6:1-5**

An often overlooked question that surrounds Isaiah's calling is how and why Isaiah finds himself in God's throne room in the first place. To this question the text gives no adequate answer. The transition from Chapter 5 to Chapter 6 is abrupt. Chapter 5 contains the Song of the Vineyard, an extended allegory that uses six images to describe the relationship between God and Israel. Suddenly the song ends; the reader and Isaiah are transported to a throne room for a direct encounter with God. The reader is not told how or why this strange vision occurs, nor does the text indicate that Isaiah himself understands why he is there.

Isaiah is the only one in the throne room who doesn't seem to belong. We would expect God to be in the throne room, as we would expect the angels. We would not expect to find an average, unknown mortal. Through some mystery, Isaiah has been given the privilege of being present to witness God incarnate.

The real wonder that we celebrate on Sunday morning is the wonder of being included in the church. Through a mystery that we cannot begin to understand, we have been granted the privilege to know God and to be coparticipants in God's plan of reconciling the world through Christ. In my Wesleyan tradition, we believe that God effects this reconciliation by allowing persons to experience the grace that is offered in Christ, which allows us to grow in response to that grace and to achieve a sanctified life.

PRAYER: Almighty and everlasting God, I rejoice at the opportunity to be included in your plan of reconciliation. May I respond to your invitation and live my life as a disciple in your name. Through Christ I pray. Amen.

---

*Student in *Juris Doctor* degree program at Harvard Law School, Cambridge, Massachusetts; ordained elder, The United Methodist Church.

TUESDAY, JANUARY 30 • **Read Isaiah 6:6-13**

The vision that surrounds Isaiah at the moment of his calling to prophesy is full of wonder and grandeur. The author goes into great detail to describe the throne room, the angels, and most important, God—seated on the throne.

We are led to consider Isaiah's emotive state at the moment that the call to ministry is given. Probably his reluctance to speak is borne out of an intimidation due to his surroundings. Confronted by all this wonder, Isaiah must feel completely mundane and unspectacular. It is likely that Isaiah would consider anyone in the room to be worthier than he to answer the call to proclaim the message. Confronted by the reality of his call to proclaim the reality of what he has witnessed, Isaiah must be struck by the contrast between how the reality of God has been presented to him and the mundane, unspectacular sight of himself relaying the message to others.

Being the church often requires that the spectacular, impressive message we have received be communicated through ordinary, unspectacular people. The next time you worship with your community of faith, take a look around the room. If you know the people sitting around you well, you know they are fallible and capable of error. You know your own fallibility. Yet God has called you and those around you to ministry anyway. This calling is a gift given to us despite our unworthiness. It is a gift worth getting excited about.

SUGGESTION FOR MEDITATION: Use me, O God, in my ordinariness to bring about your intentions for the world. May I be a channel through which your grace is communicated to a world in need. Through Christ I pray. Amen.

WEDNESDAY, JANUARY 31 • Read Psalm 138

The use of monarchical metaphors for God pervades the Hebrew Scriptures. It continues to be prevalent in our own Christian liturgical practice. Yet an analysis of the biblical texts that use monarchical imagery to describe God reveals that the Bible uses this imagery in surprising, unexpected ways. God chooses to enter into relationship with ordinary persons like Isaiah, Peter, and Paul, in direct contrast to normative behavior for ancient kings. In the New Testament, Jesus' common motif of the reign of God as analogous to a banquet where everyone is welcome suggests the radical inclusivity of God and God's plan for the world. Such biblical images would have been an insult to ancient kings who reveled in the hierarchical relationships they held over their subjects and in the right to exclude.

Responding to God's call means living as a servant, because in service we imitate the nature of the God who has called us into discipleship. Central to our faith is the notion that in Christ, God willingly humbled Godself and became as a servant to effect reconciliation and redemption. Within my own Wesleyan tradition, as well as in many other Protestant traditions, we believe that discipleship is a means of growing in grace through an imitation of Christ, who was God revealed among us.

The image of God as king is therefore ironically subversive in a cultural setting where hierarchical power is normative, because it calls those in power to behave as servants, empowering those who live their lives as servants to see themselves as imitators of God through the very role that others see as a sign of weakness.

SUGGESTION FOR MEDITATION: Today focus on the spiritual discipline of humility. Reflect upon the humility God revealed through incarnation in Jesus. Consider how you can model this humility in your own life as a disciple.

THURSDAY, FEBRUARY 1 • Read 1 Corinthians 15:1-8

I spent three years as the associate minister of a large United Methodist Church in middle Tennessee. Part of my responsibilities entailed coordinating local church evangelism efforts. My responsibility was, as ludicrous as it sounds, to market the church. Consequently, I spent countless hours thinking about why people come to church and what compels them to return.

Only late in my three-year appointment did I realize that the most common reason people come to church is, fortunately, the right one: every Sunday morning the four hundred or so persons who filed into our sanctuary, regardless of their age, gender, social location, or income, were there because they wanted to hear the good news of salvation preached to them. If I could do the appointment all over again, I would spend much more time worrying about whether or not our local church was proclaiming the gospel with passion and intensity and much less time worrying about whether we were providing visitors with the right kind of coffee.

Paul recognizes in First Corinthians that the centrality of the proclamation of the message is what gives life to the church. His task is not easy, as our task in proclaiming the gospel today is not easy. Those to whom Paul preached in the marketplace had many other demands upon their time and other distractions, just as contemporary parishioners have other places they could be and other things they could be doing. People gathered in the marketplace to hear Paul's proclamation of a story; churchgoers gather in sanctuaries today to hear the same story.

PRAYER: Creator God, may we as individuals and as the church continue the task that was set before Paul to proclaim the good news of salvation offered to us in Christ. May we proclaim your gospel with boldness, courage, and integrity. Amen.

Friday, February 2 • Read 1 Corinthians 15:9-11

According to mainstream scholarship, Paul wrote the first epistle to the church in Corinth at about the midpoint of his ministry. The letter is both reflective of the past and of the possibilities that lay ahead for the church in the future.

Imagine that you are Paul, sitting and writing the epistle. You probably can't begin to believe all the changes that have occurred in the last ten to fifteen years since the beginning of your ministry. Certainly in your time of persecuting the church, you could not have believed that you would now find yourself its most well-known proponent.

Just as Paul cannot believe all that has happened since his calling, he is equally sure that he has no idea what the future holds. Given what we can gather from Paul's journeys in Acts and the epistles, he lived a tenuous existence. Paul narrowly escaped death several times. As he sat and wrote the letter to the church in Corinth, Paul probably would not have even hazarded a guess as to where he would be a week from that time, let alone ten years.

Paul's life serves as a model for the church and for us as individual disciples. Responding to God's call requires a willingness to go to strange places, not knowing what will happen or when. Willing vulnerability is scary, unsettling, and exciting at the same time. The setting for spiritual leadership that challenged and absorbed Paul's attention remains our setting as we move into a new century of ministry.

SUGGESTION FOR MEDITATION: Today consider the meaning of the calling of Isaiah, the disciples, and Paul. What can you discover from these callings about why, how, and in what manner God calls persons to special avenues of service?

SATURDAY, FEBRUARY 3 • Read Luke 5:1-5

The lections for this week focus on three instances of persons being called to special avenues of ministry. The lection from the Hebrew Scriptures relates the calling of Isaiah. In the epistle lesson, Paul alludes to the story of his own calling as an apostle. Finally the Gospel lection presents the call narrative of the disciples by the Sea of Galilee.

On the surface, it would appear that we might distinguish Paul and Isaiah from the disciples by the Sea of Galilee on the basis of their scholarly expertise and sophistication. From what we can gather from biblical and extra-biblical sources, both Isaiah and Paul were well-educated, sophisticated, urbane. Isaiah spent a considerable period of time as the prophetic advisor to the king. Paul's Hellenistic background implied a familiarity with Greek customs and culture; he would have seemed particularly urbane in an isolated backwater province such as Israel. By contrast, the disciples were simple fishermen who have no such credentials.

However, what ties these three call narratives together is that Isaiah, Paul, and the fishermen chose to accept the call immediately after receiving a demonstration of God's power. Consequently, we can construe each of these three callings as radically experiential, rather than academic: All three callings come directly out of an immediate awareness of the reality of God and the power of God to effect change in the world. This awareness of God's power continues to sustain and revive the church.

PRAYER: **God who has called me into new life, open my heart to remember the wonder that I experienced when I first accepted your call. May this remembrance strengthen and guide my efforts to do your will today. Amen.**

SUNDAY, FEBRUARY 4 • Read Luke 5:6-11

When we trust in God's power, we can do wondrous things that would have been impossible through trust in our own instincts. When the church listens and responds to the voice of God, the church becomes a channel for a power greater than itself; and the power of God transforms the world.

The disciples in the Gospel lection are both powerful and powerless. They bring about a miracle. Certainly the locals would be impressed. Yet this act of power is only possible through the disciples' willingness to trust in a power greater than themselves. In this instance, such trust requires them to do something as counterintuitive as casting the nets on the other side of the boat. As Peter gives the order, we can imagine the others muttering to themselves about what good this could possibly do.

The Gospel lection demonstrates the odd duality of powerlessness and power at the heart of authentic discipleship. The disciples manifest power, yet this power is actually the power of God acting through them. They are able to be powerful only by allowing themselves to be channels through which a power much greater than they can manifest itself. Such power requires several spiritual disciplines: faith in the efficacy of God's power, the courage to be a conduit through which God is revealed, and patience and diligence in listening for the voice of God's direction.

PRAYER: Creating and redeeming God, may I be a vessel through which you pour out your grace for the life of the world. May your Holy Spirit enable me to do the wondrous things that you have in store for the world. Through Christ I pray. Amen.

A Light for Our Path

February 5–11, 2001 • *Barbara Grace Ripple**

MONDAY, FEBRUARY 5 • **Read Psalm 1**

This week's selections remind us that our life's journey sets our feet upon a path that is often rocky, steep, and definitely challenging. As we struggle to keep our footing, we might see a way that appears much easier. Do we continue on this steep and difficult path with no apparent end in sight, or should we try that new path, the one that looks so smooth and enticing? The temptation is to leave our difficult journey and follow the well-worn path that leads to the rewards of this world.

This week's scriptures, however, help us in our choice. We remember that it is Christ who gives light to our world, who illumines our path. We are reminded of the importance of our choices and the need to examine them in the light of Christ.

From today's psalm we learn that those who delight in God's law (who follow God's path) will prosper, flourish, and bear fruit. Their roots will go deep. God watches over the way of the righteous. When we choose to follow God's way we find the light of Christ illuminating our path, the true way for the fulfillment of God's plan for our lives.

PRAYER: Illumine my path, O God of compassion and love, and guide my feet in ways everlasting. Amen.

---

*Superintendent, the Hawaii District of the California-Pacific Annual Conference, The United Methodist Church; living in Honolulu, Hawaii.

TUESDAY, FEBRUARY 6 • Read Jeremiah 17:5-8

It sounds so easy, doesn't it? Just live right, and all will be well. Follow the rules set before you. Do not veer to the left or the right, but stay on the straight path. "Just say no" to temptation. How many of us hear these messages throughout our lives and feel like total failures because we're unable to follow them?

Our passage today clearly states that the one who trusts in God will be like a healthy, strong tree planted by streams of water. The foliage will be so verdant and full that even in times of drought there will be no anxiety, for this tree will not cease to bear fruit. By comparison, the one who trusts in mortals rather than in God will be a mere rootless shrub, growing in a parched wilderness, an uninhabited salt land. I think of a tumbleweed blowing across the Mojave desert in California.

Then why are we not all solid, fruitful trees with roots going deeply into the rich soil of faith, drinking deeply of living water? We are reminded of the words of the Apostle Paul: "I can will what is right, but I cannot do it. For I do not do the good I want, but the evil I do not want is what I do. Now if I do what I do not want, it is no longer I that do it, but sin that dwells within me" (Rom. 7:18b-20).

"Sin" is that which tries to separate us from God. We sin when we place our faith and trust in things other than God— things that are perishable and corruptible. When we place our entire lives in God's care and allow the light of Christ to guide our paths, we can find hope even in the darkness of despair.

SUGGESTION FOR MEDITATION: **What things separate you from God's love?**

WEDNESDAY, FEBRUARY 7 • Read Luke 6:17-23

Jesus came into our world to show us the way back to God. He interpreted the scriptures, the sacred words known by all devout Hebrew people, in ways that gave meaning to God's intent. Jesus' vision turned the world of his Hebrew contemporaries upside down and created enemies of the learned folk who preferred their own moralistic and legalistic interpretations. Jesus' teachings continue to turn our lives upside down today.

I recently visited a church-sponsored homeless shelter in Honolulu that serves nine hundred meals daily to the hungry and provides beds nightly for three hundred men, women, and children who have nowhere else to go. One floor of the shelter is for families. Wooden frame bunk beds and small wardrobes, arranged side by side, give each family a small area to call its own. Family pictures and children's artwork are taped to the wardrobes, and small stuffed animals lie on the beds. This one floor of wall-to-wall beds and wardrobes serves as a temporary "home" to dozens of families. These persons have little claim upon anything that we value in this world, yet Jesus would call them "blessed."

Those who today are poor, hungry, weeping, hated, excluded, reviled, defamed—those are the ones whom God honors. This goes against everything we have been taught to believe in this world, where wealth, fame, comfort, and "being liked" are the sought-after goals.

PRAYER: Help me, O God, to see those persons I despise, resent, or fear as your beloved children, my sisters and brothers. Amen.

THURSDAY, FEBRUARY 8 • Read Luke 6:24-26

"We are giving our furniture to the new pastor," a dear friend and church member said to me recently. "We are selling our home, and buying a small condo." I immediately felt sorrow for this woman and her family as I thought of the beautiful house they had built overlooking the ocean. "I know the economy has been in decline," I replied, sympathetically, "but I did not realize your business had been so badly affected by it."

"Oh no," she replied with a smile. "We are not having financial problems. You see, we have been planning this for the past few years. During the time we have been part of a Bible study and prayer group, my husband and I have realized that God has a better use for us than to live in such a big house. We are going to live more simply and use our resources for the work of the church. We have entered a program at the hospital to be trained as volunteer chaplains, and we think that God will give us guidance for the future."

Jesus' admonition in today's passage that "woe" will come to those who are now rich, full, and prosperous is not a curse or condemnation but rather a statement of fact. Those who are wealthy and comfortable often forget their need for God. They have chosen a different way. What does it mean for those of us in the Western world to know that the world produces enough food to feed all persons adequately and yet also to know that we do not want to risk lowering our standard of living to share our abundance with others? Which way have we chosen?

PRAYER: Christ Jesus, circumcise my heart, that I may be open to receive you, and with you, my sisters and brothers who cry out in need. Amen.

FRIDAY, FEBRUARY 9 • Read 1 Corinthians 15:12-20

When I lived in northeast Ohio, many symbols, especially in the month of February, helped teach about the Resurrection. The earth was frozen solid, and all trees but the evergreens were devoid of leaves. The earth seemed desolate and barren. But Ohio residents knew that within a few short weeks, that which was happening deep within the ground would be made evident. Tiny green shoots would poke through the crusted earth, and beautiful crocus blooms would appear, followed by jonquils and then tulips. At the same time, sap would begin to flow in the trees, stimulating the formation of buds on the branches. The sap could soon be tapped and boiled into delicious maple syrup! Yes, resurrection occurs each spring in the northern hemispheres.

But I now live in the tropics on an island where flowers bloom year-round, and verdant foliage is ever present. For many of our sisters and brothers throughout the world, February means the warmth of a bright sun and lush green with blooming flowers. So how can I explain the Resurrection in new ways?

On the island of Hawaii, lava covers a large portion of the land—some lava from flows as recent as five years ago. Hardened black rock stretches for miles, some smooth, some in "pillows," and some in broken chunks, reminding me of what the moon's surface might be like. However, within a few years after a new flow, a miracle takes place as plants, new green life, poke up through the black rock. New life appears where no life could seem to exist. God's plan for resurrection—true for nature, true for us!

PRAYER: Help me, O God, to find resurrection in my own life as well as in the lives of others. Amen.

SATURDAY, FEBRUARY 10 • Read 1 Corinthians 15:12-20

The Greek philosopher Aristotle, who lived about three hundred years before Jesus and Paul, used syllogistic logic to prove a point. The syllogistic method introduces two or more premises, often with the word *if*, and finally reaches a conclusion, often preceded by *therefore*. If the premises are valid (true), then the conclusion will also be valid or true.

Paul, the educated former attorney Saul of Tarsus, uses syllogistic argument in today's passage to prove the resurrection of Jesus. Interestingly, he uses a reverse argument: "If the dead are *not* raised, then Christ has *not* been raised" (emphasis added). Paul repeats the phrase about Christ's not being raised several times, spelling out the consequences of that premise: Our faith becomes futile and we remain stuck in sin; all those who have previously died in Christ will have perished, and we would be all the more to be pitied. In verse 20 Paul proclaims to all who will hear, "But in fact Christ has been raised from the dead, the first fruits of those who have died."

While a logical argument might help some believe in the Resurrection, for me belief comes through personal experience. "He Lives" by Alfred H. Ackley has been a favorite hymn of mine since childhood. The first verse affirms a risen Savior who is active in the world. The last line of the refrain speaks to me about the knowledge of the Resurrection: "You ask me how I know he lives? He lives within my heart."

Feeling Jesus alive in my heart, and seeing Jesus alive in others and in the world—these are proof enough of the Resurrection for me.

SUGGESTION FOR MEDITATION: What gives you proof of the resurrection of Jesus Christ?

SUNDAY, FEBRUARY 11 • Read Jeremiah 17:5-10

We end the week as we began, with choices before us. Paul urges us to choose between believing in the resurrection of the dead, including the resurrection of Christ, or of not believing and being among those "most to be pitied." The psalmist encourages us to be fruitful trees planted by streams of water, as opposed to being rootless, blown like chaff by the ways of the world. The prophet Jeremiah, in a passage of beautiful poetic contrast, compares those who put their trust in mortals to a rootless shrub in the desert, while those who trust in God have roots that go deep into soil fed by life-sustaining water.

Jesus, in the passage known as the Sermon on the Plain, urges us to remember that those who hold to God's way are blessed, even though despised by the world's standards, while those now honored by the world will be full of woe. We recall the words of Paul to the church at Rome: "I consider that the sufferings of this present time are not worth comparing with the glory about to be revealed to us" (Rom. 8:18).

Whether fully aware of it or not, we are all on a journey, a spiritual path, a pilgrimage. We receive no promise that it will be smooth, easy, or comfortable; in fact, it is often the opposite. The temptations of an easier life, of "winning the lottery," may pull us away from God. We put our trust in the promises of others, rather than in the promises of God. On our life's journey, let us turn from the darkness to the light that God sent into this world to illumine our path and show us the way.

PRAYER: O God, test my mind and search my heart; enable me to be firmly rooted in you. Amen.

Love Your Enemies

February 12–18, 2001 • Bass M. Mitchell*

MONDAY, FEBRUARY 12 • Read Luke 6:27a

The readings this week may not be for you or everyone. If you do not have enemies, if you never have to deal with difficult people, if you like everyone and everyone likes you all the time, then these readings are not for you. Skip them. Go to next week. But if there are persons at work, at school, in your community, at church, even in your own family with whom you are often at odds, keep reading.

"Love your enemies," Jesus says here. I imagine this sounded just as strange and disturbing to the first hearers as it does to us. Perhaps many in Jesus' day would have immediately thought of the Romans. Others thought of those not in their own group like the Pharisees and Sadducees, who were often not the best of friends. Perhaps others thought of neighbors they did not get along with or business associates with whom they were in tough competition. Whomever they thought of, it was probably not difficult for Jesus' listeners to identify some of their "enemies."

"Love your enemies," Jesus says. Before we even think about what it means to love them, we have to admit that we have them. We are naive if we think everyone is going to like us all the time. We also lack sensitivity if we think we never do or say anything that causes others pain. We will have enemies. Why else would Jesus have to tell us to love them?

SUGGESTION FOR MEDITATION: **Think back over your past. Who have been your enemies? Who are they now? Why would you consider them enemies?**

---

*United Methodist minister; curriculum writer and author of numerous articles; living in Hot Springs, Virginia.

TUESDAY, FEBRUARY 13 • Read Luke 6:27*b*-29

Got your enemies in mind? Here's how Jesus says to treat them.

First, "do good" to them. That's the opposite of what we want or feel. Do not treat them as they treat you. In all your interactions with them seek to know and do only what is best and good for them. Find something "good" that you can do for them.

Second, "bless" them. That's the last thing we want to do to our enemies. In Jesus' day one could place curses on people. Words were powerful, and to curse someone was to say that as surely as I say this it will happen. But Jesus goes against all of that. He says not only to *do* good to your enemies but to *say* good things about them. What might that imply? Do not gossip about them. Do not tear their character down with your words about them. Compliment them. Praise them to others.

Third, "pray" for them. In my own life I have found it hard to continue disliking someone if I pray daily for him or her. Prayer brings the whole matter into the presence of God, and it is difficult to hate there. The prayer of Jesus on the cross is a model. He prayed for those who had just hung him on the cross, "Father, forgive them."

Fourth, "offer the other [cheek]"—again, not our natural response. If someone strikes us, we want to strike back. If someone hurts us in some way, we want to hurt back. But Jesus rules out retaliation. Do not respond in kind. Treat your enemies as you wish to be treated.

By practicing Jesus' prescription for dealing with our enemies, our bitter, angry feelings may subside to be replaced eventually by love.

SUGGESTION FOR MEDITATION: How might you put Jesus' words into practice?

WEDNESDAY, FEBRUARY 14 • Read Luke 6:30-38

People often refer to these teachings of Jesus as "hard sayings"; that is, hard to understand and even harder to put into practice. It often seems that Jesus expects the impossible from us or at least expects behavior that does not come naturally. "Love your enemies" is exactly the opposite of how we feel or of what's been the normal human response all our history.

But Jesus expects us to do what is not normal, not easy. He thinks it is possible. He set the example to prove it is possible. In fact, his teachings reveal to us who we are called to be, the kinds of human beings God created us to be; and how we are to be in relationship with others, especially with others who make our life difficult.

How we are to relate to others is the theme again in today's reading. The normal response is to love only those who love us. We respond to love with love, to hatred with hatred; we do unto others as they do to us. In other words, we allow others' actions toward us to dictate our feelings and actions. That's the normal way of things, the cycle we so easily fall into.

Jesus' response to our desire for retaliation is not sheer passivity. Jesus requires aggressive action in answer to hostility and violence: turning the other cheek, offering the shirt, giving to one who asks. Jesus asks us to break the vicious cycle through our love for others that guides and determines all we do and say in regard to them. This love is present whether we receive love, or even hatred and hurt, in return. And as we give and forgive rather than condemn and judge, we become "children of the Most High."

SUGGESTION FOR REFLECTION: Today is Valentine's Day, a day often reserved for romantic relationships or at least friendly ones. But think of your enemies today as Valentines, as friends. How might you demonstrate your love for them?

THURSDAY, FEBRUARY 15 • **Read Genesis 45:3-11, 15**

Genesis contains a great deal of material about Joseph. Chapters 37; 39; and 45 through 50 give an overview of his life.

So much material about Joseph suggests he must have been a favorite character and hero for many generations. Maybe his popularity hinged on people's ability to identify with him. His life often mirrored their own—trials, family problems, injustice, imprisonment but also providence, wisdom, and hope.

Joseph's father, Jacob, favored him. Some have called Joseph a spoiled brat. His father gave him a coat that made Joseph's brothers jealous. Yet Joseph spied and tattled on them and even told them dreams that, in essence, announced how much greater he was. Needless to say, they hated him so much that they plotted to kill him. His brothers sold him into slavery, but Joseph eventually became an important official in the Egyptian government. Clearly we are to see in his whole story the hand of God. (See Genesis 45:7.)

A famine has ravaged Palestine, forcing Joseph's brothers to Egypt for grain. They come before Joseph but do not recognize their brother. Joseph tests and toys with them some; but as we see in today's reading, he eventually lets them know who he is. He forgives them, and they are reconciled. He models for us Jesus' teachings in Luke 6:27 and following verses. It is possible to love our enemies, to do good to them, even and especially when they are family members. And maybe that's where we need to begin—with our own family.

SUGGESTION FOR REFLECTION: **How might I follow the example of Joseph and the teachings of Jesus in regard to a painful family relationship?**

FRIDAY, FEBRUARY 16 • Read Genesis 45:5-8

Joseph's words in today's verses express years of pain, anger, alienation, and resentment between him and his brothers. He has suffered greatly, but he no longer blames his brothers for his suffering. In fact, he goes to some lengths to assure them not to be afraid, though they have reason to be. He sees a greater plan behind his pain, a greater purpose for it. He believes that God brought him to Egypt so he could be in a position to help his own family and his own people. Out of his own woundedness and healing he is now in a position to help them.

To me the image of the wounded healer has always held power. It is one of the more meaningful ways to describe Jesus, since we believe that through his stripes we receive healing. To use one's own suffering and woundedness to heal others is tremendous love.

I well remember a couple who did and said some things that really made my life miserable. In fact, they were the main reason for my leaving a place of employment. Soon after that my wife and I had our first child, born prematurely. We were so afraid, not knowing what to expect. During this time this other couple, who had been through the same experience with their child, came by. Something about them had changed. They did not seem the same people. And out of their own woundedness and pain they helped us through that difficult time in our lives. Love has a way of using our woundedness to heal, even our enemies.

PRAYER: **Lord, show me how to use my woundedness to bring healing to others, even those I do not like at all. Amen.**

Saturday, February 17 • Read Psalm 37:1-11, 39-40

The theme of this wisdom psalm is the certain judgment that will come to the wicked. So the psalm offers a word of hope to those who may suffer at the hands of the wicked. As such, it goes well with the readings this week, offering the kind of wisdom fleshed out in the story of Joseph. Joseph models the kind of trust and patience this song extols. He does not take the law into his own hands or seek retribution. He leaves the matter in God's hands. His brothers do not get away with what they have done; they experience guilt while suffering fear of punishment by Joseph. But rather than getting what they fully deserve, they receive forgiveness, mercy, grace.

Perhaps one of the most difficult things about having enemies is to see them apparently get away with their offenses against us and even prosper. What we want is to see quick and sure justice for them. And some of us take it into our hands to ensure that justice happens. As I write this meditation, yet another news story about a shooting in an office appears on the television screen. Someone was seeking retribution.

But this psalm puts our feelings about our enemies in a whole new light. It encourages us to keep on trusting in and serving God, no matter what our enemies say or do—even when their offenses go unpunished. Such matters are best left in God's hands. God will act in God's own good time and way. Best of all, God may bring about reconciliation with our enemies, as with Joseph and his brothers, for reconciliation is God's will. Peace, harmony, love are qualities God desires and works for among us.

Suggestion for reflection: How is God working for reconciliation in your life?

SUNDAY, FEBRUARY 18 • Read 1 Corinthians 15:35-38, 42-50

I recently read books about the lives of Dietrich Bonhoeffer and Father Kolbe, both of whom died in concentration camps during World War II, both persons of great faith. Their enemies held the power of life and death, and they used that power to take Bonhoeffer and Kolbe's lives. Yet from those stories arises the overwhelming sense that neither was defeated. Their faith, love, and witness live on to this day. These two men also shared with us the blessed hope that not even death can remove us from the love of God, which is ours through Christ Jesus.

Was this victory in death not also true of Christ? What powerful enemies he had. Few empires have been as powerful as Rome, an empire that placed him on a cross and gave him Good Friday. But Easter came! Good Friday was not the last word!

Today's reading reflects on the power given that is greater than any enemy can have—resurrection power. Even though enemies may take our physical lives, that is not the end of us. Love raises us up. Even in the face of death, even after experiencing the worst our enemy can deal out, we are more than our conquerors. "What is sown is perishable, what is raised is imperishable."

PRAYER: **God of love, you have created me for communion with you and with others. Neither is easy for me all the time, Lord. I know that at one time I was your enemy, and I still fall back into that role. Yet you sent Christ to forgive me, to make peace. And in him you also give me the power of love and the blessed hope of resurrection that enable me to be an agent of reconciliation in my own home, at work, wherever I go. Help me, Lord, truly to love my enemies. Amen.**

An Awe-full People

February 19–25, 2001 • John Ed Mathison*

MONDAY, FEBRUARY 19 • Read Exodus 34:29-35

How glad we are that God gives humanity a second chance. God has delivered the commandments to Moses previously. Moses has made a covenant with God, which he and the people have broken. The tablets of the commandments have been shattered.

In Exodus 34 God asks Moses to bring two more tablets on which God will write the words from the former tablets. Moses meets with God for forty days and forty nights, serving as the people's representative before God. He will return as God's representative before the people.

The description of Moses' face when he returns to the people indicates the awesome power of being in God's presence and being God's representative. The skin on his face shines. The light on his face makes the Israelites afraid to come near him, so he wears a veil on his face.

While many of us do not see burning bushes or hear God speak audibly or have our faces light up so much we have to veil them, the difference God makes in our lives should be evident to other people. It should show on our faces. Being God's representative to people ought to show in every aspect of our lives. I saw a sign recently that read, "If you have joy in your heart, please notify your face." What do our facial expressions communicate? Does my face communicate joy? Does my face communicate that I am living in the presence of God?

PRAYER: As I live today, O God, may my face communicate your presence in my life and my eagerness to share the covenant you desire to make with all people. Amen.

---

*Senior minister, Frazer Memorial United Methodist Church, Montgomery, Alabama.

TUESDAY, FEBRUARY 20 • Read Psalm 99:1-5

The psalmist reminds us of the awesome power and presence of God. He begins by saying that where the Lord reigns, let the people tremble. God is positioned above the cherubim; let the earth shake. What a humbling experience to recognize how awesome God is.

Often the word *awe* is associated with God and God's people. The first few verses of Psalm 99 fascinate me because of their close correlation with the early church in the Book of Acts. Psalm 99:1 talks about the earth's shaking. Acts 4 talks about how the people were in the presence of God praying and the place where they gathered began to shake (v. 31).

Psalm 99:3 describes how when we praise God we remember that God's name is awesome, that God is holy. Acts 2:43 describes how the early church worshiped and witnessed and "everyone was filled with awe" (NIV).

Wouldn't it be great if more of us were "awe-full" people? When society looks at what God is doing in our lives, does it stand in awe? Wouldn't it be wonderful if God raised up "awe-full" churches? What a witness to the world!

Awe-fullness begins when we discover how holy God is. It begins with worship. Psalm 99:5 reminds us that we are to exalt the Lord our God and "worship at his footstool."

The perspective must always be how awesome God is and our need as the created to worship the Creator. What an awesome experience!

PRAYER: O God, as I come into your presence this day, I am full of awe at your majesty and your dominion. I worship you. I desire to experience the strengthened power of your presence. May this be an "awe-full" day. Amen.

WEDNESDAY, FEBRUARY 21 • Read Psalm 99:6-9

The Bible records how people call on God and God answers. The psalmist specifically mentions Moses, Aaron, and Samuel as people who called on the Lord's name.

I strongly identify with them, especially when I find myself in situations where I am powerless. But I know that God wants me there, serving as God's representative in that situation. Like Moses, Aaron, and Samuel, I call upon God. It is so comforting to read that God answered them. God never leads me by turning a deaf ear to my cry. The Lord hears my plea and answers.

Today I believe that God has placed me precisely in the situation where I find myself. I also know that God will provide everything I need to accomplish the divine purpose and tasks for my life. I rely on God as my primary resource, present with me in every situation. The psalmist concludes in verse 9 that my responsibility is to extol and worship the Lord my God.

Today I will not strive to make things happen on my own but realize that my strength is in God. My joy comes in fulfilling the purpose God has given me.

Authentic strength is available when we acknowledge that the strength lies in the Creator, not the creature. Only then can we receive it.

PRAYER: O God, I get discouraged and am easily disappointed when I face tasks that seem too big. Many times I face challenges that seem as big as the Red Sea that Moses faced. I know that you are the same God who heard his cry. I know that you will hear my cry, and you will answer. Thank you for this assurance. Amen.

THURSDAY, FEBRUARY 22 • Read 2 Corinthians 3:12-18

Paul reminds us early in Chapter 3 that our adequacy for ministry does not come from our own talents or gifts but from God (vv. 5-6). The more we try to act on our own initiative, the more frustrated we become. The more we open ourselves to divine use and rely on God, the more effective and satisfying our ministry becomes.

Relying on God takes a lot of the pressure off me to perform, but it requires a lot of faith to surrender to God's leadership. This is the nature of the new covenant, a ministry that Paul describes in this passage.

One of the most exciting aspects of this concept is the liberty and freedom that God gives us in ministry (v. 17). We are not bound by the way other people do things or the way things have been done in the past. We are freed from those chains that would hinder our ministry.

A great danger resides in this opportunity when we use our liberty as license to do what we want to do rather than what God wants us to do. However, when we exercise our freedom within the context of God's leadership in our lives, we become powerful agents for teaching and tranforming others' lives. Paul affirms that this gives us hope, and that hope can help us become bold in our speech (v. 12). There is no need for timidity—we can speak with confidence and assurance because our ministry and witness are not our own but allow God to work through us.

This new covenant for ministry opens up unbelievable avenues for effectiveness, fulfillment, and purpose in our lives.

PRAYER: O God, may I experience the new covenant for ministry that brings effectiveness, fulfillment, and purpose to my life. Amen.

FRIDAY, FEBRUARY 23 • Read 2 Corinthians 4:1-2

In chapter 4 Paul resumes this theme of effective ministry given us by God. He offers a word of encouragement; we need not become discouraged or lose heart, because our ultimate success is not based on what we do but on our surrender to God.

I believe that we are to become as well trained as possible. We also need to sharpen our theological thinking and be constantly improving our skills. We must work hard at trying to present the good news of the gospel in the most appealing manner, but the prevailing factor in effective ministry is God.

I oftentimes get hung up on trying to be successful. I tend to measure success in earthly terms. Paul constantly reminds us that our success is not based on earthly evaluations but by eternal standards. My education and training can become a false strength to me, leading me to think that I can be successful in myself. My first commitment is connection to God, who is the source of power. Then I use my gifts and skills to communicate God's word to the people around me.

We live in a success-oriented society. The measure of our success comes not in secular terms but in God's terms. God does not call us to be successful but to be faithful.

Paul's teaching to the church of Corinth was consistent with his teaching to the people at Galatia when he said, "It is no longer I who live, but it is Christ who lives in me" (2:20). This defines successful and effective ministry.

PRAYER: O God, I commit my ministry to your standards of success today. Amen.

SATURDAY, FEBRUARY 24 • Read Luke 9:28-36

The life that the disciples enjoyed with Jesus was one of exciting surprises. The more they followed him, the more they came to know him and the more surprises they encountered at what he could do.

The Transfiguration is such an example. Peter, James, and John have been with Jesus and have experienced the miracles of the feeding of the five thousand and his ministries of healing. They have heard the tremendous parables that he told so simply. The three are accompanying Jesus up the mountain for prayer, a fairly common event, and they're probably expecting an ordinary prayer meeting.

But something extraordinary happens. Luke states that the appearance of Jesus' face changes, and the disciples see Moses and Elijah talking with him. Peter immediately suggests that they should make three dwellings, an expression of his commitment and devotion to what he has experienced.

One of the toughest things for me to express adequately to God is my genuine feelings. Oftentimes I make quick suggestions, which might or might not be well thought out. Amazingly God always responds regardless of the foolishness of my suggestion.

Clearly God's message from the Transfiguration experience is that Jesus is the Son of God and that we should listen to him (v. 35). Never again in the minds of Peter, James, and John would there be any serious doubts about Jesus' identity. At times in their lives they might waiver in their commitment to him, but the Transfiguration solidified in their minds the reality of who Jesus really was.

PRAYER: O God, use events and circumstances today to communicate your awesome power. May I receive these experiences and respond appropriately. Amen.

SUNDAY, FEBRUARY 25 • Read Luke 9:38-44
TRANSFIGURATION SUNDAY

It amazes me that the overwhelming experience of the Transfiguration is followed immediately by the continued ministry of Jesus among people. This was such a high visibility event, but he and the disciples return to their everyday ministry.

Each of us has high points in ministry, mountaintop experiences. I tend to want to stay on the mountaintop a long time—not coming back down into the valley where people are hurting. Jesus immediately goes back to meet people's needs.

For Jesus people are always a priority. He encounters a man whose little boy is possessed by a spirit and restores him to health. God's greatness as evidenced by Jesus' healing power astounds everyone watching.

Today the world is still full of people who are hurting emotionally, physically, and spiritually. Jesus directed his ministry to meet their specific needs. I believe that God's call to the church in the new century will be to meet people at their point of need and to minister to them in the name of Christ, offering healing, help, and hope.

Today is Sunday. Often we feel closest to God on Sunday; perhaps we have mountaintop experiences on this day of sabbath. Monday is sometimes dreaded. I pray that the Transfiguration will help us clearly know and see Jesus for who he is, renewing and refreshing us for our ministry to the hurting people in our world—not only on Monday but every day of our lives.

PRAYER: O God, thank you for mountaintop experiences. Make me as grateful for the everyday experiences of life, and may I approach them with equal vigor and commitment. Amen.

God's Boundless Love

February 26–March 4, 2001 • Nancy Mairs*

MONDAY, FEBRUARY 26 • Read Deuteronomy 26:8-11

In Moses' agrarian society the "first fruit of the ground" might have been dates and figs and olives, as well as grain. By today's standards, the life of Moses' people seems a meager existence: a brief life devoted to cultivating crops and rearing livestock in a semi-arid land. Yet Moses enjoins them to "rejoice" in the harvest—not to measure it. Not to grumble that it's too small to feed the growing number of mouths at the table. Not to fret that next year they might not fare as well—a hard freeze killing off grapevines or an infestation of locusts chomping up wheat. Just delight in what the land has produced and thank God for it.

How differently we live, bombarded with messages that whatever we have is too small, too old, too shabby, too boring. We can't simply rejoice in our possessions or else we wouldn't want more of them. *More*, not *enough*, is the operant word that drives the mad but not mysterious cycle of production, acquisition, disposal, replacement—God doesn't enter this loop. God might be thought to send a parching wind that shrivels the first sprouts or a rain that rescues the crop at the last moment, but Bill Gates sends the software that keeps our lives humming along.

No one wants to go back to the subsistence living of biblical times, but we can't sustain our current rapacious habits either. We need to bring forward into our own world the sense of sufficiency, even abundance, felt by those who believed they had been given "a land of milk and honey." We need to cultivate in ourselves the habit of gratitude for the plenty we have.

PRAYER: Teach me, O Holy One, to recognize and rejoice in life's bounteous sweetness. Amen.

---

*Poet and essayist; Roman Catholic; member of the Community of Christ of the Desert, which emphasizes commitment to issues of peace and justice; living in Boston, Massachusetts.

TUESDAY, FEBRUARY 27 • **Read Deuteronomy 26:1-7**

Moses instructs the Israelites not just to feel good about the crops they've raised and gathered in, not even just to sing God's praises for providing the land and the conditions that have resulted in such plenty but actually to put some of the produce in a basket and take it to the priest as an offering to God—the *first* fruit, mind you. No hanging back to see if there will be a surplus and offering the leftovers. Through this offering, Moses says, "you shall rejoice in all the good things the LORD your God has given to you and your household" (26:11, NIV). *And what would have become of the offering*, I wonder. Perhaps it would have been left to rot, but such waste seems unlikely. Might not the priest have taken it to feed himself and his family or to share with the poor?

In any case, the message seems clear: Although gratitude for God's bounty puts us into right relation with our possessions, it doesn't fulfill our responsibility for them. As Moses enjoins, we need to give some of them away—and not our junk either but real goods for which people might have some use. But no act seems harder in a society premised on scarcity rather than abundance. If we believe that no matter how much we own, more will make us safer from any possible want, then we can't bear to part with the least thing. We need to practice feeling safe when others have more.

We could start simply, as a way of observing Lent. If every affluent household regularly bought enough food for one more member, giving that "spirit" member's portion to a poor person, either directly or through a community agency, soon hunger would cease to be the social scandal it is throughout the world. God expects me to celebrate my abundance through giving. Who am I to disappoint God?

PRAYER: Yahweh, I am fortunate to live in a place and time of plenty. May I trust in your goodness enough to keep only what I need and use the rest to further your work in the world. Amen.

WEDNESDAY, FEBRUARY 28 • Read Psalm 91:1-2

ASH WEDNESDAY

Watching my daughter stroke my grandson Trevor's feathery head as he nurses, I am struck anew by how essential a sense of safety is to human well-being. The infant craves it from the moment of birth (and even before) and achieves it initially through being amply nourished and cuddled close to a large, warm, sheltering form. For years of my adulthood, I was puzzled by a sensation I often felt, generally just after I had curled up under the bedclothes: a firm pressure, from the back of my neck along my spine and around the curve of my body. Out of the blue one night it occurred to me that this was a hand—the hand of a giant to accommodate my present size but only that of a normal adult if I were a newborn—providing the protection and support I had enjoyed in infancy.

Such comfort is withdrawn gradually, as it must be if we are to mature. Trevor's brother Colin is no longer given the breast but must sit at the table and chase his spaghetti around his plate himself. One day he'll have to earn the money to buy the spaghetti and learn to cook it too. One day he may nurture new beings. The world will seem a colder, scarier place than it did when a parent's arms could engulf him. No wonder one of our strongest images of the holy invokes a parent's loving care: shelter, shadow, refuge.

Yet much as we yearn for God's steadfast protection, we tend not to rely on it. In pondering the tension between scarcity and plenty, for example, I'm aware of how easy it is to acquire new possessions and hang onto the ones I have for fear that I'll suffer without them. If only I can say with the psalmist, "my God, in whom I trust," I will feel the confidence of a well-nurtured child no matter what I own or do not own.

PRAYER: Abba, you give unbounded care to the least of your creatures. Increase in us all the sense of safety we gain from trusting your love. Amen.

THURSDAY, MARCH 1 • Read Romans 10:8*b*-13

In view of our human craving to be cradled in protective arms, it's hardly surprising that the words *safe* and *save* share the same root. To be saved is to be made safe and, in the theological sense, to be made safe forever: from sin and from death, those terrors that harrow us as soon as we can grasp their universality and inevitability. We all stand in desperate need of salvation. Ironic, then, that Christianity has from early times reduced salvation to a commodity, creating "haves" and "have-nots" in the spiritual as in the material economy, as though God, the All-Embracing Parent, would gather some children into safety and shut the rest out in the cold (or the eternal flames, depending on your image of hell).

Saint Paul seems to exhibit this kind of thinking when he writes, "If you confess with your lips that Jesus is Lord and believe in your heart that God raised him from the dead, you will be saved," as though only by fulfilling certain conditions can you escape damnation. But I believe God's love to be unconditional. God loves us to distraction no matter what we "confess" or "believe," making "no distinction between Jew and Greek; the same Lord is Lord of all and bestows his riches upon all who call upon him" (NIV). The difference between the believers and the nonbelievers lies not in God's treatment of them but in the way they experience themselves in the world.

Those who know that God can be called upon and who trust in God's unstinting affection and mercy are not necessarily better, purer, more favored by God, more deserving of "salvation." They are saved in that they feel safe: cherished and supported whatever happens to them. Those who can't sense God's presence don't need to be threatened with an eternity in hell for their skepticism. They are there already.

PRAYER: Thank you, God, for the gift of faith that saves me from loneliness and fear. May I live in such a way that others come to believe in the richness of your love. Amen.

FRIDAY, MARCH 2 • Read Luke 4:1-4

Lent, like Jesus' prophetic career, begins and ends in temptation. "If you are the Son of God," whispers the small voice of doubt that Luke characterizes as the devil, "command this stone to become bread." "Let him save himself!" shout the doubting people as he hangs on the cross. Throughout, Jesus is not immune to these enticements, but he steadfastly resists.

I love the homeliness, the apparent harmlessness, of the first temptation, which must have attracted Jesus. If he was the Son of God, why not find out what his special status had to offer? Who would ever know, out here in the wilderness? And really, after forty days without eating a bite, not even locusts and wild honey, he was famished. Just one stone, a little one .... Imagine how convenient it would be to possess the power to turn one substance into another. When your stomach rumbled, you could pick up any old rock and transform it into a nice chunk of rye or sourdough. And if bread, why not a little something to go with it? A handful of pebbles could mutate into a bunch of grapes. And then, why stop with food? A cave could become a castle, a pumpkin a Rolls-Royce—ah yes, such visions are the stuff of fairy tales, not the facts of life. And it's a good thing too, since the temptation to transmogrify the world would doubtless run away with you, and a geology made out of bread would lack a certain necessary structure and stability. Stones need to be stones.

But Jesus understood that neither stones nor bread, the things of the world, matter very much. Though necessary, they are not sufficient for "life" as Jesus intends the word. He has nothing against feeding hungry people, as the tale of the loaves and fishes makes clear, but the crowd fed that day had gathered not for a picnic but because they were starved for the word of God. That was nourishment to live by.

PRAYER: Help me, Jesus, to discern and discard life's trivialities and to sustain myself on the truth in your teaching. Amen.

SATURDAY, MARCH 3 • **Read Luke 4:5-13**

Who is this "devil" Jesus encounters at the end of his lonely desert sojourn? Is he (and I've always heard him referred to as "he," even though historically women have been thought to embody evil more often than men) an actual entity? If so, does he have a red body, a horned head, a barbed tail, and cloven hooves like the figure on the tin from which my mother made me many a lunch in my childhood? Or is he beautiful and proud and furious like Milton's Lucifer, a fallen angel? And whatever his appearance and behavior, do I need to fear him?

From the way we talk about him, the devil certainly seems like a real and rather menacing figure, lurking as he does in the details, capable of trapping us between himself and the deep blue sea, taking the hindmost, making us pay. Accused of a sinful act, we protest our helplessness: "The devil made me do it!" In Luke's account, he is so powerful a being that he can confer authority over all the world to whoever worships him.

Yet Jesus shows no fear as he resists the devil's blandishments, and upon his composure we can model our own behavior. For many people the devil is a bogeyman who materializes out of some nether world to lead us astray. But some of us discover that the devil is a projection of our own worst dreams and desires. If we worship these, enslave ourselves to them, insist upon their fulfillment regardless of the cost to others, we may feel a torment worthy of the devil's dwelling place. But we don't have to live in thrall to greed and ambition, Jesus shows us. We can choose to serve God instead.

PRAYER: Teach me, my God, to relinquish my own limited aims, focusing instead on the ways I can best shape my life to your worship and service. Amen.

SUNDAY, MARCH 4 • Read Psalm 91:9-16

FIRST SUNDAY IN LENT

Psalm 91 resonates with reassurances of God's watchful benevolence, yet the devil chooses a passage from just this text to tempt Jesus. "Go ahead," he taunts at the top of the temple, the place reserved for praising and worshiping God. "Jump! Surely God won't let his own little boy splatter all over those stones down there like a squashed pomegranate." As usual, his thinking is laughably literalistic. He's taken the words of a song, a poem, the most figurative form of human expression, to be a realistic description of what God will do to protect the faithful.

I'm always puzzled by people who think of God in this way, as a worker of miracles great and small on our personal behalf. My husband has survived an advanced and deadly form of cancer, an outcome so unlikely that some ascribe it to God's intervention. Many of the friends in our Living with Cancer support group have died, however. Are we to think that God elected to save George from the disease but abandoned them? The eleven-month-old grandchild of dear friends was electrocuted in a freak water accident. If God can prevent such accidents, what are we to think of Shane's death? That God blinked?

The devil's simplistic approach to God's power may tempt us to "test" God as Jesus forbids. "If you really love me, God," it urges us to say, "then you'll give me an *A* on my test, send me the rent money, cure my cold, make a fine day for my wedding...." And then the failed test, the eviction notice, the pneumonia, the nuptial tornado prove that God's love has failed.

God's love never fails. But we do. If we think of God as a powerful figure who hands out or withholds divine favors, we'll never grasp the reality celebrated in Psalm 91. But if we sense God as a constant presence with us through all life's vicissitudes, we'll begin to understand what it means to be so loved.

PRAYER: Thank you, Holy Spirit, for accompanying me with tenderness and sympathy through all the events of my life. Amen.

The Goodness of the Lord

March 5–11, 2001 • Louis Jordan*

MONDAY, MARCH 5 • Read Luke 9:34-36

It's a terrifying experience. While driving along a mountain road at night, you move into a dense, pea-soup fog that the headlights fail even to illumine, much less penetrate. Or perhaps a mild snowstorm suddenly turns into a blinding blizzard, blending the landscape, the highway, the sky, and everything outside the car's interior into a solid, dimensionless white haze. At these moments, stark terror overwhelms us as we brake.

We take comfort in thinking of God as the light of the world that beats back the darkness and enlightens us with wisdom and the warm love of gentle grace. We want God to make us feel good. We want our experiences of God to be revealing and uplifting. We want to stand on the mountaintop, to know our destiny, and to see the world with clarity and perfect vision.

On the unknown mount of the Transfiguration, Peter, James, and John awake to a moment of glory and splendor. Peter, the ever-fallible, does a very human thing: He tries to take control. Suddenly a cloud envelops them, and they are terrified. In the terror and darkness, God exerts ultimate control. God speaks, leaving no doubt as to Jesus' divinity.

In other biblical accounts, God is also concealed and shrouded in dark clouds. Sometimes we have to venture into the terrifying blackness of loss, mystery, and the unknown. Indeed, revelation and truth often come in times of darkness and terror because, in those moments, we have no control and must surrender to our base nature—and to the grace of God.

PRAYER: God, when I cannot see the way, may I rely on you. Amen.

---

*Sunday school teacher, active layperson, businessman; member of Belmont United Methodist Church, Nashville, Tennessee.

TUESDAY, MARCH 6 • Read Luke 9:28-33

Travel through the South and you see the monuments. At Appomattox, Chickamauga, and Andersonville, there are dozens of them, tall spires commemorating the fallen heroes of the Civil War. I often wonder whether marble and stonemasons were cheaper and more plentiful at the turn of the last century or our grandparents and great-grandparents had a greater sense of history.

Even if postmodern society has diminished our propensity to build monuments, humankind still has the instinctive need to commemorate special times. When we experience a historic moment or an extraordinary event, our reaction is the same as that of Peter and his companions when they see Jesus talking with Moses and Elijah. We want to take a picture, write a history, edit a videotape, or do something to record and preserve the special significance of the moment.

This is our human way of dealing with sacred mysteries, with things that we cannot comprehend or understand. How can Moses and Elijah be conversing with Jesus? How can Jesus' face change and his clothes become dazzling white? How can our human minds process the reality of such a divine encounter? Simply put, they can't; but they do recognize its significance. So we try to position the unknowable in a particular place and time by constructing a shelter or a monument.

And like Peter, we really don't know what to say or do after an intense encounter with God. Our impulse is to stop time and hold onto the miracle. Only Jesus knew the true significance of this sacred moment called the Transfiguration. It completed his preparation and empowered him to fulfill his destiny—not on a holy mountaintop but on a worldly hill named Golgotha.

SUGGESTION FOR MEDITATION: **Envision a monument. Imagine its builders and the special events they were trying to commemorate. Sense the meaning of that moment and arise with power and determination to enter your everyday world.**

WEDNESDAY, MARCH 7 • Read Philippians 3:17–4:1

I find both the tone and theology of this passage troublesome. Paul seems arrogant ("join others in following my example," NIV) and condemning ("their destiny is destruction," NIV). The underlying theological concept of "earthly things" coveted by the "enemies of the cross of Christ" (NIV) in contrast with those who have "citizenship in heaven" (NIV) resonates of Platonic dualism and calls into question the sacredness of God's earthly creation. Furthermore, Paul's contention that Christ has "the power that enables him to bring everything under his control" (NIV) doesn't exactly reinforce the concept of free will or contemporary theories of faith development.

Others may react in a totally different way to this passage. In their quest to escape unpleasant worldly conditions, they may find solace in envisioning the kingdom of heaven. They may look forward to a day of transformation. They may desire authority figures like Paul who emphasize strict codes for living. Globalization and pluralism create daily examples of differences in theology and Christian beliefs.

So is it enough to say that one person's theological discards are another's treasure? Hardly. Recognizing and accepting diversity is only the first step. True growth and spiritual development occurs only when we examine the context of different beliefs and when we accept the reality that our personal views may not always be absolutely right. We must ask—and answer—hard questions. Spiritual growth requires an open heart and prayerful attitude. When I consider the historical realities of Paul's letter and the zeal and dedication of his ministry, I begin to understand his position. Perhaps I could even cast aside *my* arrogance and learn. I still might differ with Paul, but I would have a richer faith.

PRAYER: Help me, God, to move beyond acknowledgment of differences and to reach the point of understanding. Encourage my willingness to relinquish beliefs in order to grow. Amen.

THURSDAY, MARCH 8 • Read Luke 13:31-35

Jesus' remark that "no prophet can die outside Jerusalem" (NIV) is a puzzling one. Certainly this statement cannot be taken literally, and Jesus refers to Jerusalem symbolically as the seat of religious authority. He has just dismissed concerns about danger from Herod. He knows that his approaching conflict is with religious, not secular, powers and that his destiny can only be fulfilled at the heart of his society. It is time to move out of the wings and onto center stage. He must play this final scene in Jerusalem. Jesus also knows that the timing is not yet ripe for his ministry to end. He will choose the time and place of his final journey.

Others in history also have sensed the appropriate moment and place to move from preparation to action. Imagine what might have happened if Luther had written his ninety-five theses but not nailed them to the Wittenburg church door. Imagine the difference if Martin Luther King Jr. had studied Ghandi and written eloquent essays but failed to take to the streets of Montgomery, Selma, and Birmingham. Imagine also if Luther, King, and countless other great men and women had rushed into action without preparation or a keen understanding of the importance of their actions. No doubt history would be far different.

Few persons change history so dramatically. Yet, like Jesus, we all face moments when we must decide a course of action. Sometimes we can choose the time, sometimes the place. Sometimes we can control our destiny, sometimes not. However, we can be spiritually and mentally prepared for these moments. Then, with God's help, we will be ready to decide and act.

SUGGESTION FOR MEDITATION: **Reflect on a time when you faced an important decision. Consider the time, the place, your preparation, and the outcome. Prayerfully think about the outcome of this moment and its impact on subsequent actions.**

FRIDAY, MARCH 9 • Read Genesis 15:1-12, 17-18

Okay, it's stupid. But I bet I'm not the only one who does it. On holidays when the U. S. Postal Service doesn't deliver mail, I still meander to the mailbox to see if anything is there. Even though I realize that no mail will be delivered, I still need a visible sign to believe the mailbox is actually empty.

Perhaps the same psychological need leads Abram to say, "O Lord God, how am I to know…?" after God tells him that he will possess the land that will become Israel. Abram certainly wants to believe God, but he still needs a visible sign. Hearing the word of God is not enough. Abram, like most of us, wants something that he can see or touch.

One key to this story is the nature of the signs that God then provides. A notarized deed doesn't drop from the sky. Nor do road signs appear on the caravan trails saying, "Welcome to Abram's Land." God asks Abram to prepare a ritual sacrifice. After dark, a smoking firepot with a torch mysteriously passes through the prepared sacrifice. God becomes real through ritual and mystery, not from the headlines of the morning paper.

Abram was fortunate; afterward God again spoke directly to him and reiterated the promise. Few people hear God's voice so clearly. For most, it's a matter of interpreting signs, which can only be done with hearts and minds attuned to God through practicing spiritual disciplines, performing charitable acts, and participating in the ritual of worship. Once we have prepared ourselves in this manner, we will discover the signs that God has set before us. Like Abram, we then can claim our heritage and destiny.

SUGGESTION FOR MEDITATION: **Quietly contemplate the ways you keep your heart and mind attuned to God. Reflect on the opportunities ahead in the next week that might enable you to better understand signs from God.**

SATURDAY, MARCH 10 • **Read Psalm 27**

Luckily, the psalmist did not have access to a thesaurus built into a word processor. Mine lists the antonyms of *faith* as *doubt* and *distrust*. To the psalmist, the alternative to faith is not doubt; it is fear. His faith provides courage and confidence to overcome the fear of defeat by evildoers, adversaries, and foes.

More often, doubt, distrust, and uncertainty are presented as the killers of faith. Accordingly, the questioning of doctrines, traditional beliefs, and scriptural authority diminishes faith. In truth, those who assert that doctrines and scriptures should not be challenged have succumbed to the very fear that the psalmist depicts as the opposite of faith. They stand behind a false wall of authority rather than growing their faith in the garden of life.

The Spanish philosopher Miguel de Unamuno said, "Life is doubt, and faith without doubt is nothing but death." Clearly we affirm certain fundamental, unchanging truths about God's love for us and about our relationships with others. At the same time, medical and technological advances, encounters with other cultures, emerging social issues, and life changes all challenge our personal beliefs. In this rapidly changing world, few people have the same beliefs at sixty that they had at age twenty. We need not fear the questions raised by new, complex issues and retreat to dogma. Rather we can welcome the opportunity to examine and refine our faith.

It's impossible to box our faith up in a neat package and decide that it's a finished product. That's what the Pharisees did before Jesus began telling parables, asking questions, and raising doubts in people's minds. Thank goodness a few disciples were willing to doubt the conventions and established wisdom of that era. Can we do less today?

SUGGESTION FOR MEDITATION: **Take a moment to list three beliefs that you held dear as a youth or young adult. Reflect on how these beliefs have changed or been challenged.**

SUNDAY, MARCH 11 • Read Psalm 27:13

SECOND SUNDAY IN LENT

Popular theologians argue that God has a game plan for our lives, and if we play the game of life successfully we will know the glory of God in heaven. Perhaps I'm just impatient, but I can't wait until then to see the glory of God. Therefore the psalmist truly speaks to me when he states, "I believe that I shall see the goodness of the Lord in the land of the living."

Rewards in heaven may come, but, like Hamlet, we honestly cannot know what shape or form our existence might take once we have "shuffled off this mortal coil." Therefore, I'm more interested in what might happen now rather that what might happen then. I need to feel the presence of God today.

Thankfully, God provides bountiful opportunities to do so. It might come in the innocent smile of a child, an act of kindness by a youth, or the gentle compassion of a lover. It could come through a brilliant sunrise or a refreshing rain. The Lord's goodness is present in acts of justice or vibrant social dialogue. We don't have to wait to see the goodness of God; it permeates the land of the living.

Of course, so do evil and the failures of humanity. They bombard us in the evening news and our everyday experience. How do we react? One option is to do nothing, to become cynical and pessimistic, perhaps to decide that goodness can only come at the end of time. I believe it is far better to allow God to empower us to perform our own humble acts of love. Then we shall find God in the land of the living.

SUGGESTION FOR MEDITATION: **Recite this verse from Psalm 27 three times. Empty your mind and reflect on the goodness of God on earth today. Close by again reciting the verse three times.**

Precious Memories

March 12–18, 2001 • Roger K. Swanson*

MONDAY, MARCH 12 • Read Isaiah 55:1-5

"Ho, everyone who thirsts, come to the waters; and you that have no money, come, buy and eat! Come, buy wine and milk without money and without price." What a gift of grace to impoverished pilgrims on their way home to Zion with few possessions except the hope of a different and more abundant future. My first remembered experience with grace occurred early in my life, as a boy with a voracious appetite for the adventures found in books. A frequent visitor to the city library, I was always late returning the books. I often delayed because I had no money, which made the late fees even higher.

One day I returned long-overdue books with no money in my pocket. I thought I would lose my borrowing privileges, and I should have. Instead, the librarian did an extraordinary thing. She opened her pocketbook and paid the fine for me. I had trouble understanding her action, except—as I have since figured out—she was giving me a gift of grace.

I later came to understand that God is in the grace-giving business. Grace offers something with no cost involved except acceptance. The Zion-bound pilgrims had few resources to fall back on. What they had was an awesome God who had adopted them by grace, led them to a promised land, forgiven them the sin of rebellion, and promised to be with them through all their future. What is your first remembered experience of God's grace?

PRAYER: O God, for all the remembrances of your grace toward me, incarnated in human kindness and generosity, I thank you. May I be a living remembrance of your grace to someone today. Amen.

---

*Director of Operation Evangelization, Florida Annual Conference of The United Methodist Church; living in Lakeland, Florida.

TUESDAY, MARCH 13 • Read Isaiah 55:6-9

"Seek the Lord while he may be found," counsels the prophet Isaiah to the exiles returning from Babylon. "Call upon him while he is near." These words seem to imply that there is a particular time and place where God is to be found. The exiles are encouraged to seek God "while he may be found" and "while he is near." Mystics and scholars are always debating how God reveals Godself. When and where has God chosen to be available to us? When and where have you been most aware of God's presence? Some people discover God's presence in the grandeur and diversity of the natural world. For others God is most present in deep quietness, whenever and wherever found. Still others find God in the gathered community of faith.

However, my own experience calls me to attentiveness to whatever is happening in my life at the moment, whether in any of the above or in some other setting. In other words, God is to be found and is available to me in the here and now!

What is happening in your life today through which God might be seeking to reveal Godself to you? Is it a celebration of sorts, a day of work, or perhaps some difficult passage in your life? God has promised to be a daily presence. As disciples of Jesus, our daily discipline is to seek God's nearness and to pray.

A year ago I had surgery for the removal of a cancer. My mind kept pushing me into the future. *Am I about to become a statistic? Am I ready for my death?* Family and friends, however, kept me in the present with their constant demonstration of love and care until I realized the importance of the present moment. Today I am persuaded that serious illness can be a means of grace as it keeps us focused on the God who comes to us in each and every moment.

PRAYER: O God, keep me attentive to my need for the "daily bread" of your presence, that I may receive all you have to offer and give to others all I have to give. Amen.

WEDNESDAY, MARCH 14 • Read Psalm 63:1-4

"O God, you are my God, I seek you, / my soul thirsts for you; / my flesh faints for you, / as in a dry and weary land / where there is no water." Tradition says that Psalm 63 is a prayer of David while he was hiding from Saul in the wilderness of Judah. We can feel the discomfort of the desert in his language. He "thirsts" for God; the emptiness in his soul mirrors the "dry and weary land" of the vicinity of the Dead Sea where he hides. The familiar places of prayer, the tabernacle and the shrines, are not accessible to David in his desert refuge. What he does have available to him are the precious memories of past times of rich, spiritual blessings.

What are the landmarks of your spiritual journey? Where have you looked upon God? Some may recall the family dinner table of childhood and youth or the summer church camp where early decisions for Christ were made around a closing campfire. My landmarks, like David's, center around sanctuaries in which I have gathered with a congregational family that celebrated God and prayed together. Prominent among the several sanctuaries I have called home is the first one, where I experienced the richness of acceptance and joy of Christian community. In that sanctuary I received the embrace of Christian hospitality and heard the "good news" of God's incredible love in Jesus Christ preached. Here also I met with other youth and explored, in frank and open discussion, the questions that my mind posed to the faith I had been offered. But what I most treasure about this sanctuary is that here I was offered a way to respond in celebration and commitment to Jesus. I have traveled many miles through many sanctuaries, but the memory of that first sanctuary remains fresh.

PRAYER: I thank you, God, for the ways you led and blessed me even before I knew your name and that you continue to lead and bless me even when I forget your name. Amen.

THURSDAY, MARCH 15 • **Read Psalm 63:5-11**

"You look like you could use some help!" he said, as I struggled with a carton too big for one person to carry. I could, and he did! Whoever he or she may be, one who helps us in our need is blessed indeed! Hiding from Saul in the Judean desert, David remembers that God has been his helper in times past. Was he thinking, I wonder, of the years in which he had been a shepherd, living alone much of the time and by his wits? As a shepherd he had faced "the paw of the lion and...the paw of the bear" (1 Sam. 17:37), as well, I'm sure, the demons that often visit the lonely. In those days, he confesses, God had been his help.

This was even truer with the greatest challenge of his young life, his meeting with the gigantic Goliath, the Philistine champion. No Israelite would answer the challenge to settle the differences of the two armies by a single Israeli doing battle with Goliath. "Give me a man!" (1 Sam. 17:10) taunted Goliath. David, only a young man, stepped forward and offered himself. "You are just a boy" (1 Sam. 17:33), said Saul. "The Lord," David answered, "who saved me from the paw of the lion and from the paw of the bear, will save me from the hand of this Philistine" (1 Sam. 17:37).

"You come to me with sword and spear and javelin," the young warrior said to Goliath, "but I come to you in the name of the Lord of hosts, the God of the armies of Israel, whom you have defied" (1 Sam. 17:45). As we know, David prevailed that day with only a sling and a stone—and an incredible trust in God. Undoubtedly this remembrance of God's faithfulness remained with him as a keystone of his faith as he was called to face other giants, including the building of a nation and his own sin! What giants have you and God faced together?

PRAYER: Helper God, you have been there when I have needed you the most, when I have needed wisdom, healing, and direction. I rest confident that I will never have to face any adversary alone. Amen.

FRIDAY, MARCH 16 • Read 1 Corinthians 10:1-7

My recent change of jobs has required a move to a different state as well as to a different primary mode of transportation. Instead of flying, as I did previously, I now drive to most destinations over still unfamiliar roads. In other words, I have to pay attention both to maps and road signs along the way.

I seem to see two signs more than others. One reads "Construction Ahead." America is busy rebuilding its road system. The other sign, new to me, declares in flashing lights: "CAUTION." The particular reason for caution varies. Sometimes lanes change up ahead, or the sign warns of unusual traffic congestion. No matter the reason, those flashing letters always get my attention.

In his first letter to the Corinthians, Paul cautions these new Christians to remember the hard lessons that others have learned before them. "Do not become idolaters," he counsels. Do not, in other words, put anything God has made in God's place. Idolatry worships the creation rather than the creator. It settles for second best! It attributes ultimate value to things that are penultimate, throwing the proverbial "monkey wrench" into our value system, which—as Paul recounts—can be disastrous. "God was not pleased with most of them," declares the apostle, "and they were struck down in the wilderness." When we get our values out of order, chaos results.

PRAYER: Today, O God, help me to keep the main thing the main thing, to live a godly day, honoring you in all that I do. Amen.

SATURDAY, MARCH 17 • Read 1 Corinthians 10:8-13

"God is faithful, and he will not let you be tested beyond your strength, but with the testing he will also provide the way out so that you may be able to endure it." Because many of us experience life as a continual test of core values and of faith, these words offer comfort. Even Jesus began his ministry with a forty-day period of severe testing of his motives and his goals. However, Paul's words reflect more than a bit of apostolic experience and wisdom. He offers the promise of God. God will not allow any test of our faith to outdistance the resources God has provided. God has provided the way out.

What is that "way out"? What are the resources available to us? First, there is God, accessible to us through prayer and fasting, through the reading of scripture and participation in the sacraments, and in the worship and daily life of the community of Christ. Historically, these disciplines, called the "means of grace," have helped God's people access and experience the daily presence of God. Jesus was able to turn aside the tempter through prayer and fasting and with the word of scripture (Matt. 4:1-11). He answered the tempter each time, "It is written...."

We now observe the Christian season of Lent, a period of preparation for baptism for persons new to faith and a time for all Christians to remember the suffering and death of Christ and to draw closer to God. God has provided the means. It falls to us to employ them for our spiritual benefit.

PRAYER: O God, you have provided everything I need to stay in daily touch with you. As a disciple, help me lead a disciplined life, following the means of grace. Amen.

SUNDAY, MARCH 18 • Read Luke 13:1-9

THIRD SUNDAY IN LENT

We conclude this week where we began, with an offer of a gift of grace. In the story Jesus tells in Luke 13, a three-year-old fig tree has yet to produce fruit. "Cut it down!" orders the land-owner to his gardener. Good land, after all, is at a premium; and though they might be pleasant to look at, fig trees are expected to bear fruit. Earlier in Luke, Jesus has warned that "every tree…that does not bear good fruit is cut down and thrown into the fire" (Luke 3:9).

Jesus also expects his disciples to bear fruit. "My Father is glorified by this, that you bear much fruit and become my disciples" (John 15:8). Does he speak of the fruits of the Spirit listed in Galatians 5:22: love, joy, peace, patience, kindness, generosity, faithfulness, gentleness, and self-control? Or does he speak of making other disciples through the witness of word and deed? In either case, Jesus expects there to be some fruit, some observable difference in the lives of his disciples.

Whatever was in Jesus' mind, the fact is that none of us measures up to his expectations. However, the good news is that God is patient. In this story the gardener asks for a one-year grace period, during which he promises to give the tree special attention. The tree is given a second chance. One of my precious memories is of such a second chance in which disaster was turned aside. It is Jesus' way to give us another chance. Yet this story also makes it clear that there is a last chance—not when God shuts us out, but when we shut ourselves out by our unwillingness to act on the grace we are offered.

PRAYER: O God, I confess that I have at times grieved your spirit, but your grace has been constant. Grant me remission of my sins, true repentance, and amendment of life, through Jesus Christ my Lord. Amen.

Changed by God's Love

March 19–25, 2001 • Timothy L. Bias*

MONDAY, MARCH 19 • Read Psalm 32

Be glad in the Lord and rejoice, O righteous;
and shout for joy, all you upright in heart.

David is happy. His sin has been forgiven. For David and for us, there is no greater blessing or happiness than to experience God's forgiveness. In this psalm, David goes from disobedience to repentance to worship. He experiences both spiritual release and physical healing, which are the gifts of true forgiveness. He has strayed from God's purpose. When he repents, God no longer sees him as off the path. When he accepts God's promise of forgiveness, God puts him back upon the path of righteousness.

Just like David, when we do not turn from our disobedience, we feel emotional pain, alienation from God, and even physical heaviness or weakness. But when we repent, we experience release from our sin and an assurance of God's acceptance. When we repent, we turn from our way and open ourselves in obedience to God's way and instruction.

God not only shows us the way but guides us in the way. Then like David, we shout for joy, for God is our salvation. Our hearts are renewed with the presence of God's plan and purpose. True repentance is a work of the heart. When we experience the forgiveness of God, respond by turning away from our sin, and come to know God's mercy, we are glad in the Lord and our hearts are full of righteousness.

PRAYER: O God, I have felt the heaviness of your hand upon me. Today I turn from my disobedience. I do not want to hide any longer. Make me righteous in my heart. Amen.

---

*Pastor, First United Methodist Church, Peoria, Illinois.

TUESDAY, MARCH 20 • Read Joshua 5:9-12

On the day after the passover, on that very day, they ate the produce of the land, unleavened cakes and parched grain. The manna ceased on the day they ate the produce of the land, and the Israelites no longer had manna; they ate the crops of the land of Canaan that year.

Can you imagine how the Israelites felt? As soon as they celebrated the Passover, the manna ceased. As soon as they ate the produce of the land of Canaan, things changed. The Passover celebration provided a bonding experience and tied the people to their history as well as their future. But as soon as they celebrated the Passover, God no longer provided the miraculous daily appearance of manna. They must have been frightened as their circumstances changed.

As our circumstances change and as we grow beyond one kind of provision to another, God knows what to provide. Our response is to trust and obey. We are to keep ourselves open to God's provision. Part of what makes our congregations dull to many people is that we have accommodated ourselves to the status quo. Change is upsetting, so we do not want anyone to rock the boat. As circumstances change, we become frightened. Instead of turning to God in trust and obedience, we often turn on one another.

Joshua reminds us that change is a fact of life and that God's provision always suffices. For the Israelites to enjoy the fruit of Canaan, they had to change their methods of gathering food. God will provide.

PRAYER: **O God, you are my hiding place. When I turn to you in the midst of change, I trust you to provide and to surround me with what I need to live into tomorrow. Amen.**

WEDNESDAY, MARCH 21 • Read 2 Corinthians 5:16

From now on, therefore, we regard no one from a human point of view; even thought we once knew Christ from a human point of view, we know him no longer in that way.

Paul believed that Christ acted on behalf of all the human race. The act of Jesus' dying on the cross became the foundation of Paul's thinking and action. When the implication of the statement "He died for all" began to get hold of Paul, it changed his feelings about every person in the world.

Paul had been shaped by a religious world that glorified the deed and ignored the motive. But in his relationship with Jesus Christ he came to realize that fear or guilt or a sense of duty or a desire to impress God and others were inadequate reasons for sharing the gospel. The fact that every person he met was the object of God's eternal love and was someone for whom Christ died defined the nature of his ministry.

Paul did not exploit or manipulate people. He loved them the way Christ loved them. The moment we become Christian we no longer have the right or the luxury to pick and choose whom we love. We begin to see people as God sees them. Each and every person is someone for whom Christ died and someone we love.

Sometimes we think we cannot love certain people for any number of reasons; but as new creatures in Christ, we have the presence and power of God's transforming love within us. Accepting and loving others becomes a matter of heart. Just as the psalmist has reminded us, it becomes a matter of righteousness. For Paul, a new humanity was being created. As Christians, we act as the new humanity.

PRAYER: O God, help me love people as you love them. I offer myself to you for that purpose today. Amen.

THURSDAY, MARCH 22 • Read 2 Corinthians 5:16-17

So if anyone is in Christ, there is a new creation: everything old has passed away; see, everything has become new!

There are few words filled with more hope than these from Paul. He announces that the new order that will last forever has already begun. His good news is that when persons become Christians, followers or learners of Jesus Christ, then God makes them part of that new creation. Paul is not talking about a cosmetic change. He speaks of an inner change that only God can make. It is a newness that ties together our past, our present, and our future. It is a newness that, while not seen immediately, will eventually reflect itself in every area of life.

When Christ comes into our lives, he creates a new unity, a new direction, new goals, and a new commitment. Just as the psalmist reminded us earlier this week, God welcomes us home. God cleanses us and makes us new. God restores us to God's self. Paul understood God's work to be in Christ Jesus. God, through Christ, is the loving Father who welcomes us home. God cleanses us with the blood of Christ. If we are in Christ, we are freed from guilt and reconciled to God. We are new people with a new hope and a new focus.

PRAYER: O God, thank you for your transforming love that makes us new people in Jesus Christ. As you renew our hearts, give us faith and courage to risk becoming the people you created us to be. Amen.

FRIDAY, MARCH 23 • Read 2 Corinthians 5:17-21

In Christ God was reconciling the world to himself, not counting their trespasses against them, and entrusting the message of reconciliation to us. So we are ambassadors for Christ, since God is making his appeal through us; we entreat you on behalf of Christ, be reconciled to God. For our sake he made him to be sin who knew no sin, so that in him we might become the righteousness of God.

Paul inspires and challenges us as he answers his critics in defense of his ministry. Through these words he describes the work that God has given Christians to do in the world—the work of bringing God and people together. Authentic religion, particularly the Christian faith, is always interested in the nature of humanity's relationship with God.

Everyone lives in some kind of relationship with God. It has been God's intention from the beginning for people to live in a relationship of trust and obedience. But sin (a basic distortion of and disconnection from God) entered the world and created a mistrust of God and a basic disobedience of God's plan and purpose for all creation.

God took the initiative, through Christ, to reach out in love to reestablish the relationship. To define his ministry and ours, Paul took a phrase from the world of politics, "So we are ambassadors for Christ." In Paul's world this statement would be clearly understood as describing the act of representing Christ in the Roman Empire. Our role is to represent Christ in the culture in which we live. We are new creatures in Christ. The world will know of Christ through our living in a loving relationship with God and with one another.

PRAYER: O God, use me as an instrument of reconciliation. Empower me to represent you in all my relationships today. Amen.

SATURDAY, MARCH 24 • Read Luke 15:1-3, 11-24

So he set off and went to his father. But while he was still far off, his father saw him and was filled with compassion; he ran and put his arms around him and kissed him. Then the son said to him, "Father, I have sinned against heaven and before you; I am no longer worthy to be called your son."

When the prodigal son comes "to himself," he decides to say no to his old way of life and to return home. He is broken and discouraged by his pursuit of the world's empty promises. When confronted by the holiness of his father's love and forgiveness, he speaks freely of his sinfulness and is free to repent.

When we are honest with ourselves, we know we are not holy people. On the outside we put on masks and act as if everything is fine and we have no real problems; but on the inside we feel phony and begin to dislike ourselves. When we repent, we name the truth of who we are. We name it to God, to the world, and to ourselves. We know that God already knows it; but our conscious confession that we are in need of God's help frees us from the self-imposed prison of guilt and self-hatred as well as the misguided desire to hide them.

When we drop the mask of dishonesty, we take a step toward a life of faith-filled integrity where the exterior life reflects the interior life. We know ourselves and repent, returning to the loving parent who has already met us with unconditional love and forgiveness in Jesus Christ.

PRAYER: O God, help me be honest with myself and meet me with love and forgiveness when I decide to return to you. Amen.

SUNDAY, MARCH 25 • Read Luke 15:25-32

FOURTH SUNDAY IN LENT

Now his elder son was in the field; and when he came and approached the house, he heard music and dancing. He called one of the slaves and asked what was going on. He replied, "Your brother has come, and your father has killed the fatted calf, because he has got him back safe and sound." Then he became angry and refused to go in.

As the younger son returns from a pen of rebellion, the older son reveals he is in a pen of self-pity. On the outside the older son is everything a father could want in a son. But on the inside he is overcome by jealousy, consumed by anger, and blinded by bitterness. His younger brother returns home, and dad throws a party.

The older son is bitter because he is focusing on what he doesn't have and has forgotten what he does have. Unable to accept the fact that his brother has been received with love and forgiveness, he refuses to come to the party.

For David there was no greater blessing or happiness than the experience of God's forgiveness. To enjoy the fruit of Canaan, the Israelites had to change their way of thinking about gathering food. Because of Christ, Paul began to see people as God sees them.

The younger son has experienced the love and forgiveness of a loving father, but the older son has not. Even though he has been with the father on the outside, he has not experienced this loving relationship on the inside. The older son's repentance will come by attending the party. Think about it! Would you go to the party?

PRAYER: O God, remind me again today that I am yours and that I can celebrate with all others who experience your love and forgiveness in Christ Jesus. Amen.

A Way in the Wilderness

March 26–April 1, 2001 • Kathleen Crockford Ackley*

MONDAY, MARCH 26 • Read Isaiah 43:16-21

On our first day of vacation in the Arizona desert, surrounded by the majestic red rocks of Sedona, my husband and I arose before dawn and headed for Bell Rock. Something powerful seemed to pull our travel-weary bodies out of bed, so that we would not miss the first rays of sunlight glinting off the towering rock formations. We found the perfect spot and waited for God's show to begin. We watched, enchanted, as the sun inched higher and higher in the sky, playing off the rocks in a spectacular array of reds, oranges, and golds.

Still wrapped in a sense of wonder, we decided to walk some of the trail around the rock to view the sun's continuing journey. Before we knew it we were hiking in earnest. Initially the trail was wide and obvious. We felt confident that we could navigate without a problem, relying on our memories of the trail map. Soon we were frozen with indecision; another trail crossed the one we were on, and the way back seemed ambiguous.

Then, by the side of the trail at the crossroads was a pile of large stones neatly stacked like a tower. A sign? Yes! Someone had been here before us, someone who knew how confusing this intersection would seem to those who didn't know the way. Like God, who promised to "make a way in the wilderness," there was help to guide our way. Relieved, we followed the stone-marked trail, giving thanks to God for the one who had gone before us.

PRAYER: O God, sometimes my wilderness wanderings take me to desert places where I become confused and fearful. Help me recognize the signs you place along my way. Amen.

---

*Director of Marketing for United Church Press and The Pilgrim Press; clergy in The United Church of Christ, Cleveland, Ohio.

TUESDAY, MARCH 27 • Read Psalm 126:1-3

The Lord has done great things for us.

As you read Psalm 126 imagine a group of faithful pilgrims singing the words of this psalm as they travel together to Jerusalem for a festival celebration. This psalm is one of a collection of "pilgrim psalms" (Psalms 120–34) people sang or recited as they made their way on a pilgrimage to the holy city of Jerusalem. A pilgrimage for the ancient Hebrew was a significant event—a call from the ordinary, everyday routines to a journey to the sacred, the holy. It was a search for meaning, purpose, restoration, renewal, and transformation.

People of all ages gathered in the main town in their region on the eve of the pilgrimage, spending the night in the open air to avoid the risk of exposure to anything that might make them ritually "unclean," which would prevent their journey to the Temple, the most sacred place in the most sacred city.

The journey might take days, but the hopeful and reflective words of the song express the expectation of what could happen: "When the Lord restored the fortunes of Zion, / we were like those who dream. / Then our mouth was filled with laughter, and our tongue with shouts of joy."

When have you dreamed of making a "pilgrimage" to a new and different place, hoping to be refreshed, changed, renewed? How has God spoken to your dreams? Where is this sacred place to which you are called to travel? What practices will you adopt to keep your life in the "open air," so that you are ready to meet the Holy and be transformed? What could lead you to say, "The Lord has done great things for us, and we rejoiced"?

PRAYER: **God of a pilgrim people, you know the places in my life that have become stale and dry. When I dream of becoming new again, you invite me with a stirring breeze of fresh air to make a pilgrimage to the sacred center of my life with you and discover what truly gives meaning to my life. Stay close, O God. At times the way is rough. Amen.**

WEDNESDAY, MARCH 28 • Read Psalm 126:4-6

Those who go out weeping...shall come home with shouts of joy.

Dear friends of mine longed to be parents. After two pregnancies that ended in miscarriage after the first trimester, they were convinced that their hearts' desire to have children would never become a reality. Tears of sorrow and grief overflowed, a strong contrast with the feeling of being dried up. Prayers of lament, commingled with unspoken hopes of someday nurturing children of their own, filled the nights and days.

But the tears did water the ground where seeds of promise were buried. When a friend encouraged them to think about adoption, the idea took root in their hearts. After filling out mountains of paperwork and receiving approval from social services, they completed the application. Now it was time to wait.

During the difficult time of waiting, the sustaining force of prayer brought my friends through the seemingly endless time. They prayed for the child who was to become theirs. They prayed for her birth parents. They prayed for the persons who would care for her until she came to be with them.

What a joyous day it was when our friends got word that the time had come for them to travel to China to bring their daughter home. The long days and nights of waiting were over. The prayers that sustained them became shouts of joy!

God's compassion sustained our friends during the tearful times of sorrow and grief. God's mercy brought together these loving parents and this amazing child. God's love continues to grace their days as they become a family, with all of its blessings and challenges. God hears the desires of our hearts.

PRAYER: God of grace and mercy, knowing the desires of my heart, help me discern what is right for me. You help me face my sorrows, disappointments, and the things that hold me captive. Release me from all that binds me so that I can know the joy you want for me. Amen.

THURSDAY, MARCH 29 • Read Philippians 3:4b-11

If anyone else has reason to be confident in the flesh,
I have more.

Paul had everything going for him—the right lineage, the right upbringing, the right attitude about this upstart religious movement threatening the status quo of the traditional faith of Israel. Then an encounter with Christ turned his life upside down. He confesses to the followers of Jesus in Philippi: "Yet whatever gains I had, these I have come to regard as loss because of Christ. More than that, I regard everything as loss because of the surpassing value of knowing Christ Jesus my Lord."

Paul attests to the amazing paradox of letting go to gain all. When he lets go of the idea of his own righteousness based on externals such as family background, social status, religious purity, and legal rectitude, he finds something far more valuable—God's righteousness.

It may seem that Paul has replaced one obsession for another, being as compulsive in his pursuit of Christ as he was in his keeping of the law. But we can learn from the difference in his focus. Paul now knows that the righteousness he seeks to live out is from God. His encounter with Christ changes his values. He willingly participates in God's loving pursuit of him.

Have you ever stopped long enough in your pursuit of what you value—friends, family, job, financial security, leisure time—to face the sobering fact that God loves you totally and completely, without reservation? No matter how you think you have succeeded or failed, no matter how you think you have accomplished what you have on your own, God wants you to know more than anything that you are loved simply because you are you. Can you live with that?

PRAYER: Some have called you "the hound of heaven," O God. You pursue me with a fierce and tender love if I will open myself to the pursuit. Help me let go of my defenses so that I may experience the joy of being loved unconditionally by you. Amen.

FRIDAY, MARCH 30 • Read Philippians 3:12-14

I press on toward the goal for the prize of the heavenly call of God in Christ Jesus.

These words of Paul are so vivid in their description. Imagine a runner pushing with every ounce of muscle and determination to reach the finish line and complete the race. But the goal, as Paul elaborates, is not necessarily to win the prize for being first but to be faithful to God's call.

Discerning what God calls us to is a lifetime endeavor. As we change, grow, and develop new skills and interests, we may experience God's call in different and challenging ways. Sometimes we express the call through our career choices, our family relationships, our community involvement, or our financial commitments.

When Osecola McCarthy, an elderly woman who made her living as a wash woman, gave $150,000 to the scholarship fund of the University of Southern Mississippi, the amount may have surprised her friends and neighbors but not the spirit of the gift. Years of spending little on herself, trusting the words of scripture, and believing in the power of God's call to do something big as she shared her wealth to "help the children" resulted in an action consistent with a lifetime of pressing toward the goal.

What is God calling you to press on to do? Where are you called, not to be first, but to be faithful? What obstacles seem to be in your way? How can you find the strength to "press on"? Who or what is near to help you? Perhaps it is time to take an inventory of what you enjoy doing, what you value, what gives you a sense of joy for God's sake. What consistency do you evidence among your actions and where you spend your time, energy, and other resources?

PRAYER: When I need coaching or coaxing, Holy One, you are there to help me stretch my spiritual muscles if I will trust your lead. Help me be open to your call today. Amen.

Saturday, March 31 • Read John 12:1-3

Mary took a pound of costly perfume...anointed Jesus' feet, and wiped them with her hair.

What an amazing and extravagant gesture of love and gratitude Mary expresses to Jesus at the Passover celebration in her home when she anoints his feet with perfume. The act may seem strange or quaint to our twenty-first century sensibilities; but in first-century terms, the height of hospitality included welcoming guests and providing them an opportunity to wash the dust of the road from their feet. Mary's elaboration of this courtesy, using costly perfume made of pure nard to anoint Jesus' feet and wiping them with her hair, conveys the depth of her devotion to her friend, teacher, and Lord.

A friend told me about a Lenten discipline that she practiced out of a need to express her devotion to Jesus. She took some prayer time to ask God how she, like Mary, could do something extravagant. What emerged from the prayer was a sense that she needed to simplify her life and do "more with less." She decided to awaken each day during Lent, look around her house, and select a belonging that she would give away to someone. She did not want discard things that had little value but to see what she possessed of value that would bring joy to someone else. She discovered that she had as much fun figuring out to whom she would give an item as she had deciding what items to give away. Built into this practice was the fact that she did not expect or want anything in return. Sometimes the recipients were friends, family members, or colleagues. Sometimes they were total strangers. When asked "Why?" and "Why me?" she replied, "It is my way of saying thank you to God for all that God has done for me." Extravagant? You decide.

Prayer: Ever-giving God, anoint my heart with your fragrant perfume so that I may be able to give with humility the gifts that express your extravagant love for all creation. Amen.

SUNDAY, APRIL 1 • **Read John 12:4-8**

FIFTH SUNDAY IN LENT

"Leave her alone....You always have the poor with you, but you do not always have me."

The sweet fragrance of Mary's devotion to Jesus fills the first half of this story in John's Gospel. But the tone shifts dramatically when Judas Iscariot, also one of the dinner guests, questions Mary's actions: "Why was this perfume not sold...and the money given to the poor?" A laudable concern? Perhaps, if it were genuine. But Jesus can see into Judas's heart, and he challenges his motivations. Jesus clearly perceives that Judas's words do not match his true intentions.

To varying degrees, we all have a piece of Judas in us. Our words are not always consistent with our deeds or intentions. Indeed the softness of the words we choose may serve only to mask the hardness of our hearts. A careful examination of our souls will surface our lack of authenticity. Without question, examining one's conscience is difficult work of the soul.

The good news is that we are not left to do this hard work alone. In Jesus we have a trusted friend and teacher who can help us see into our own hearts and make sense of what we find there. Facing hard truths about ourselves can be daunting, but the unique power of faith can help. The tool of faith can help us face truth without fear.

With this tool of faith prayer can be a time of deep listening. Coming into a time of prayer with complete trust, we might ask the question, "What would you want me to understand about my life right now, God?" Count on hearing God's response and receiving the power to reconcile even the most tangled places.

PRAYER: **Gracious and loving God, you know me more deeply than I know myself. What would you want me to understand about my life right now? Prepare me to hear your answer. Amen.**

Let This Mind Be in You

April 2–8, 2001 • William H. Willimon*

MONDAY, APRIL 2 • Read Philippians 2:5-11

Some days the world is a tuxedo,
and you are a pair of brown shoes.

Is there anything worse than being out of step? A fellow campus minister learned this the hard way. At the first meeting of his campus ministry group in the fall, someone thought it would be cool to engage in a little game where everyone was to keep in rhythm with the leader. If you fell out of rhythm, you had to stand up and tell the group about yourself. The next week two students who had visited told the follow-up callers, "We're never coming back. We didn't come to church to be made fun of just because we can't keep in step with you."

Think of this week and the story we are enacting as a kind of dance whose rhythms do not come naturally. Jesus' path turns toward Jerusalem. When he says to his disciples, "I'm going to Jerusalem," he is not only going up to the big city; he is dancing toward his death.

Jesus enters a city full of raucous excitement. Passover, Israel's Fourth of July, is in full swing and Jesus rides in on…a donkey! Bobbing along, out of step. His disciples expect him to enter on a war horse like a conquering hero, but he bounces in on a donkey, humbling himself. And we, his would-be disciples, must also be out of step, keeping time to a countercultural syncopation if we are to waltz with him.

PRAYER: Lord Jesus, help me obediently follow you down that narrow path toward doing God's will rather than my own. Amen.

---

*Dean of the Chapel and Professor of Christian Ministry at Duke University, Durham, North Carolina.

Tuesday, April 3 • Read Philippians 2:5-11

There is a movement in Philippians 2. It begins low, then goes high. Watch where Jesus walks—downward. Here is a way against our natural inclination. Downward mobility.

The call is not to keep time with your own beat, your own subjective inner drum; to devise your own rhythm and stick to it. The call is to hear a different drummer, Jesus. He walks down a narrow path toward a cross. Furthermore, he bids us to walk that way as well. "Let this mind be in you, which was also in Christ Jesus" (KJV). This beat is to be lodged so deep in our brains that we walk as he walked.

A friend of mine spoke of someone who had risen high in his organization, a man whose ambitions had been mostly realized.

"In a way, I've always been grateful to that man," said my friend.

"Grateful? Why?" I asked.

"He helped curb my own ambition. He showed me the limits of success and the goals I thought I wanted. To watch him, to observe the price he has had to pay for what he has gotten, the way he has had to compromise and flatter has helped me decide that I don't want what I thought I had to have."

The call to the upward path is seductive. It often begins with, "I hope that we can count on you to be a team player," or someone will firmly assert, "Of course, you've got to face facts, go along to get along, right?" And why be out of step?

But because you belong to Christ and not to the firm or to the ambitious desires of this world, you may have the grace to say, "Sorry, I've promised this dance to someone else."

PRAYER: Lord, give me the grace to resist the subtle temptations of this world and to follow you. Amen.

WEDNESDAY, APRIL 4 • Read Luke 22:21-27

We have only been with him at the table for a short time on Thursday night when Jesus drops the bombshell. "But see, the one who betrays me is with me, and his hand is on the table." And with that, everyone raises his hand off the table. "Is it I?" we all begin to ask.

And well we should. For one verse later (Luke 22:24) an argument breaks out among us over who will be the greatest in the kingdom of God. "When we get him elected Messiah, and the kingdom is come, who will get to be on the cabinet?" And in this dispute over greatness, we reveal that all of us have our power-grubbing, little hands on the table. If Jesus seeks his betrayer, he need look no further than the faces of those who stare at him around the table. Jesus is preparing to submit to suffering and death in obedience to the will of God; and here we are, arguing over who is the greatest.

What irony that at the end, Jesus' twelve best friends, the ones who have heard him teach and who have witnessed all of his work, demonstrate through this dispute that we have not the slightest notion of what he has been talking about.

Patiently he again tells us that we ought to be different, that his way is counter to the world's way, that we are to be those who serve rather than who seek greatness. Even as we dispute over greatness, preference, empowerment, and dominance, he is among us as one who serves. He passes the wine, his very blood; he offers bread, his broken body.

The hour is late. The journey is almost ended. When will we get the point?

PRAYER: Teach me, O Lord, your way of service so that I may be faithful to your way. Amen.

THURSDAY, APRIL 5 • Read Luke 22:15-30

"I have eagerly desired to eat this Passover with you before I suffer," he says to us huddled about the table with him.

Jesus' hospitality at the table this night is rather amazing, considering that he knows his betrayer is with him. Later on the cross, he will look down on the ones who have betrayed him and pray, "Father, forgive" (23:34). But Jesus' forgiveness does not begin at the cross. Even here at the table with his disciples, he gathers with the ones who will forsake him. There is no way for a person like Jesus to eat with people like us without a great deal of forgiveness. What a group of people with whom to spend your last night before execution!

Earlier Jesus' critics have charged, "This fellow welcomes sinners and eats with them" (15:2). The charge is well documented in the many meals Jesus has eaten with sinners of all stripes in the Gospel of Luke. "I have come to seek and to save the lost," he has responded to those who so severely have criticized the company he keeps.

Whenever we gather, in your church or mine, for the Lord's Supper or for a covered-dish supper, we cling to the memory of this Thursday night. I like the way the old service of Holy Communion put this matter in the Prayer of Humble Access: "We are not worthy to gather up the crumbs under thy table." How true. And therefore how gloriously redemptive that Jesus says to sinners such as we, "I eagerly desire to eat with you"—with you, and you, and you.

PRAYER: Lord Jesus, continue to welcome sinners to your gospel feast, for that is the only way we will ever be with you. Amen.

Friday, April 6 • Read Luke 23:18-23

Pilate goes to the people for a verdict on Jesus. And with one voice we scream, "Crucify!" So much for democracy in action.

Of all the moments of worship in Duke Chapel, few are more memorable than Palm/Passion Sunday. As the long, violent, dramatic story is read before the congregation, tension builds. We know how this story ends.This is always the way it ends—betrayal, violence, and death. Having raised so many crosses in the just passed bloody century, if we ought to be able to comprehend anything, it is a crucifixion.

The same crowd who yelled, "Hosanna!" when Jesus marched into Jerusalem a few days before now yells "Crucify him!" When we dramatize this reading on Palm Sunday, the voices arise from out of the congregation. "Crucify him!" They are our voices. They are the voices of fellow students, friends, faculty; the violent voices are our own. It is a stunning moment of terrible realization—the voices that scream for the crucifixion and death of Jesus are ours.

The good news is that Jesus does not flinch from the murderous mob. He does not sidestep the terror or miraculously escape *deus ex machina* into some divine world, hermetically sealed from human pain and terror. He comes among us. He passes through the waving palm branches (branches waved either to welcome him or to ward him off, I know not) and marches with us up to The Place of the Skull. He embraces all the terrible, horrifying, painful ambiguity of human existence. "Brothers and sisters, I love you still."

Prayer: Jesus, help me acknowledge my complicity in the pain of the world. Then, O Savior of my soul, forgive. Amen.

SATURDAY, APRIL 7 • Read Luke 23:26

I had asked a talented student, a drama major, to memorize the entire Gospel lesson (longest of the year!) for Palm/Passion Sunday. We met on the Saturday evening before to go over his part in the Sunday service.

"Am I free, when I recite this tomorrow morning, to change anything?" he asked.

"Well, we usually don't do that. What do you want to change?" I responded.

"It's where this guy Simon comes in."

"Simon of Cyrene?" I asked.

"Yea, him. It just doesn't fit. It messes up the flow. Jesus has just been given over for crucifixion. He has his cross, and he is on his way, and then there's this Simon who is asked to help him carry his cross. It seems an intrusion to me."

"Please, don't edit out Simon," I said quietly. "He's there for us."

"There for who?"

"For us, all of us ordinary, forgettable little people who sometimes get enlisted to help Jesus with his cross. Maybe you think Jesus, because he's the Son of God, doesn't need any help. But look at Simon! He gets enlisted to carry the cross of Jesus. And he does. And then he disappears."

"So then maybe I'm like Simon," said the student.

"You got it," I said.

Only one man, only one verse in the longest Gospel lesson of the year, yet how we love Simon. He is the best you and I can hope for, that we might be enlisted to carry the cross, to help Jesus take back the world for God.

PRAYER: Lord, as you go the way of the cross, embolden me to walk that way with you. Amen.

Sunday, April 8 • Read Luke 22:39-46

Palm/Passion Sunday

In the Garden of Gethsemane, Jesus tells us to wait for him while he prays. We can't. We simply fall asleep. On Palm Sunday we are asked to wait. There is Jesus' triumphal entry into Jerusalem where palm branches wave amid shouts of "Hosanna!" But we must not yet sing Easter songs. We must wait.

Jesus parades into Jerusalem to go head-to-head with the powers that be. Who will win? Caesar or Jesus? The Prince of Darkness or the Prince of Peace? We must wait for victory.

Modern people find it hard to wait. We are most happy when we are most active. Control is our goal. We want the future in our hands to make tomorrow turn out right. Tragedy for us is merely a problem to be solved, a temporary obstacle to be overcome.

All of that sounds rather silly as we plod toward the cross. We have gotten organized, taken matters in our hands, acted, and where has it led? Up Golgotha, to a cross. We have acted. And now there is nothing for us to do but wait.

The wait is difficult, not just because we have spent weeks waiting for Easter, but also because preparing gives us a hint of our deepest fears. What if, after this final act of gore enacted on Golgotha, God at last leaves us to our own devices? What if this is the end of the road in our dealings with God? What if God abandons us to ourselves?

There is now nothing to do but wait. If there is to be a move in our relationship with God, the next move is God's.

PRAYER: Lord God, do not leave me to my own devices. Come, save me by your life-giving love and power. Amen.

The Heart of the Christian Mystery

April 9–15, 2001 • *Ted A. Campbell**

This week's readings take us to the heart of the Christian mystery: "The mystery that has been hidden throughout the ages and generations but has now been revealed to [God's] saints" (Col. 1:26). The Gospel lesson recounts the anointing of Jesus by Mary, an act that points to the mystery of Christ, for the word *Christ* means "the anointed one." Jesus' words in the Fourth Gospel also connect this event with his approaching death: The perfume that anoints would be used for his burial.

The Book of Hebrews further expounds the mystery of Christ, using the imagery of sacrifice. In the ancient world, a worshiper brought a pure offering to God, which represented the worshiper's giving of self to God. The offering, not its destruction, was the primary idea in the notion of sacrifice. In this week's Bible lessons, we shall see how the events of Holy Week encompassed this and other aspects of sacrifice. We see that Christ's life and death (together) were his pure offering to God.

At the heart of the Christian mystery lies Christ's self-offering. But we do not contemplate Christ's self-offering abstractly. We might recall that on this spring day, April 9, 1945, Nazis executed Dietrich Bonhoeffer. He joined the Christian saints and martyrs through the ages who were empowered by Christ's grace to offer their lives to God. At the heart of the Christian mystery is Christ's eternal sacrifice and Christ's call for us to follow him.

PRAYER: Eternal God, give me grace to discern the mystery of Christ, even if I cannot fully comprehend it. Empower me to follow his example of loving sacrifice. Amen.

---

*Professor of the History of Christianity at Wesley Theological Seminary, Washington D.C.; elder in The United Methodist Church.

TUESDAY, APRIL 10 • Read John 12:20-36

The Gospel lesson from the twelfth chapter of Saint John includes this short narrative about Greek people visiting Jerusalem who wished to see Jesus. It is not a trivial story in John's Gospel, for clearly the Fourth Gospel intended to speak to people from the Greek or Hellenistic world.

The Gospel begins with the words, "In the beginning was the Word, and the Word was with God, and the Word was God" (John 1:1). The term used here for "beginning," *arche*, was the term for the "stuff" of which the universe is made. Greek philosophers before Socrates had argued about what this primordial stuff might be. The term translated "Word" here, *logos*, was a central notion in Greek thought after the time of Plato, denoting the "reason" or "thought word" that gave structure to the universe. The Gospel of John appealed to Hellenistic people by using terms drawn from their own culture to expound the mystery of Christ.

Saint Paul expresses a similar notion in First Corinthians, and he also uses Greek concepts: "For Jews demand signs and Greeks demand wisdom [*sophia*], but we proclaim Christ crucified. A stumbling block to Jews and foolishness to Gentiles, but to those who are the called, both Jews and Greeks, Christ the power of God and the wisdom [*sophia*] of God."

We find this scripture inscribed over the apse of the Greek cathedral of St. Sophia in Washington, D.C. But "St. Sophia" was no human saint: The term refers to Christ as the eternal Wisdom of God. The Christian mystery, then, is a mystery intended for all peoples. It is a mystery that cannot be fully explained in any human language but demands expression in every language and every culture.

PRAYER: Eternal God, give me grace to discern the mystery of Christ, even if I cannot fully comprehend it. Empower me to perceive beyond the limitations of my own tongue and culture the glory of the mystery of Christ transcending all human limitations. Amen.

WEDNESDAY, APRIL 11 • Read John 13:21-32

The reading for today points us again to the mystery of Christ's sacrifice. In John 13 Jesus foretells his coming betrayal by Judas. Verse 21 says that Jesus "was troubled in spirit." We would say that he was upset. But how could this be? Was he not the very Word who "in the beginning was with God" and "was God"? How could this One be "troubled in spirit"?

It is not a new question for Christians. Through the fifth Christian century (the 400s C.E.) Christians pondered the mystery of how God could become a human being. A central verse for them was John 1:14, "The Word became flesh and lived among us." But verses like John 13:21 and John 11:35 ("Jesus began to weep") make it clear that the mystery of Christ was not simply a divine mind inhabiting human flesh. Christ's sacrifice involved his very real, very human mental and spiritual anguish, as well as his bodily suffering. The lesson from Hebrews 12 makes the same point: that "for the sake of the joy that was set before him [Jesus] endured the cross, disregarding its shame" (Heb. 12:2). The Savior's sacrifice involved "shame" as well as bodily suffering.

This passage calls us to follow the example of Jesus' self-offering. "Therefore…, let us also lay aside every weight and the sin that clings so closely, and let us run with perseverance the race that is set before us, looking to Jesus the pioneer and perfecter of our faith" (Heb. 12:1-2a).

At the heart of the mystery of Christ is the mystery of incarnation: the mystery of the infinite God who takes on the limitations of a human body and soul for our sake. The scriptures call us to follow him as "the pioneer and perfecter of our faith."

PRAYER: Eternal God, give me grace to discern the mystery of Christ, even if I cannot fully comprehend it. Empower me to follow Jesus, and in following him to offer my own life as a reasonable, living, and holy sacrifice, acceptable to you. Amen.

THURSDAY, APRIL 12 • Read John 13:1-17, 31*b*-35

MAUNDY THURSDAY

In the narrative of the supper given in each of the four Gospels and in 1 Corinthians 11, the mystery of Christ is associated with the sacrifice of the Passover lamb. In the account in First Corinthians and in Matthew, Mark, and Luke, the meal occurs at the Passover seder on Thursday evening ("on the night when he was betrayed"). In this case, the body of the sacrificed lamb would have lain on the table when Jesus said, "This is my body that is [broken] for you" and "This cup is the new covenant in my blood" (1 Cor. 11:24-25).

John's Gospel suggests that the supper took place on the evening before the Passover (see John 13:1). This chronology would place the crucifixion at noon on the day when the Passover lambs were offered in the Temple, again associating Jesus' death with this most central of Jewish sacrifices.

Ancient sacrifices involved a pure offering that represented the worshiper's self-giving to God, often involving a ritual meal in which worshipers consumed part of the sacrificed offering. In their understanding, the meal represented restored fellowship between themselves and God. With this same understanding, Charles Wesley wrote about the Lord's Supper,

> *See him set forth before your eyes;*
> *behold the bleeding sacrifice;*
> *his offered love make haste to embrace,*
> *and freely now be saved by grace.*

At the heart of the Christian mystery is the sacred meal through which Christians participate in the Savior's sacrifice, receiving his sacred body and blood.

PRAYER: Eternal God, give us grace to discern the mystery of Christ, even if we cannot fully comprehend it. Empower us to discern in Holy Communion a means of divine grace, indeed the presence of our Savior. Amen.

FRIDAY, APRIL 13 • **Read John 18:1–19:42**

GOOD FRIDAY

We now come, literally, to the crux of the matter, for *crux* means "cross." The Gospel narratives echo an older account of Jesus' work that comes from within a decade or two of the crucifixion: "that Christ died for our sins in accordance with the scriptures" (1 Cor. 15:3). The very first words that testify to Jesus associate his death with the forgiveness of sins.

Protestant spirituality often has focused on Jesus' death as the central moment in salvation history. But the mystery goes deeper, because Jesus' sacrificial death is the culmination of his whole life and is linked to his resurrection. The crucifixion is part of the great mystery of the self-giving of God in Christ. Perhaps the poetry of Charles Wesley better expresses such an idea.

> *'Tis mystery all: th'Immortal dies!*
> *Who can explore his strange design?*
> *In vain the first-born seraph tries*
> *to sound the depths of love divine.*
> *'Tis mercy all! Let earth adore;*
> *let angel minds inquire no more.*

The image of "sounding the depths" suggests the practice of making a sound on the surface of a deep body of water, then timing the echo that comes in response. The longer the wait for the echo, the deeper the water. In Wesley's use of this image, Christ tries or proves the depth of divine love. His cry on the cross goes down into the depths of the divine being, and we wait for the echo. And we wait. And we are waiting still. But the echo never returns, for the divine love shown in the cross is simply unfathomable, immeasurable, bottomless.

PRAYER: Eternal God, give me grace to discern the mystery of Christ, even if I cannot fully comprehend it. Empower me to find in Christ's sacrificial death the assurance of the depths of divine love for all humankind. Amen.

SATURDAY, APRIL 14 • Read Matthew 27:57-66

HOLY SATURDAY

The Gospel for Holy Saturday recounts the burial of Jesus. Christ experienced a real human death. "He descended into hell," in the traditional words of the Apostles' Creed. But this does not mean that Christ went to the place of eternal punishment; it means that he went to "the place of the dead" (Hades). It is another way of saying that Christ died as truly as any other human has died or surely will die.

Paul's words in Romans 6 suggest a deeper meaning to the Savior's death and burial. By way of baptism, we are buried with Christ. Paul surely has in mind the practice of baptism by immersion. Immersion involves the twofold motion of going down into water and rising out of the water again. So Paul writes, "Therefore we have been buried with him by baptism into death, so that, just as Christ was raised from the dead by the glory of the Father, so we too might walk in newness of life" (v. 4).

At the heart of the Christian mystery is the sacrament of baptism. In many churches anointing accompanies baptism, which shows how the Christian has become like Christ. Remember that *Christ* means "the anointed one." In their own ways, both of the sacraments commanded by Christ proclaim his sacrificial death and resurrection. Through them we participate in the mystery of Christ.

But Paul doesn't allow Christians to get too far into the depth of the mystery without calling us back to its ethical implications. We have been buried with Christ and will rise with Christ not for any esoteric purpose but to the end that "we too might walk in newness of life."

PRAYER: **Eternal God, give me grace to discern the mystery of Christ, even if I cannot fully comprehend it. Empower me to recall my identification with Christ's death, burial, and resurrection in my baptism, and give me grace to walk in newness of life, following him. Amen.**

SUNDAY, APRIL 15 • **Read John 20:1-18**

EASTER SUNDAY

We considered on Good Friday Paul's recollection of the terms in which he himself heard the message about Christ. In recounting these words, Paul focused on the message of Christ's bodily resurrection, for some persons in the Corinthian congregation had denied it. Paul recounts the witnesses to the Resurrection and makes the point that if Christ were not raised from the dead, our faith would be vain (1 Cor. 15:14).

Here is the final element in the mystery of Christ's sacrifice. We have already seen that in the ancient world, a sacrifice involved an offering to God and often a ritual meal. A third element was the burning of the offering. Ancient people believed that the burning of the offering showed God's acceptance of it. So Genesis 8:21 refers to God's smelling the "pleasing odor" of Noah's sacrifice and accepting his offering. The New Testament uses this same imagery to describe Christ's sacrifice: "Live in love, as Christ loved us and gave himself up for us, a fragrant offering and sacrifice to God" (Eph. 5:2).

The Resurrection denotes God's acceptance of Christ's offering. "The last enemy to be destroyed is death" (1 Cor. 15:26), and Christ's resurrection makes God's victory clear. The heart of the Christian mystery is the self-giving of God in Christ. The Resurrection completes God's perfect offering and sacrifice in Christ. The joy of Easter, then, is a solemn joy. It is a joy that comes at the end of wrenching pain, pain in which the very heart of God was broken for us. On Easter morning we recall the depth of God's suffering love. Together with all the company of heaven and with Christians of all generations, living and dead, we sing, "Alleluia! Christ is risen! Christ is risen indeed!"

PRAYER: Eternal God, give me grace to discern the mystery of Christ, even if I cannot fully comprehend it. Empower me so to live in this mystery that my life may be a pure and perfect offering to God. Bring me at the end to see Jesus, my risen Savior. Amen.

Resurrection Continues

April 16–22, 2001 • Arthur Gafke*

MONDAY, APRIL 16 • Read John 20:19-31

Jesus' appearance on the evening of the first day of the week echoes God's creation on the first day. "Then God said, 'Let there be light'; and there was light" (Gen. 1:3). Into the dark chaos before creation, God spoke the light. Into the fearfulness of the disciples, Jesus spoke the peace. "Peace be with you."

What an amazing speaking that brings light and peace. Even while we delight in the day and seek for peace, we wonder if this speaking light and peace can be quite as real as the darkness and the fearfulness.

The resurrection answer is, "The light shines in the darkness, and the darkness did not overcome it" (John 1:5). Jesus delivers the answer physically in a locked room, where he appears, speaks, breathes, and invites touch. In this astounding moment for the disciples, darkness and fear are overpowered with light and peace. Their belief in the darkness is replaced by their belief in Jesus.

In the dark and fearful times we need one another to speak the light and peace of Jesus. A parent's reassurance on a stormy night, a friend's counsel without rancor or judgment, a leader's empowering words to an anxious group can be resurrection speech. In such times and places belief in darkness is replaced by belief in the light and peace of Christ.

SUGGESTION FOR MEDITATION: When have you received the light and peace of Christ? When have you spoken them to others? Rejoice in such times. Resurrection continues.

---

*A United Methodist elder serving with The General Board of Higher Education and Ministry as Director of Clergy Supervision and Support Systems, Nashville, Tennessee.

TUESDAY, APRIL 17 • **Read John 20:21-23**

Again today our scripture takes us to that locked room with the disciples. Jesus enters and bids us peace. He commissions us, "So I send you." He breathes on us and bids us receive the Holy Spirit. Finally Jesus announces for us the power of forgiving or retaining the sins of others. What does this mean for you and me?

Unfortunately we of the disciple community can exercise the forgiving or retaining of sins with much arrogance, drawing judgments and announcing opinions. Yet we are measured and bound by the counsel of the Holy Spirit that Jesus breathes into us. Our actions are to extend the peace of Jesus. Humility replaces arrogance.

Several years ago a preacher spoke to the congregation about an issue that deeply divided the local community. He counseled that all judgments are first self-judgments. In the years since, I have discovered that all my judgments about someone else do indeed first apply to me. Such discovery forces humility.

Jesus offers the same insight in the Sermon on the Mount. "You have heard that it was said to those of ancient times, 'You shall not murder'; and 'whoever murders shall be liable to judgment.' But I say to you that if you are angry with a brother or sister, you will be liable to judgment" (Matt. 5:21-22). Who among us has not been angry with another person?

Jesus sends us as his agents. We speak words of peace. We forgive or retain sins.

PRAYER: **God, who in Jesus is my measure of judgment and grace, help me measure myself even as I measure others. May I know that all accusations are first self-accusations. And may I continue to know the guidance of your Holy Spirit. Amen.**

WEDNESDAY, APRIL 18 • **Read John 20:24-29**

Today's story from John again places the disciples in a house with the doors shut. This time Thomas is with them. Absent when Jesus appeared before, Thomas has declared that he will not believe unless he sees the marks on Jesus' hands and touches the wounds. Hence he has become known as doubting Thomas.

Fortunate for us that the story includes Thomas, because he represents so many of us who doubt. He expresses with refreshing clarity what he needs to believe—to see and to touch. Perhaps we would do well to be so clear about what we need for our own belief. We too often simply swim in our doubt of Jesus, offering him no opportunity to help move us from doubt to belief.

Thomas names what is necessary for his belief, and Jesus appears with the opportunity for Thomas to fulfill the conditions for belief. Other scriptures invite us to take the actions that let Jesus enter our lives. "Listen! I am standing at the door, knocking; if you hear my voice and open the door, I will come in to you and eat with you, and you with me" (Rev. 3:20). "Ask, and it will be given you; search, and you will find; knock, and the door will be opened for you" (Matt. 7:7).

Today if you have any doubt, what is necessary for your belief in Jesus? Is there a door to be opened, a request to make, a search to begin?

PRAYER: God of the risen Jesus, too often I close myself in, doubting the power of your resurrection in my life. Aid me in using my doubt as a pathway to belief. Aid me in asking, searching, knocking. Amen.

THURSDAY, APRIL 19 • **Read Psalm 150**

Blow the trumpets; play the lute and harp; shake the tambourine; hear the strings and pipe; dance. We praise God. Let the praise break forth in the most unlikely places and in silly ways. Let the laughter be deep, for we are God's people.

Two people in their late sixties meet, fall in love, and marry. After a few weeks the woman, laughing, reminds me of the story of Sarah and Abraham and says that she has been having morning sickness. Could God's liveliness express itself through pregnancy? We laugh with the wild thought of it.

In the sixth-grade church school class we practiced reading scripture aloud as a group using various tones, inflections, and moods to convey the sense of the passage. Psalm 150 invites a bright reading—sometimes breathless and always a bubbly and extravagant mood. Read it aloud and try different tones, inflections, and moods, or try a tambourine or drum as an aid.

Open the windows and doors of your soul, and let stale odors escape. Smell the sweet scent of God's love. Feel the tender touch on your skin that whispers of God's life with you. In quietness hear melody, rhythm, and beat in your own heart and soul. This is the praise of God. This gives reason for a bubbly and extravagant mood.

SUGGESTION FOR MEDITATION: **Name the places and the times in your life and in the lives of those you love when God bubbled with laughter, mirth, dance, and song. Name the persons for whom you pray this day that they may be able to praise God in simple or extravagant ways. Picture these precious persons dancing in the delight of God. Read Psalm 150 aloud as though you are a solo performer before an audience of angels, calling them to dance.**

FRIDAY, APRIL 20 • Read Acts 5:25-27

These verses in Acts offer dramatic confrontation between the apostles and the religious leaders of Jerusalem. The apostles proclaim Christ risen. The leaders, seeking to protect society from risk, have arrested the apostles, imprisoned them, sanctioned them not to speak; but to no avail.

John McPhee writes about the "principle of least astonishment" in his volume about geology entitled *Annals of the Former World*. The principle in geological terms states that all previous earth movement occurred for the purpose of yielding the current formation; there will be no subsequent movement of importance. Plate tectonics and the continued shifting of the earth's surface have shown the folly of the principle of least astonishment. Yet in our religious, political, and social lives many of us live by the principle. We believe that all previous movements were for the purpose of yielding the current situation and that any movements to change the current balance are dangerous and evil.

In the story of Acts the religious leaders stand against the radical message of the apostles, seeing it as evil. Similarly, leaders across the world today stand against proclamations that challenge current configurations. Such stances, as in the biblical accounts, are expressed with reverence and piety. Yet the Holy Spirit as the gift of Jesus continues to blow into people's lives. Bold witness will not be suppressed in the home, the workplace, the church, the courts and legislative halls, the stores and shops.

The vision of Christ's victory has been imprinted upon the world. It will not be obscured in jail, in suffering, in death.

PRAYER: Lord, may I feel the wind of your spirit, the courage of your grace, the healing of your love, and the joy of your hope this day. Amen.

Saturday, April 21 • Read Acts 5:27-32

The story in Acts continues with the drama of the apostles' arrest. The high priest clearly states the situation: "We gave you strict orders...yet here you have filled Jerusalem...and you are determined to bring this man's blood on us." The small, three-letter word *but* speaks volumes as it introduces Peter and the apostles' reply.

In English grammar the word *but* contradicts what has preceded it. When the scripture says, "But Peter and the apostles answered," it forces the reader to consider another depiction of the truth.

The high priest does what people in authority so often do: He states the situation of fact followed by attributing motive. "You are determined to bring this man's blood on us." How often do we, in our authority roles as parents, teachers, professionals, or leaders, state the situation and then give negative motive to those whom we cannot control? We may experience such situations beyond our control as personal affronts.

In the Acts account the apostles do not try to attack the religious leaders. Rather they simply proclaim the risen Christ. Nevertheless, the religious leaders choose to take their proclamation as a personal attack.

When have we gotten so stuck in our authority roles that we cannot see or hear a word of God? When do we define the dramas of our lives in personal terms? How can we transcend our roles enough to feel the movement of the Holy Spirit?

PRAYER: Christ, who did not count equality with God but became a servant, teach me today to hold my authority lightly so that in my use of power I may extend your healing and protecting presence in the world. Amen.

SUNDAY, APRIL 22 • **Read Revelation 1:4-8**

The lengthy salutation in today's scripture contrasts with current writing styles that shorten introductions in order to get to the point. We are taught to use action verbs and concise sentences and to give clear direction. Yet in today's passage grace and peace are offered with a diffuse affirmation of God who is timeless and Jesus Christ who is the faithful witness.

Following this extended introduction is the short but striking verb "look!" The weight of the word *look* often tempts a reader to draw eyes in the *oo*, as if the word itself looks and sees. As readers of the letters to the churches, we are admonished in this introduction to John's revelation to look, to see, to perceive the prevailing power of Jesus Christ who was dead but is alive.

This looking, this seeing, does not come automatically, because so many earthly powers still believe in the force of fear, the intimidation of bullying, the sweetness of bribery. The predominant perspective that saturates our eyes can make the seeing of Jesus Christ's power seem tame and irrelevant.

John's message to the churches in Asia reminds us to "look!" We need to help one another see Jesus Christ's power. Sometimes we may need to retreat from the world in order to rest our senses and renew our perceptions. At other times we may find ourselves in chaotic storms of life that hamper our looking and distort our seeing. When our eyes grow heavy, we may need reminders to look again.

We live our lives as though time is a string we can trace from yesterday through now to the future. This passage of scripture reminds us twice that God is the one who was, who is, who is to come. God hugs and encompasses all time simultaneously.

SUGGESTION FOR MEDITATION: Play with the verb "look" and explore ways you can use the verb to invite others to see God's presence with them.

God's Grace in Action

April 23–29, 2001 • Evelyn Laycock*

Evangelical Christianity uses the story of the Damascus Road experience as the paradigm of conversion. The first thing we might note is Luke's placement of Saul's experience; it is not the beginning of the biographical section on Saul. Saul's conversion fits within the context of other conversions. Beginning with Acts 8:4 we read about the conversion of the Samaritans, then the Ethiopian eunuch, then Saul. Each of these dynamic experiences takes us farther away from the original community of believers in Jerusalem to seeing the command of Jesus, "Go therefore and make disciples of all nations," a lived reality. These are the watershed events of Christianity.

Saul, a Pharisee, appears on the scene at the stoning of Stephen (Acts 7:54–8:1). After Stephen's death Saul "was ravaging the church by entering house after house; dragging off both men and women, he committed them to prison" (Acts 8:3). Near the city of Damascus there is an abrupt interruption of Saul's itinerary. Believing he was God's defender by persecuting the followers of Jesus, he comes to see himself as a persecutor of God. The one who intended to enter Damascus like an avenging fury enters powerless, passive, helpless, childlike. Isn't it awesome that in such a condition Saul receives his vocational call?

PRAYER: **O God, how easy it is to be on the road consumed with plans that are contrary to your will. I pray for your divine light to flash around me and strip from me anything that separates me from you. I am willing to become broken in order to be whole. Amen.**

---

*Professor Emeritus of Hiwassee College; Director of the Lay Ministry Center for the Southeastern Jurisdictional Administrative Council; layperson in The United Methodist Church, Lake Junaluska, North Carolina.

TUESDAY, APRIL 24 • Read Acts 9:10-20

In a vision the Lord calls Ananias to go lay hands on Saul so Saul may receive his sight. Ananias raises reasonable doubts and reminds God that he has heard from many about how much evil Saul has done to the saints in Jerusalem. The voice does not argue; the command "go" is simply repeated.

Then comes the bombshell! How difficult it must be for Ananias to understand that Saul is a chosen instrument of God to "bring my name before Gentiles and kings and before the people of Israel." Saul has been chosen to be God's witness to persons he formerly considered unworthy and unclean (Gentiles).

Next comes a moment in history when I wish I could have been present. Ananias could have approached Saul with suspicion, doubt, and even recrimination, but he does not; he obeys the vision. When he reaches Saul, his first words are words of welcome to the family, "Brother Saul." In Christ previously bitter enemies become brothers.

When teaching in Israel I often visit with a rabbi who is a treasured friend. I value his wisdom, his understanding of scripture, and his deep love of humanity. On one visit I asked, "Rabbi, when will the hatred, injustices, and fighting stop between the Jews and the Palestinians?" He looked at me with intense eyes and a heart filled with pain and replied, "When we love our children more than we hate our enemies, peace will come." What a statement of understanding!

Think for a moment. What would happen if we had the spirit of Ananias? Don't you think the words "My brother, my sister" would demolish dividing walls, restore families, end ethnic cleansing, eliminate violence and hunger, and bring God's reign on earth?

PRAYER: Let there be peace on earth, dear God, and let it begin with me. Amen.

WEDNESDAY, APRIL 25 • Read Psalm 30

Who has not experienced the emotions expressed in this psalm: suffering, rejection, fear, hope, and thanksgiving? The psalmist has experienced recovery from a grave illness. When God "brought up my soul from Sheol, restored me to life from among those gone down to the Pit," the psalmist tells us he was near death. Sheol and the Pit are familiar names for what the Jews called "the land of the shadows." The Hebrew Scriptures do not contain a fully developed doctrine of life after death; that comes with the resurrection of Jesus. Many Jews believed (some still do) that after death one went to Sheol or the Pit and there experienced a shadowy existence until eventual annihilation.

From Sheol the psalmist cries to God for help, and God answers his prayer. The psalmist confidently affirms that "weeping may linger for the night, but joy comes with the morning" (v. 5b). Was he made well? We do not know, for in the Hebrew mind wholeness did not necessarily mean wellness. The Hebrews saw life as having four dimensions—the mind, body, soul, and relationships. Salvation or wholeness integrated these four areas, since each flows into and affects the other. Wholeness did not necessarily imply physical wellness.

We do know the psalmist was made whole, for God "turned my mourning into dancing." Life was filled with joy, so much so that he could "not be silent."

Even with limitations in any of life's four dimensions, a full life is possible through God's grace and power.

PRAYER: O God, I want to be open to your reign in every area of my being. This openness is demanding and difficult. Please help me desire your will more than I desire anything else. I know what it is to be in Sheol, but now I want wholeness. Amen!

THURSDAY, APRIL 26 • Read Revelation 5:11-14

The Revelation, while one of the most meaningful writings in the Bible, is also the most misunderstood and misinterpreted. After addressing the seven churches, the author writes a transitional chapter that describes heavenly worship. This early chapter in the book of the Revelation becomes the recurring theme for the remainder of the writing.

What a magnificent picture! The throne of God is there, the twenty-four elders, the four living creatures; unnumbered hosts of heaven sing a chorus of praise. The angels sing of the seven great possessions of Christ in his glory: power, wealth, wisdom, might, honor, glory, and blessing. Each of these possessions serves to bring humanity into right relationship with God.

The song of the redeemed offers thanksgiving for the person and work of Christ. The chorus of praise continues but goes even farther, as it encompasses the whole of the universe and all of creation. The one seated on the throne is identified as Jesus Christ, the Eternal Truth of God.

I heard a story years ago that I have never forgotten. Several seminarians played basketball in the evenings after study. An old janitor whose job it was to close the gym never seemed to mind how late they played, for he used this time to read his Bible. One evening one of the seminary students approached the janitor and asked, "What book of the Bible are you reading?" "Revelation," came the reply. "Do you understand what you are reading?" asked the student. "Of course," said the janitor. "It says Jesus wins!" What a profound insight he had into this marvelous book of hope.

PRAYER: Forgive me, Jesus, for forgetting who you are and allowing fear, hopelessness, and despair to rent space in my life. I want to sing with the choir of angels. Amen.

FRIDAY, APRIL 27 • **Read John 21:1-8**

As John begins his Gospel with a prologue, so he ends it with an epilogue. The prologue meaningfully presents the doctrine of the incarnation—God was in Christ. The scripture lessons for the next three days come from the epilogue, which affirms Jesus' presence among those who believe in him.

John 20 locates all the resurrection appearances in Jerusalem, but in John 21 the appearance takes place in Galilee at the Sea of Tiberius. The opening sentence contains an important phrase: "Jesus showed himself again." The verb *showed* is associated with the revelatory dimension of Jesus' miracles in 2:11 and 9:3. The Gospel writer also uses that verb to summarize the purpose of Jesus' ministry in 1:31 and 17:6. Use of this word underscores for the reader that the miracle story to follow is an epiphany, and we are to interpret it in light of the revelatory acts of Jesus' ministry.

Seven of the disciples are by the sea, including Nathanael, the first mention of him since the call narrative of John 1:45-50. At that time Jesus promised Nathanael he would see "greater things," and his being present at this closing epiphany affirms the promise's fulfillment. When Peter announces he is going fishing, the others join him for a night of casting the net, only to have it come up empty each time.

In the early morning when it is too dark to see, a stranger calls from shore, "Children, you have no fish, have you?" The phrasing in Greek implies the negative question. Note the use of the word *children*, a word that implies a teaching moment. When Jesus receives the answer he expected, he then tells the little group to cast the net on the other side. They obey and cannot haul the net in because there are so many fish.

PRAYER: O living Christ, I know what it is like to cast my net in the sea and have it come up empty. Make me aware that you are always with me by my Sea of Tiberius. Amen.

SATURDAY, APRIL 28 • **Read John 21:9-14**

The fishing miracle focuses on Jesus' identity as the source of life for the disciples. The abundance of the fish caught and Jesus' preparation of the meal confirm that he is the giver of gifts and the source of life-sustaining nourishment. This meal is reminiscent of the feeding of the five thousand around the same sea at the beginning of the disciples' association with Jesus.

The Gospel describes the magnitude of the catch threefold: "full of large fish"; "a hundred fifty-three of them"; and "though there were so many, the net was not torn." This confirms that Jesus has performed a great miracle and is, as previously mentioned, the generous giver of gifts.

Give close attention to the use of the verb "to haul." The mission of the disciples does not seem to lie in the great number of fish but in the fact that Peter "hauled the net ashore." The disciples now join God and Jesus in drawing (hauling) people to Jesus.

Jesus invites the disciples to breakfast and serves as host. He takes bread, gives it to them, and does the same with the fish, actions that echo the feeding of the five thousand (6:11) and the Cana miracle (2:1-11) The early church saw eucharistic symbolism in the breakfast by the sea. Indeed, an epiphany!

PRAYER: Jesus, thank you for being the giver of God's gifts and offering life-sustaining nourishment. Help me always be aware of your invitation to breakfast. Amen.

SUNDAY, APRIL 29 • Read John 21:15-19

These verses narrate a private conversation between Peter and the risen Christ. Jesus' initial question compares Peter's love for Jesus and that of the other disciples ("more than these"). Though Jesus uses the new gospel word for love, *agape*, Peter's reply uses the more familiar and weaker word *philo*. Essentially Peter says, "Yes, Lord, I have a friendly affection for you." Peter is not ready to say *agape*: I have an undying commitment to you. Getting the *philo* response twice, Jesus asks the question a third time using *philo*. Peter finally responds, "Lord, you know everything; you know that I love you." Whether these gradations of meaning are pertinent, Jesus now replaces Peter's three denials with three affirmations.

Jesus charges Peter to "feed my lambs," "tend my sheep," "feed my sheep." The heart of these verses lies in the relationship between Peter's love for Jesus and the command to "feed my sheep." These words echo 13:34-35: "Just as I have loved you, you also should love one another. By this everyone will know that you are my disciples, if you have love for one another." Peter is called to love Jesus' sheep as he has loved them.

In verse 18 the expression "Very truly, I tell you" marks the introduction of a new teaching, Peter's martyrdom. The agape level of living will require sacrifice. Jesus uses a parable whose general meaning contrasts the freedom of Peter's youth with the captivity that will mark his old age and death.

Jesus closes the conversation with the words "Follow me," knowing that Peter's love for him will result in his keeping the command "Feed my sheep."

PRAYER: O Jesus, help me to love with *agape* so that I too may feed your sheep. Amen.

The Lord Is My Shepherd

April 30–May 6, 2001 • *Steve Dawson Blaze Blazina**

MONDAY, APRIL 30 • **Read Psalm 23**

Psalm 23 was the first passage of scripture my mother taught me. It identified well with the print of Jesus that hung over the headboard of my childhood bed. The portrait was that of a gentle, peaceful shepherd who lovingly cared for his flock, an image that gave me a real sense of security as a child.

I did not leave the significance of Psalm 23 behind in my childhood. It has become a catalyst, helping me to understand the relevancy of Christ in my adult life. Some of the most often asked questions I hear from Christian adults are shrouded in this one: Is Jesus still relevant for my life as an adult?

We must realize that our dependence upon the Lord does not make us less than adults. The journey of adult discipleship requires that we see Jesus as more than capable of being the Good Shepherd in all of life's situations. The journey also teaches us that we can only accomplish his purpose for us with his help. Jesus does more than protect and save the members of his flock. He enables them to live to their fullest capacity, accomplishing his good purpose, in his good time. Only when we commit to becoming disciples of Jesus can we begin to understand him as our Good Shepherd.

PRAYER: Lord, help me recognize you again as the Good Shepherd of my life. In your grace allow me to see that you have been at work in my life and continue to work even to this day. I give you thanks. Amen.

---

*Minister of Congregational Life, Cook's United Methodist Church, Mt. Juliet, Tennessee.

Tuesday, May 1 • Read John 10:26b-28

Like so many people of my generation, my grandparents were farmers. Visiting my grandparents at the farm, even frequently, did not give me the same insight that they garnered from actually living on the farm. A few years ago I learned the value of today's scripture passage. I had just accepted a United Methodist camp position in the mid-West, and the board of directors neglected to tell me until I moved that the job included the care of forty-five horses.

My first day on the job I could not tell one horse from another. But the more time I spent with those horses, the deeper my relationship with them became. Knowing the herd went far beyond simply identifying them. I learned each horse's personality and social group. I discovered what each horse feared and how to encourage and handle them all. I knew each horse's ailments and remedies. Those horses were much more than simply trail ride animals. They were my friends; we shared a devotion, knowledge, love, and respect.

The mutual love and admiration that Jesus talks about in this passage also goes far beyond being able to pick us out of a crowd. As our shepherd, Jesus knows who we are and where we have been. He understands our needs and ailments. He too longs for our healing. He knows how to handle us so as not to hurt others or ourselves as we grow in our relationship with him. Finally he loves us more than we are capable of understanding. If by God's grace we can extend this love to other parts of God's creation, how much more does God know and care for us?

PRAYER: Lord, I am joyfully overwhelmed by your love. Thank you for blessing me. Help me honor this sacred gift by being a blessing to those around me, even the smallest parts of your creation. Amen.

WEDNESDAY, MAY 2 • Read Acts 9:36-43

Societies around the globe have evidenced a fascination with stories of the afterlife. We have heard testimonies from people who were for all practical purposes dead, if only for a few moments, being revived and sharing that the Lord wanted them to come back to earth and complete a plan he had for them. Whether you agree with this testimony or not, it is an important and convincing message for the person who hears from the Lord. Tabitha ministered to the poor and the widows. Her life enabled life for the outcasts in her community. Her untimely death now caused a real crisis in the lives of those to whom she had ministered. The scripture tells us that Peter knelt, prayed, and then said, "Tabitha, get up." The next verse tells us her eyes opened, and she sat up.

At first we tend to focus on the miracle of Peter's bringing Tabitha back from the dead. Luke does not spend a great deal of time on the details of the miracle of her resurrection. He quickly moves past it to a more significant event: the empowered lives of ordinary people because of the gospel of Jesus Christ.

Peter, a fisherman, becomes an itinerant preacher; Tabitha changes the world by graciously touching the lives of people who will never be able to repay her. Death does not have the last word in this situation. Tabitha's resurrection proclaims a message of hope to a desperately needy world. No longer is life a formula of cause and effect or an accumulation of hopeless philosophies. The Christian faith offers something new to Peter and Tabitha and ageless for us. It has authority in this life and the next. It has the power to make the ordinary sacred.

PRAYER: **Lord, I stand amazed at the things you do in the lives of the people who love you. Help me gracefully touch the world by reaching out to those people you place within my reach. Amen.**

THURSDAY, MAY 3 • Read Mark 6:30-44

Have you ever felt exhausted only to find that the Lord was calling you to go the extra mile? According to this day's scripture, the disciples are having that kind of day. They are on their way to a much needed place to rest. Their plans, however, do not pan out as they hope. A crowd awaits their arrival, compounding their hunger and exhaustion.

Scripture tells us that Jesus has compassion for the crowd, because "they were like sheep without a shepherd." In spite of the disciples' frustration, Jesus teaches the crowd, ministers to them, and then chooses to feed them. The disciples suggest that Jesus do the practical thing about supper: Send the people out to neighboring towns to find something to eat. Instead of granting their request, Jesus turns to his disciples and makes a seemingly impossible request: "You give them something to eat."

Jesus does not free his disciples from the burden of responsibility. He asks them, "What do you have?" They respond, "Five barley loaves and two fish." Jesus uses what the disciples have to offer to the crowd. He blesses it and the food feeds the five thousand men and their families. The crowd seemingly has no idea of the miracle Jesus has just performed.

Jesus clearly intends this miracle for the disciples' benefit. This is an opportunity for the disciples to see Jesus in all his glory. What does the passage tell us about being a disciple? It tells us that the Lord sometimes calls us even when we are tired. He calls us to do the impossible by human standards. Jesus does not ask us to do it all by ourselves, but he does ask us to offer him what we have. And remember that sometimes the miracle he performs is for our benefit.

PRAYER: Lord, help me trust you. Remind me that you know what you are doing, even if I do not completely understand. Help me to be obedient and make myself available to you. Amen.

FRIDAY, MAY 4 • Read John 10:22-30

The Gospel of John concludes the public ministry of Jesus at the Feast of Lights (Hanukkah). During this celebration great expectation centered around the coming of the Messiah. Accordingly, the Jewish leaders find themselves hard-pressed to get some answers from Jesus. Here is a man who has greatly impressed the crowds, and the Jewish leaders simply cannot explain him away. They confront Jesus with the statement, "If you are the Christ, tell us plainly" (RSV), implying the idea that "we may be sharing the same tongue, but we are not speaking the same language." Jesus cannot answer the question in their terms because to know Jesus as the Messiah requires a deeper understanding of him. Jesus states that the evidence they look for lies in the changed lives of the people to whom he has ministered.

Clearly this passage is concerned with the cost of discipleship. The Jewish leaders weigh a living faith that Jesus offers against the institutionalized religion to which they are committed. The Jewish leaders are more concerned about the future of their own careers.

Contrast the demands of the Jewish leaders with the mutual devotion of Jesus and those who belong to his flock. Jesus suggests that those who belong to him accept his word; the miracles he does only affirms those who already know and love him. For the Jewish leaders, it doesn't matter how many signs and wonders Jesus performs; they always need one more to prove that Jesus is who he says he is. This passage calls for commitment from the Jewish leaders and offers a word of caution for the people of the Lord who occasionally want to put Jesus to the test. What things in our lives keep us from moving beyond the contemplation of the cost of discipleship toward a stronger commitment to our Lord?

PRAYER: Lord, I want to do my best for you, yet I continue to carry that which keeps me from accomplishing this goal. Help me, as an athlete in the race of life, focus on you. Amen.

SATURDAY, MAY 5 • **Read Revelation 7:9-17**

Most of us can remember a time of testing, a trouble-filled experience and the pain that it caused. We can also recall the closure that eventually came and the excitement of a new beginning. This is the cycle of life: a beginning, a time of growth and maturity, a time of testing, a call for endurance, and finally a new beginning. Trials and tribulations are nothing new; they have been a part of the Christian faith since its beginning.

This passage in Revelation is about completion and fulfillment. It is about gaining closure on the hard times and rejoicing over the beginning of something that has been anticipated for a long time. This passage describes the second of two visions that take place in chapter 7. In the first of these visions God places a seal of spiritual protection on those who remain on earth and are about to go through the Great Tribulation.

The second vision describes the magnificent outcome of the first vision. Every one of the Lord's people has made it, and there is great rejoicing in heaven. Here Jesus is portrayed as royalty, a righteous champion, the conquering Lamb who has enabled the completion of God's plan of salvation. Contrast this image with the passage about Jesus' triumphal entry into Jerusalem during his earthly ministry. (See John 12:12-16.) Jesus is no longer the mysterious prophet wandering into Jerusalem on a donkey but the Lamb of God, sitting in his rightful place. As well, the people are no longer the curious and fickle crowd waving palm branches amid the hoopla of a Passover festival. They know without a doubt who they are and to whom they belong. This passage is a source of hope, reminding us that the Lord is with us, providing spiritual protection for God's people while they endure hardship.

PRAYER: Lord, let me look back over my life and see how you have worked for my good. Help me remember your faithfulness during times of trial. Grant me the strength to endure and overcome life's obstacles until I arrive at the new beginning you have for me. Amen.

SUNDAY, MAY 6 • Read Psalm 23

"The Lord is my shepherd, I shall not want"(RSV). As a child, I read the first verse of Psalm 23 as if it were a commandment. In my thinking, it was more like "You shall not want." I confused it with "You shall not covet"; and for a long time, I felt guilty about wanting anything. I believe that this confusion is not just limited to me. Learning to live a balanced life between our wants and needs is one of the most difficult tasks we face today as Christians.

Advertisements bombard us on a daily basis, telling us that the latest item is better than what we have and that acquiring it will fill the void in our life. Sadly, marketing schemes are not the only place from which poor notions of success come. Some within the Christian community promote "name it, claim it" theology as well as the idea that accumulated wealth testifies to a life lived right in the eyes of God. Don't be fooled. Unless an individual has a clear understanding of the differences between success according to scripture and success as defined by things, such schemes will leave an individual tossed about between the worlds of abstinence and addiction.

This first verse sets the tone for the rest of the psalm, and we may better understand it by reading from another version of the Bible. For example, "You, Lord, are my shepherd. I will never be in need" (CEV). The psalmist declares that God is sufficient to meet his needs. This understanding liberates the psalmist from the pressures to seek out and accumulate things, because in the end it is only his relationship with God and others that will give him the peace and happiness he seeks.

PRAYER: Lord, help me discern the difference between worldly success and the satisfaction only you can offer. Enable me by your spirit to bring my requests to you, granting me the wisdom to ask with a pure heart, and helping me believe that you really are able and willing to look after me as a faithful shepherd does the sheep. Amen.

Glory from the Unexpected

May 7–13, 2001 • *Dwyn M. Mounger**

MONDAY, MAY 7 • **Read Acts 11:1-3**

Electronic doors sealed us within the prison. Nervously we church folk contemplated the service we were to lead in this facility that once housed James Earl Ray, convicted assassin of Martin Luther King Jr. Would our captive congregation pose danger, especially to our female companions? Would the worshipers be hostile or open?

The packed chapel and expectant, Bible-clutching prisoners who welcomed us quickly dispelled our fears. Soon we thrilled to their fervent singing, testimonies of conversion to Christ, reverent partaking of the Eucharist, and finally "thank-yous" and "come back soons!" Our surprise resembled that of the "circumcised believers" (law-abiding Jewish Christians) in Jerusalem, when they learn that Peter has dared dine with "unclean" Gentiles and welcomed them as fellow Christians.

Who are the "uncircumcised" in your community? Whom do some respectable churchgoers shun as being almost beyond redemption: teenagers with hairstyles and apparel that suggest a contempt for tradition, newcomers who speak little or no English, men and women whose moral lives provoke raised eyebrows and lifted noses?

For two thousand years believers often have adopted society's pecking order instead of Christ's. And yet the gospel shatters stereotypes, bridges gaps. Like startled Peter entering the world of Gentiles and witnessing God's spirit upon them, we stand amazed at holy glory from the unexpected.

PRAYER: God of astonishments, thank you for showing us your powerful saving grace among those whom we blindly see as beyond it! Amen.

---

*Minister, First Presbyterian Church (U.S.A.), Oak Ridge, Tennessee.

TUESDAY, MAY 8 • Read Acts 11:4-18

In nearly thirty-six years as a pastor, I have been troubled most by a few sanctimonious parishioners. In contrast, adulterers and depressed teenagers have proved far easier to reach and to help!

While in seminary I served as a student minister one summer for a mission church. Before returning to campus, I vainly searched for someone to lead the youth fellowship group I had organized. Meeting refusals from others, in some desperation I turned to a friendly, middle-aged couple with my request, trying to ignore the constant smell of alcohol on their breaths.

Accepting with great enthusiasm, they did wonderful work for weeks with the youth, who loved them. But late one Sunday night, back in seminary, I received a telephone call from an irate father. The couple had arrived at the fellowship meeting quite drunk. Young people were puzzled, distressed. Some parents were outraged.

"Naturally, they're through as youth advisors," boomed the father. "Oh, we'll let them come to church, if they want to! But that's it!" I was horrified. What an opportunity missed—a wonderful chance to guide the youth in understanding the tragedy of alcoholism, and maybe through them help the couple too.

Self-righteous people are truly lost. They rarely get beyond condemnation of those they deem less holy than themselves. That's why, in our lesson, the about-face of the conservative Jewish Christians of Jerusalem startles us so. When they hear from Peter's story of the Holy Spirit's moving among even uncircumcised Gentiles to praise Jesus as Lord, they cease complaining about his dining with them. And they give thanks that the gospel is proving far more broad than they ever had dreamed.

PRAYER: God, teach me that not even the holier-than-thou are beyond your mercy and your reach, through Jesus Christ. Amen.

WEDNESDAY, MAY 9 • Read Psalm 148:1-10

Our psalm begins in the highest heaven—but soon descends to the depths. With soaring spirit one can envision the angels raising their voices in praise to the Lord, with the sun, moon, and stars joining in.

The intrusion of ancient Levantine cosmology, with its picturesque "waters above the heavens" (v. 4) that help to swell the music, in no way detracts from the drama. On the contrary, it adds a note of delight to the whole oratorio.

Our psalmist obviously takes an almost childish joy in the adoration of the Maker by the entire cosmos. The pattern of his song seems to spring largely from the Hebrews' first creation story, Genesis 1:1–2:4.

But how do "sea monsters and all deeps" lift their praises? And "fire and hail, snow and frost, stormy wind" and "creeping things"? The victims of real-life monsters and of ocean disasters, as well as those of us who shudder at all sorts of creepy beings, wonder.

And what about those who have suffered loss of their homes or even their loved ones through fire, blizzard, hurricane? Do devastating tornadoes, tsunamis, and clouds of locusts that destroy crops receive the Lord's hearty welcome into the expanding choir? Surely our psalmist must be kidding!

Not so. This singer worships not only a Creator but a Restrainer—one to whom even the scariest creatures and forces are subject. And, far more important, he adores the almighty Sustainer—one who enables God's children, despite the worst of experiences, still to lift voices, minds, hearts, and hopes in such glorious hymns of acclamation.

PRAYER: God, I often shut my ears to the magnificent chorus of praise that rises all around me. Mercifully keep them open, that I may hear and add my own adoring voice. Amen.

THURSDAY, MAY 10 • **Read Psalm 148:11-14**

For nearly sixty years our city has been a major center for nuclear research. The public knows it chiefly as a site for World War II's Manhattan Project, which produced the atomic bomb. This puts our citizens under obligation to further world peace through such projects as the "International Friendship Bell" that adorns our main municipal park.

Moreover, a few miles from where I now sit, humanity's first permanent reactor in 1946 produced the earliest isotopes for the treatment of cancer. For these reasons some people see Oak Ridge as a dangerous place to live because of radiation hazards.

Nothing could be further from the truth! The rate of malignancy among our citizens is lower than in most other U.S. cities. Wildlife flourishes here—Canada geese and woodchucks, known in Appalachia as "whistle pigs," and also skunks and squirrels. And in virtually every neighborhood one often can see at night healthy, relatively tame deer emerging from woods, crossing the roads.

Occasionally one encounters a buck—noble, with his antlers high. Such a sight remarkably resonates with some striking imagery in our psalm: the Lord "has raised up a horn for his people, praise for all his faithful."

To the ancients, horned animals, particularly rams, wild goats, and bucks, possessed great dignity and strength. Thus the Jews colorfully spoke of the Lord as having crowned God's loyal children with a horn, to mark them as special and to protect them.

How fitting for this chorus of praise, sung by the voices of all creation, to end in this way! Our highest reason to give thankful adoration to the Maker is for the glory we enjoy in being God's children—redeemed by grace, shielded from our enemies, enfolded in unending divine love and care.

PRAYER: Thank you, God, for this glorious horn! Amen.

FRIDAY, MAY 11 • Read Revelation 21:1-4*a*

In John's magnificent vision of a transformed heaven and earth, why does he seemingly rejoice that "the sea was no more"? To the many beach lovers in our twenty-first century a world without oceans is unthinkable!

Some theorists cite John's exile on remote, insular Patmos as an explanation. Banished there by the Roman government, which was then severely persecuting Christians, he wishes the sea that separates him from the beloved churches in Asia Minor (1:4) would dry up.

A more likely explanation is the ancient, inbred Jewish dread of great bodies of water. The Hebrews of Jesus' day were landlubbers. Even their cherished "Sea of Galilee" was just a lake. Nowhere is the ancient Jewish fear of the ocean better expressed than in Ecclesiasticus (Sirach), in the Apocrypha: "Those who sail the sea have tales of its dangers / which astonish all of us who hear them; / in it are strange and wonderful creatures, / all kinds of living things and great sea monsters" (43:24-25, REB).

What more horrible disaster could befall anyone than that which Jonah experienced? Cast into the whitecaps and swallowed by a "great fish" (Jon. 1:15, 17, RSV)! Moreover, the Jews knew that the unpredictable Mediterranean could spawn terrifying storms to assault their land and hurl down the trees of the forest (Ps. 29:9). Thus God's coming new creation, without an ocean in sight, signifies a great blessing.

How glorious to envision life in the eternal, divine presence! No towering billows of sorrow to seize us and plunge us to the depths. No terrifying ebb tides to drag us far from shore. No typhoons with tidal waves to drown us. No seas of tears.

PRAYER: Ruler of the fiercest oceans, comfort me with the knowledge that in your coming realm your peace will calm all chaos. Amen.

SATURDAY, MAY 12 • Read Revelation 21:4*b*-6

Introduced by dazed television reporters, they appear from several nations: refugees in shock. The lucky have found shelter in crowded camps; exhausted others stumble along roads or shiver in the rain in open fields. Victims of "ethnic cleansing," they've known rape, massacre, mutilation, genocide—just because they differ in tribe, language, or religion from the majority. Eyes of old and young, of parents and children, have witnessed horrors never to be erased in this life.

Some of the hearers of the words of John here are like those refugees. Roman Emperor Domitian (81–96 C.E.) insists that all subjects call him "Master and God" and burn incense before his statue. Refusal to do so results in torture and death to Christians who acknowledge only Jesus as Lord. Indeed, some members of the seven churches in Asia Minor, to whom John writes, have met this fate (1:9; 2:10, 13; 6:9; 13:15).

For this reason it must be hard for their surviving relatives and fellow believers to grasp this vision of a "new Jerusalem." (Domitian's brother Titus had utterly destroyed the old Jerusalem, slaughtering its citizens, in 70 C.E.) After what they've seen, how can they believe in a coming heavenly capital where "death" and "mourning and crying and pain will be no more"? Yet John assures them that the Lord is still "on the throne" (v. 5; see also 1:8) and God's "words are trustworthy and true."

Our own encounters with suffering and death, if less outrageous than those of the persecuted, are still real. How reassuring to know that God rules despite everything and that one day we ourselves shall find peaceful refuge in the perfected holy city!

PRAYER: God of mercy, bring soon your great community of peace on earth for all your children, through Jesus Christ. Amen.

SUNDAY, MAY 13 • Read John 13:31-35

Nowhere else does the greatest Christian paradox more clearly express itself than in today's Gospel reading. Judas has just bolted from the Last Supper to betray his Lord (vv. 21-30). To the remaining apostles Jesus declares, "Now the Son of Man has been glorified."

How can any glory come from double cross, torture, crucifixion? More puzzling, how can God be "glorified" through such a fate for Jesus? Do we worship a celestial monster?

This glorification is incomprehensible only if we forget two points crucial to Johannine theology—and to all of Christian faith: the Incarnation ("the Word became flesh and lived among us, and we have seen his glory," John 1:14) and the "new commandment" ("as I have loved you, you also should love one another," John 13:34).

For our salvation God dares to become one of us, to suffer the very worst that evil can devise, and to triumph over it in the Resurrection. Thus the divine nature stands revealed gloriously for everyone who looks at Golgotha and the empty tomb.

Few, however, raise their eyes to see Golgotha and the empty tomb until first exposed to the love of transformed Christians for one another. Nearby is a Korean congregation composed mainly of immigrants. Although some were reared in the faith (Korea is the most nearly Christian nation on the Asian mainland), others were once agnostic, secularized. Locally many are university scientists, chemists and, nuclear physicists.

The initial attraction to the congregation came from exposure to the sacrificial love displayed by members to one another—and extended to the seekers. After all, for two thousand years such has proved, for outsiders, to be the most surprising glory of all about sincerely practicing Christians.

PRAYER: Help me, O God, always to see in the cross of Christ and in his resurrection your greatest glory—and mine. Amen.

Heart-Opening Experiences

May 14–20, 2001 • Dolores H. Henderson*

MONDAY, MAY 14 • Read Acts 16:9-12

"Come over to Macedonia," the man tells Paul in a vision—what a magical and mystical invitation! Make a change, enter new territory, relate to different people. After this vision, Paul and his party immediately leave Asia Minor and set sail for Europe, reaching Philippi, a leading city in Macedonia, which had been named for Philip, father of Alexander the Great.

Paul has just experienced an attempt to preach in Asia Minor while constrained by the Holy Spirit. He has just passed through a sharp disagreement with Barnabas about John Mark, Barnabas's nephew. This invitation to Macedonia may have seemed like a breath of fresh air: to begin spreading the good news in a new place. Paul and his companions are sure God is calling them to spread the gospel message, and they find their travel easy.

Have you ever tried to initiate something, such as a program or a new way thinking, only to find one thing after another standing in your way? In your discouragement, you abandon your plan. Perhaps later you return to that plan or take up a new approach, only to discover that the going is so smooth you can hardly keep up with the pace. Perhaps you might choose the procrastinator's watchword and put off doing anything until everything goes smoothly, but then on another day or at another time, a new approach leads to your fulfillment of the aim.

SUGGESTION FOR MEDITATION: Come over to Macedonia! Meditate on those times when you tried to accomplish something and could not, but upon returning to the project, you found that things went smoothly. What made the difference?

---

*Superintendent, Metropolitan South District, New York Annual Conference, The United Methodist Church; living in Brooklyn, New York.

TUESDAY, MAY 15 • Read Acts 16:13-15

Having been in the city for several days, Paul and his group go outside the gates on the Sabbath. There they find a group of women. Paul speaks to the group and catches the ear of Lydia, a businesswoman and a dealer in purple dye. She heads her household and is probably quite wealthy. The scripture also describes her as a worshiper of God. The Lord intervenes and opens her heart; Lydia becomes the first Christian convert in Europe. After she and her household are baptized, she opens her home to missionaries, and it becomes the center of Christian fellowship in Philippi. Surely Paul is speaking about her when he writes in Philippians: "I thank my God every time I remember you, constantly praying with joy in every one of my prayers for all of you, because of your sharing in the gospel from the first day until now" (1:3-5).

Lydia, as the first Christian convert in Europe and the founder of a church, is important to me as an African-American clergywoman. The church has kept women from exercising their call to ordained ministry, and I find it comforting to have the biblical example of Lydia to back up our rights to orders. God calls who God wills, and this call should be encouraged, not denied.

We find the elements of the heart-opening experience in this account: The person is close to God or is a God-worshiper, who is in community on the Sabbath, listening to the preached word. Finally, the Spirit of the Lord intervenes. If we make ourselves available to God through worship, prayer, study, and meditation, we too can have heart-opening experiences. We will be changed and open to sharing the gospel.

Open my heart and let me prepare
love with thy children thus to share.
—From "Open My Eyes, That I May See," by Clara H. Scott

SUGGESTION FOR MEDITATION: What have I shared after my heart-opening experiences?

WEDNESDAY, MAY 16 • Read John 5:1-9

This miracle by the pool of Bethesda ("the house of mercy") is one of seven recorded miracles on the Sabbath. The others are the man born blind (John 9:1-14), the demoniac in Capernaum (Mark 1:21-27), Peter's mother-in-law (Mark 1:29-3 1), the man with the withered hand (Mark 3:1-6), the bent-over woman (Luke 13:10-17), and the man with dropsy (Luke 14:1-6).

I find the conversation between the man and Jesus very interesting. First I can think of several irreverent replies to Jesus' question, "Do you want to be made whole?" such as, "Why do you think I've been lying here thirty-eight years?" or "I just come here to watch the others get the prize of healing." But the man responds, "Sir, I have no one to put me into the pool when the water is stirred up." Even though the man does not answer Jesus' question, he replies respectfully (*kyrie* in the Greek), and Jesus swiftly goes into action. He tells the man to stand up, take up his mat, and walk. The man obeys and is made well instantly. Imagine his feelings and thoughts after being ill for such a long time—he was cured.

I too have experienced healing as a liberating experience. I wasn't paralyzed, but a severe backache had forced me to my bed. Prayer and the laying on of hands relieved the pain dramatically; I was then able to get up and resume a normal lifestyle.

Heart-opening, life-changing experiences involve closeness with our Lord. The elements of the cure for this man by the pool of Bethesda included presence, communication, and obedience.

SUGGESTION FOR MEDITATION: Do you feel close to Jesus? How has this closeness brought healing to your life? How do you maintain this closeness?

THURSDAY, MAY 17 • Read John 14:23-29

"Let not your hearts be troubled." How many times has that sentence run through your mind, especially during a troubling time? Leave-taking of any sort is usually troubling. Jesus' disciples are troubled and full of questions, wondering how life will be without Jesus in their midst. Throughout history, there have been many famous and not-so-famous farewells. Most of the time the person leaving or retiring sought to comfort followers. George Washington, when bidding farewell to his troops at Fraunces' Tavern in New York City, advised them to return home and live free, for their freedom had been bought for a price— the lives of those who died in the war.

Jesus reminds his disciples of their call; that is, if you love me, keep my commandments and rejoice that I am returning to the Father. Now of course, they are sad and confused. The internship is ending; they feel unsure of their roles.

The time they have spent with Jesus might have opened their hearts; and in the closeness of that experience, comfort might have made its home with them. Usually at a leave-taking, our hearts are conscious only of our pain at the departure of the beloved. We wish to prolong the time of being together. It is hard to let someone go in peace—and it is even harder to be left behind.

SUGGESTION FOR MEDITATION: **Consider your feelings at departures such as moving away, taking a new job, divorce, or the death of a loved one. Did these leave-takings offer you an area of growth? How are you better or worse for having had these experiences?**

FRIDAY, MAY 18 • Read Revelation 21:10, 22–22:5

John the Revelator, while in the Spirit, sees the holy city, the new Jerusalem coming down out of heaven. This vision, reminiscent of Ezekiel's vision, has one important difference: There is no temple in the city. The Lord is the temple, and people will worship God—not a building, no matter how beautiful or large. The light for this city comes from God and the Lamb. The Christians to whom John writes have only a dim memory of the Temple—if they have ever seen it. Persecution is their sad reality and the Christian community is their comfort. So a new and sparkling city, full of light from the Lamb, offers a beautiful and uplifting image, something to give them courage to continue in the faith.

The image of the new Jerusalem also comforted black slaves in this country. The new Jerusalem, a city with twelve gates, welcomed them to a new home where there was no persecution, hatred, or back-breaking labor.

Any who suffer can take comfort in this vision; God's kingdom will have no end and will be a source of joy for God's people. John, who offers this vision, beholds it while in the Spirit. Many persons today achieve this state of closeness to God through prayer, fasting, or meditation. This transcendent view of the kingdom of God and its people may shine before those who are in the Spirit, holding out an image of hope.

The hymn "I Want to Walk as a Child of the Light," by Kathleen Thomerson, tells us that Jesus is our light and our salvation. When we have completed this earthly race, we shall know the joy of Jesus. The hymn's refrain closes with the reminder that the Lamb lights the city of God.

Shine in my heart, Lord Jesus.

SUGGESTION FOR MEDITATION: **How do you picture the new Jerusalem? How do you try to be "in the Spirit"?**

150

SATURDAY, MAY 19 • **Read Psalm 67**

At this time of the year, when I think of heart-opening experiences, I think of the Wesleys in the year 1738. They had returned from an unsuccessful missionary trip to America, and John was quite discouraged. They expected that God would show kindness to them and bless their mission, so that the colony of Georgia would acknowledge God's ways and saving power. Their intentions were sincere, and they were sent with prayers to the new world; but John felt far from blessed.

Nothing seemed to go right. A dispirited John occasionally went through the motions of preaching. On Pentecost Sunday, May 21, Charles was very ill with pleurisy and John had a preaching engagement. When he returned, he found Charles both laughing and crying and telling him that he was convinced Jesus loved him and died for him and that he knew he was saved. John now felt truly alone; he could not join in with Charles's feeling. But why not?

On May 24, John attended a small chapel on Aldersgate Street. A group was studying Romans, reading aloud Martin Luther's treatise on that letter. John Wesley understood justification by faith for the first time, and he stood up and testified openly to all.

This was thirteen years after Wesley's ordination as a priest. He went on to spread the good news of Jesus Christ for almost fifty-three years until his death in 1791. John Wesley was blessed to be a blessing to others. His observation of slavery in Georgia strengthened his abolitionist beliefs from which he never wavered. His antislavery sermons and writings aroused great opposition in England, especially in Bristol. A heart-opening experience paved the way for the people called Methodists to be doers of the gospel and social activists.

SUGGESTION FOR MEDITATION: **What is the fruit of your beliefs? How are you a blessing to others?**

151

SUNDAY, MAY 20 • Read Psalm 67

"May God be gracious to us and bless us / and make his face to shine upon us." I feel that God is calling us to be evangelists by inviting, witnessing, and, more importantly, acting out Christ's love for humanity. People hunger for spiritual experiences. We Christians should be happy to tell them about our friend Jesus and act in such a way that they can see Jesus in us. We are the means by which all the peoples will praise God. We need to be busy about God's work.

I know that we are blessed and, according to the psalmist, God intends blessing for all the people of the world. God wills justice for all. "The land will yield its harvest," and all peoples of the world will have enough to eat. We Christians in North America need to hear the words of this psalm. We are not persecuted for being Christian; we are free to go to church and worship. But the blessings of God involve equity among all peoples, so that all benefit from the blessings of peace and prosperity, justice and righteousness.

Only a God who rules as sovereign of all can bring about worldwide renewal and blessing. The promise of blessing to all may come through those with open hearts, open to receive the promises of God. May our hearts be strangely warmed, and may we be generous with our praise of such a gracious God. May we extend God's blessing to "all the ends of the earth."

PRAYER: Pray the words of Moses to the Israelites:

The Lord bless you and keep you;
The Lord make his face to shine upon you,
and be gracious to you.
The Lord lift up his countenance upon you,
and give you peace (Num. 6:24-26).
Amen!

Hope in God

May 21–27, 2001 • Thad J. Rutter Jr.*

MONDAY, MAY 21 • Read Acts 1:1-11

The high school principal's response to my question still sticks to my ribs. Our church was considering building a youth facility. So I visited the high school principal to get his thoughts. I asked him, "What do kids need today?" His answer was short and immediate. He said, "Hope! We can't motivate our students because they lack hope."

The principal's remark both jars and challenges me. I appreciate the power of hope in God because I have known the paralysis of despair. And what shines forth from Jesus' exiting earth and ascending to God is undying hope.

Hope is what this small band of Jesus' followers exhibit as they watch "a cloud [take] him out of their sight." And hope is what Luke wants to inspire in us, his readers. This week the Christian church celebrates Jesus' ascension, a multifaceted event. The focus of this week is the facet of hope in God.

These followers were not eternal optimists. Recall their despair on Good Friday. Hope was gone because Jesus was gone. They had nothing and no one in which to hope.

With the resurrected Jesus, hope in God has been restored to them. Now at Jesus' departure, they find reason to live again, believe again, hope again, love again. They have been touched by the unfading hope of God. May it be so for all of us, including those high school kids.

PRAYER: O God, amidst so many broken relationships in my life, it is hard to hope. Help me remember that nothing can separate me from my relationship with you in Christ. Amen.

---

*United Methodist pastor serving a two-point charge; interest in the area of contemplative prayer; living in Antigo, Wisconsin.

TUESDAY, MAY 22 • Read Psalm 47

Kallistos Ware, in his book *The Orthodox Way*, tells a story in which the actress Lillah McCarthy came in great pain to George Bernard Shaw. Her husband had deserted her. She sat shivering before Shaw's fireplace. After a period of time she walked, with dragging steps, up and down Adelphi Terrace with Shaw at her side. She wept. Then Shaw gently and tenderly said, "Look up, dear, look up to the heavens. There is more in life than this. There is much more." His words restored the actress's hope.

For the psalmist, the "much more" is "the Lord, the Most High, [who] is awesome, a great king over all the earth." This psalm probably celebrated God's ascension in the annual enthronement ritual. The ark, representing Yahweh, was removed from the Temple. The Temple and the people received cleansing. The ark was then returned, symbolizing Yahweh's reenthronement.

The psalm also reminds us that the purpose of God's people is to worship, praise, and serve the one who is "Most High" and "awesome" and who gives us hope. The followers of Jesus have become part of this heritage.

We who have been touched by the light and power of Jesus Christ are called to praise God through worship for the hope that is ours. A sacred part of us knows that "there is more in life than this. There is much more." God reigns beyond the darkness of this earth. Through Jesus, God reigns amidst the darkness of this earth.

PRAYER: O God, when I feel low of heart, grant me the grace to look up and catch a glimpse of the expanse of your glory. Amen.

WEDNESDAY, MAY 23 • Read Ephesians 1:15-23

The author of Ephesians offers a prayer for his readers, asking "the Father of glory" to give his readers a "spirit of wisdom and revelation." Through a heart enlightened by the glory of God we may come to know (1) the hope to which we are being called, (2) the riches of the inheritance given to the community of faith, and (3) the immeasurable greatness of God's power.

Several years ago I met a man whose heart was enlightened by the glory of God. He knew the hope of God to which we all are called. His wife was dying of breast cancer. (His first wife had died of the same disease.) He told me two things that have helped enlighten my heart.

First, he said, "Thad, you are going to have to do my believing for me." I did not hear despair or unbelief in this remark. I felt that it was a mature and wise acknowledgment that faith comes to us through community. In moments when the darkness overwhelms us and cripples our capacity to believe, the profoundly faithful thing to do is to let others do our believing for us.

Second, he offered this observation: "Karen and I know less about God and feel closer to God than we ever have in our lives." The cancer had diminished the man's knowledge of God, but it had not diminished God. In some deep, mysterious way, my friend and his wife had grown closer to God, now knowing and hoping in the God who had grown close to them.

SUGGESTION FOR MEDITATION: **Call a person of faith and thank him or her for what he or she brings into your life.**

PRAYER: **O God, I thank you for faithful people who nurture and form my faith. Amen.**

THURSDAY, MAY 24 • Read Luke 24:44-53

ASCENSION DAY

Today marks the end of Jesus' earthly presence. Jesus' followers will soon experience his presence in an entirely new form—that of the Holy Spirit. Jesus has been *among* them as the resurrected Lord. At Pentecost, Jesus will be *in* them as the Holy Spirit. But the fact that he ascends to God in heaven means that he will be in all believers throughout the ages, for the historically bound Jesus becomes the eternally available Christ. On Ascension Day, Jesus becomes part of all eternity so that on Pentecost eternity can become part of us through the Holy Spirit.

I have always been struck by the disciples' preparation of their hearts for the gift of the Holy Spirit. In today's passage we read, "And they were continually in the temple blessing God." They spent this time of preparation in prayer.

Glenn Hinson tells of the important role prayer played in the life of Douglas Steere. Prayer helped shape his outlook of hope, which he maintained through dire circumstances. Hinson quotes Steere on what prayer meant to him. It included 1) tears down the eyes, 2) tasks given and strength to do them, 3) linking with others in intercession, 4) change of mind, 5) rest, 6) awakening from sluggish rest, and 7) preparation for life. Finally in his own words Hinson states, "Prayer has fortified me…to feel the Presence of the One who can bear me [in life] and bear me [in death]."* In terms of this week's theme, we can say that those who know hope pray and those who pray know hope.

PRAYER: Holy Spirit, teach me to pray, teach me to hope. Amen.

---

* E. Glenn Hinson, "Relentless Optimist", *Weavings: A Journal of the Christian Spiritual Life,* 14, no. 6 (November/December, 1999): 34–40.

FRIDAY, MAY 25 • **Read Revelation 22:12-14, 16-17, 20-21**

The story of the Ascension reveals the hope to be found in Jesus Christ. It also reveals the fault lines in human life. Today's Revelation passage does the same thing.

Many of us find the Book of Revelation hard going. In an unblinking way, the book reminds its readers that madness is afoot on this earth and in the human heart. John, the author, does not try to frighten us into submission to a terrifying God. Instead he confronts us with our vulnerability and offers the hope that will not betray us—the faith, hope, and love found in Jesus Christ.

The late Lee Morical gave witness to this truth. She had everything—a good job, success as an author, recognition as a lecturer, and a happy marriage. Then rather quickly it all came apart. Her husband contracted cancer, and her own cancer returned, forcing her to resign her job.

While dying of cancer, Morical wrote these remarkable words: "I can honestly say that through God's grace I have received...gifts beyond any price that was paid. I learned that it is not in the getting and having it all but in the letting go we begin to find the peace that passes understanding. It is only when we realize that life has no safety nets—never had, never will—that we begin to know that out of God's love we cannot fall."*

To those of us who know the fault lines are out there and in us and who thirst for a hope that will not betray us, John says, "The Spirit and bride say, 'Come.'"

SUGGESTION FOR MEDITATION: **The Spirit says, "Come."**

---

*Haelen, Summer 1989 (Detroit, Mich.: Ecumenical Theological Seminary, 1989).

SATURDAY, MAY 26 • Read Psalm 110

Martin Luther's words give reason for reading Psalm 110 during Ascension week: "This is the high and chief Psalm of our dear Lord Jesus Christ in which His Person and His Resurrection, His Ascension, and His whole kingdom are...clearly and powerfully set forth."*

It was a psalm to which the early church turned to express its understanding of Jesus as Messiah. This psalm is referenced in twenty-two different places in the New Testament. To enrich your reading of this psalm, look at some of the verses that refer to it or reflect on its theme.

Peter quotes Psalm 110 in his Pentecost sermon: "The Lord said to my lord, sit at my right hand" (Acts 2:34b). We are probably familiar with the concluding verses of Romans 8: "For I am convinced that neither death, nor life, nor angels, nor rulers, nor things present, nor things to come, nor powers, nor height, nor depth, nor anything else in all creation, will be able to separate us from the love of God in Christ Jesus our Lord" (vv. 38-39). This magnificent verse is preceded by "Who is to condemn. It is Christ Jesus, who died, yes, who was raised, who is at the right hand of God, who indeed intercedes for us" (v. 34). Finally we find this description of the stoning of Stephen: "But filled with the Holy Spirit, he gazed into heaven and saw the glory of God and Jesus standing at the right hand of God" (Acts 7:55). This passage returns us to our week's theme of hope in God.

SUGGESTION FOR MEDITATION: **In light of these passages, reread the psalm and look for a verse that draws you into a prayer of praise to our Lord Jesus Christ.**

---

*W. Steward McCullough, "Psalms," *The Interpreter's Bible,* vol. 4 (Nashville, Tenn.: Abingdon Press, 1955), 588.

SUNDAY, MAY 27 • Read John 17:20-26

The Last Supper in John begins with Jesus' washing the disciples' feet and concludes with this prayer. What is the last thing Jesus prays before he goes forth to die? He thinks of those present and those who will become believers in him. He asks "that they may all be one." He wants his followers to be in the Father as he is in the Father. He wants them to know the glory that comes from being in the Father's love, for in the glory of divine love, they will know oneness. And through the harmony and oneness they share, others will come to believe in God.

Jesus' prayer is definitely a work in progress, but there are moments when believers experience this oneness. When these moments occur, they forever mark us and give us hope.

On July 18, 1996, the church I served in Oakfield, Wisconsin, my home, and a good fifth of the village were destroyed by an F-5 tornado. I don't know where all the people came from who worked in that village the next few days clearing the debris. The workers included executives, farmers, blue-collar workers, teachers, sheriff's deputies, prisoners, Salvation Army workers. One afternoon I took a break and walked around. I felt the oneness present in that wounded village. I remember uttering, "This is God's reign in our midst." Along with the much appreciated Salvation Army sandwiches, all present dined on the oneness of God's love.

Despite knowing one disciple would betray him, another deny him, and most desert him, Jesus acknowledged the possibility of their being one in him. So do I. It is Jesus' final prayer and humankind's last great conquest. That is what hope in God is and will do.

PRAYER: Christ, make us one in God's love. Amen.

Creation and Re-Creation

May 28–June 3, 2001 • E. Glenn Hinson*

MONDAY, MAY 28 • Read Psalm 104:24-34

I could have entitled this week's meditations "Renewing the Whole Creation," which is what Pentecost signifies. The Spirit renews nature, human society, and individual men and women. Because of the Spirit we can again dream dreams and bring them to reality. And how greatly we need the message of Pentecost today!

Science and technology have done wonderful things with nature in my lifetime. I'm thankful for antibiotics. In 1938 I spent a month in a near coma with double pneumonia. At that time your body had to pull you through without much help. All the doctor gave me was some thick syrup to keep me from coughing too hard. Although penicillin was invented ten years before, it wasn't used to cure pneumonia until 1940. Today penicillin can conquer pneumonia in a few hours.

That same science and technology have created immense threats to human survival. The circle of nations with nuclear power grows as our own nation ponders how to clean up the deadly waste left by cold-war production. Others build lethal biological arsenals. A growing number of physicists warn of the dangers of "global warming." Uncontrolled and careless use of pesticides in agriculture puts food consumption at risk.

Psalm 104:30 offers a hopeful word to us: "When you send forth your spirit, they are created; and you renew the face of the ground." God renews the earth.

PRAYER: Thank you, dear God, for your re-creation and renewal of our earth and sea and sky. May I today treat your gifts with greater awareness, care, and respect. Amen.

---

*Baptist minister, teacher for thirty years at The Southern Baptist Seminary, Louisville, Kentucky.

TUESDAY, MAY 29 • Read Acts 2:1-21

According to the ancient story told in Genesis 11:1-9, at the beginning and by God's intention "the whole earth had one language and the same words" (v. 1). Understanding one another was a key to the community God wanted humankind to enjoy. But runaway human ambition—the tower of Babel—resulted in confusion of languages and lack of understanding (11:7). The first Christian Pentecost signaled God's effort through the church to reverse Babel.

Luke understands what happens at Pentecost as a gift of foreign languages through which the hopeful message about God's restoration of human community will reach all people everywhere. Spirit-controlled, the people in the Pentecost crowd speak "in the native language of each" (2:6). Not drunkenness but dreams are the meaning of the "divided tongues." In this strange event and in the church lay the promise of restoration of human community.

Recent world events show our desperate need for reminders of this promise. With our own eyes we've watched tens and hundreds of thousands of people flee their homes in Kosovo to take refuge wherever they can find it. Homes looted and burned; families scattered. We hear stories of massacres, and the mass graves confirm them. Yet this is not the whole story. In crisis and despair we experience Pentecost anew, as nations transcend their diversities. They find sanctuaries, supply food for the hungry and drink for the thirsty, and take strangers into their homes. They unite to force withdrawal of military forces. As in the first Pentecost, so again God pours out God's spirit on all people. People have visions, dream dreams, and act on those dreams.

PRAYER: Dear God, forgive me when I let Babel pride and ambition create divisions. Fill me with your Spirit that I may find ways to attain the community you desire for all humankind. May I seek not so much to be served as to serve. Amen.

WEDNESDAY, MAY 30 • Read Romans 8:14-17

In Romans 8:14-17 the Apostle Paul reminds us that God has done something utterly astonishing. Through the Spirit, God adopted us as children so that we can address God in the same intimate way Jesus did, as "Abba" (Mark 14:36). By God's own action we have become full-fledged members of God's family and not household servants. We can approach God with the boldness of a child running toward a loving parent, crying, "Daddy! Mama!"

That's what *Abba* means. As modern scholarship has shown, it is a very intimate way of addressing God. I think we might also use *Imma*, "Mama." But gender's not the point; approachability is, just as Jesus portrayed so beautifully in the parable of the Loving Father (Luke 15:11-32). The prodigal, who had broken all ties with his family, intended to return home and be taken back as a slave. That's all he could expect. But he didn't even have a chance to get out that part of his plea. The Father took him back as a son, instructing the servants to put the best robe on him, a ring on his finger, and sandals on his feet and to prepare the party of all parties by killing the grain-fed calf to celebrate the return of "this son of mine."

The pouty elder brother was just burned up. He refused to go inside and join the party. He'd slaved for his father and never had so much as a goat to celebrate with his friends. He spewed anger. Yet the father "came out" to him (15:28).

Just so, Paul assures us, God comes out to each of us. No matter how we have strayed or what we have done, still God welcomes us not as slaves but as beloved children. How will we know this? As Paul states in Galatians 4:6: "God has sent the Spirit of his Son into our hearts, crying, 'Abba! Father!'" Not we, but the Spirit in us speaks.

PRAYER: O God of infinite love, fill me with your Spirit that I may know I am your child and act like it. Teach me to love as you love, to pardon as you pardon, to give as you give. Amen.

THURSDAY, MAY 31 • Read John 14:8-17

The Jesus presented by John blows my mind when he says that "the one who believes in me will also do the works that I do and, in fact, will do greater works than these, because I am going to the Father." Who can believe that we, the church through the ages, can perform works of a more exalted nature through prayer and obedience? But that's what Jesus says. How can it be?

Jesus offers a twofold answer: "because I am going to the Father" and because the Father "will give you another Advocate, to be with you forever." Jesus' "going" means that he has accomplished the redemptive mission for which the Father sent the Son (3:16). That redemption is the foundation on which anything the church does must rest. Through prayer and obedience we continue his mission. John sees the key in the sending of the Holy Spirit as our eternal Advocate.

The Spirit does not experience the geographical limits the Son experienced during his earthly sojourn. Through the Spirit the Incarnation continues in the lives of those who have believed in him; that is, committed themselves to him. Wherever they are, he is. Does a look at the Spirit's work in history not lend at least a modicum of support to John's conviction about equal and greater works?

Whereas Jesus confined his ministry to his own people in Palestine, a small slice of the earth's populace in an obscure point on the globe, today at least a fourth of the people in every part of the earth claim his name. While he taught hundreds in his homeland for whom he spoke with authority, later generations of Christians have founded thousands of colleges and universities and brought the light of Christ to millions the world over. The Paraclete we celebrate in Pentecost lives!

PRAYER: Dear God, may I not forget this day your assurance that you are doing greater works through us, and may I never slacken in love and attentiveness and obedience. Here are my hands; use them in your service. Here is my life; make it your dwelling. Through Jesus Christ. Amen.

FRIDAY, JUNE 1 • Read John 14:25-27

The Christians who first read John's Gospel raised a question every generation has had to ask: How will we know what Christian life requires now that Jesus is not with us anymore? It may have been tougher to answer before Mark, Matthew, Luke, and John composed their Gospels, but John says what all generations have had to conclude: We have had the Word of truth with us, but we must trust the Paraclete, the Holy Spirit, to teach us everything and to help us understand who Jesus was and what he means now (John 14:26).

From early on some Christians have found John's answer threatening. They have felt comfortable only with a fixed body of unshakable dogmas. In dispensationalist theory revelation ceased when the last apostle died. Subsequently, Christians have had to rely on the truth delivered once for all to the saints in written form.

In better times, fortunately, Christians have concurred with John. The Spirit Jesus sent is available in every generation as the Advocate, Comforter, and Teacher. One facet of the Spirit's guidance focuses on the interpretation of scripture. At the time of John's writing, Christian scriptures consisted of the Old Testament. Christians had to listen as well to what Clement of Alexandria called "the living voice" of the risen Christ. The Spirit has always had to direct the faithful through unmapped territory: what faith requires in different circumstances, how to live faithfully in community, how to face life's arduous trials, and numerous other challenges.

Here is where prayer as listening to God comes in. Prayer is, in essence, response to God's besieging love, opening to let the love of God flow in and generate deep-down security, peace not like the world gives but the peace only Jesus gives.

PRAYER: Fount of all wisdom, guide me today in all my endeavors. May no moment pass when I fail to be attentive to your Holy Spirit. Through Jesus Christ. Amen.

SATURDAY, JUNE 2 • Read Acts 2:14-21

Not all observers of the first Pentecost interpreted it positively. Some thought those speaking in different languages had drunk too much wine. Peter had to remind them that it was only 9:00 A.M., so they couldn't have gotten tipsy yet. He found an explanation for what was happening in the prophecy of Joel that "in the last days" God would pour out the Spirit upon all. Sons and daughters would prophesy, young men see visions, and old men dream dreams.

In the early Christian view Pentecost lifted human experience to a new level. Subsequent generations, however, have debated about the length of the era. Did the age of the Spirit last only so long as the apostles lived or does it continue even now? Did the prophecy, visions, and dreams promised by Joel happen only in the past, or do they still happen today? Did God speak only in one brief span or does God speak to us as God spoke to the prophets and apostles? Many have boldly held onto the conviction that every generation of Christians has prophets, visionaries, and dreamers.

Most of us would willingly acknowledge some persons of an earlier day, but have we had any in our generation? Would we not cite Martin Luther King Jr. for his leadership in the nonviolent civil rights movement in the United States? Or Clarence Jordan for his experiment in community at Koinonia Farm, which has inspired Habitat for Humanity and Jubilee Partners? Or Mother Teresa for embodying compassion for the poorest of the world's poor, which brought the Sisters of Charity of Calcutta into being? There are such persons in our churches—those with prophetic insight, vision, and dreams; open, attentive, and yielded to the Spirit. Our world needs such persons.

PRAYER: Dear God, I know that you still pour out your Spirit upon all persons everywhere. Forgive me when I fail to pay attention and to open to your gentle knocking. I pledge myself to a new level of awareness. Through Jesus Christ. Amen.

SUNDAY, JUNE 3 • **Read Psalm 104:33, 35b**

PENTECOST

Our meditations this week have focused on God's renewal of the whole creation—nature, human community, and individual men and women. In concluding, it seems fitting to think about our response to the One who creates, invites us to participate in the stewardship of creation, and then, when we fail, recreates and restores. No response, surely, is more appropriate than the psalmist's: "I will sing to the Lord as long as I live; / I will sing praise to my God while I have being....Bless the Lord, O my soul. / Praise the Lord!"

Praise! An act of our whole being. An expression beyond all speech. "Oh, for a thousand tongues to sing, my great Redeemer's praise," we sing with Charles Wesley. That's why we feel compelled to join with others in corporate praise. Our personal benediction is too tiny. It's not enough to let the world know the joy erupting deep within us. We want our small voice to join in the chorus of those who praise God.

Some think religion is what we do with our solitude. Surveys show that "baby boomers," persons born between 1946 and 1964, and "GenXers," persons born between 1965 and 1977, often discount the importance of public worship. While I have a high regard for individual commitments, I believe we express to God our transcendent joy within community. True, our corporate praise will not be perfect. It will have flaws because we who come are flawed. Nevertheless, the spirit of God will fill it with life and make of it something greater than all our expectations.

There is an integral connection between our individual and our corporate praise. The prayers we have prayed throughout the week have prepared us for corporate worship today, and our worship today will inspire our attentiveness to God in everyday life.

PRAYER: **Hallelujah! Praise God! Bless the Lord, O my soul. Amen.**

Wise Words for the Morning After

June 4–10, 2001 • LeeAnn Inman*

MONDAY, JUNE 4 • Read John 16:12-15

"I still have many things to say to you."

What happened the day after Pentecost? Did the disciples of Jesus and all those new converts (Acts 2:41) awaken with a spiritual hangover? Life among the Jerusalem believers eventually settled into "praising God and having the goodwill of all the people" (Acts 2:47), but that first new day of the church may well have felt like a letdown. With the church still reeling in the windy wake of the Pentecost birthday bash, Trinity Sunday approached, challenging Christians to receive the gift of God's Spirit. Trinity comes not with exploding fireworks but as an unfolding mystery of God, a gift for life.

In his farewell discourse to the disciples in John's Gospel, Jesus speaks of the "Spirit of truth" and of the Spirit's ownership and authority over all things with the Father. The job descriptions of each person of God as expressed in the Trinity overlap. The lines of authority may be hazy, but one thing is clear: Our God is inherently relational.

As creatures made in the image of God, we too are inherently relational: with God, with others, with the earth. The point of Jesus' message to his friends just prior to his death, resurrection, and ascension is that, through the Spirit and the community of believers, they will not be left alone. God, the ultimate parent, will never leave them orphaned. Blessed by the Spirit, in the community of the church, may we hear the truth Jesus promises in this season after Pentecost.

PRAYER: May your Spirit come to me today, God, and guide me into all truth. Amen.

---

*Pastor, Hyde Park United Methodist Church, Tampa, Florida.

TUESDAY, JUNE 5 • **Read Proverbs 8:1-4, 22-31**

The Lord created me at the beginning....

God, the *one* God of the Hebrew people, shares an elusive name with Moses: "I WILL BE WHAT I WILL BE" (Exod. 3:14, AP) and comes with a promise: "I will be with you." From the beginning of creation, God has desired intimacy with humanity.

God's nature and name find confirmation in the form and character of wisdom. The existence of wisdom with God at the beginning of the universe indicates God's concern for order and purpose at the core of creation. When we consider all biblical references to creation, this presence with God at the beginning includes Spirit, Wisdom, and Word (Gen. 1; Prov. 8; John 1). This range of descriptors of the Creator expresses the completeness, wholeness, and goodness of creation.

Wisdom, both in Greek and Hebrew, is a feminine noun. To attribute wisdom's existence to God "at the beginning" offers a woman's touch to the creative process without depersonalizing or objectifying God. Instead, God's intimacy with creation and humankind and God's own relational being are revealed and shared with the world and its inhabitants.

I recall a chapel service in 1976, the first time I received the bread and cup of Holy Communion from the hand of a woman —a sacramental moment. My emotion in that moment had little to do with the particular woman; it had to do with all the women who had prepared and served me meals: my mother and grandmothers, neighbors and countless "church ladies." These ordinary meals were given extraordinary worth. Mealtime and Communion, provision for my physical and spiritual growth, became holy ground for me, for those who served, and for those who are served. We are all beloved children of a loving God.

PRAYER: Holy God, thank you for the completeness of your love and provision for me. Open my eyes and my heart to know the many ways you are with me; help me share your presence. Amen.

WEDNESDAY, JUNE 6 • Read Psalm 8

What are human beings that you are mindful of them,
mortals that you care for them?

My favorite praise chorus affirms the sentiment of Psalm 8. "Our God is an awesome God!" God's creation, amazing and awesome, defies our best adjectives. When we attempt to take it all in, we find that we cannot even begin to do so. The universe and its creator are above us and beyond us.

So where does that awe leave us? Are we left beyond hope of knowing the God who is so "above and beyond"? The psalmist asks this question directly, a sign of a good relationship in both human and divine communication: "What are human beings that you are mindful of them, / mortals that you care for them?"

The answer comes as directly as the question: "You have made them a little lower than God, / and crowned them with glory and honor." No cowering critters, we are made by God for God and blessed with a place next to God in the divine order.

Remember the childhood need and desire to be "next to" a special friend in line? We don't often admit it, but that need continues throughout our lives. I feel good when someone saves a place for me at a meeting—and even when the children fight over who gets to sit next to me in the car or at a restaurant.

A place is saved for us, for all humanity, right there next to God. We did nothing to earn it. That's just the way God seems to want us. Close. It's an honor to have God save us a place, an honor that calls us to respond in praise:

O Lord, our Sovereign,
how majestic is your name in all the earth! Amen.

THURSDAY, JUNE 7 • Read Romans 5:1-5

God's love has been poured into our hearts through the Holy Spirit that has been given to us.

Some of my best friends are Presbyterians. They often refer to "Wesleyan theology" as a contradiction in terms. I object! I find the practicality of John Wesley's writing and preaching challenging. Wesley's description of the developmental stages of faith pictures faith as a house. He calls the front porch *prevenient grace*. This is where God always waits, beckons, invites, and welcomes us to faith. The second stage is the doorway of *justifying grace*. Here we come around to faith, choose to step into the threshold of God's love and forgiveness, and begin a new life of discipleship. *Sanctifying grace* is the living room, where God's presence is known and enjoyed in holy living.

Romans 5 finds us within the doorway of justification. Paul makes it clear in the first four chapters that righteousness is not something we achieve on our own. It is a gift of God that, when received, changes lives. I avoided this text in my early years of preaching. Carrie, our first child, was born with Down's Syndrome. I suffered, grieving the loss of the perfect child I had expected, wondering if I would ever find my way back to God, much less the pulpit.

My mother, a wise woman of faith, showed me the way through the doorway of God's grace. Carrie, her long-awaited first grandchild, was clearly a gift of God to my mother, who held her tenderly and talked to her in the unique and loving language of grandmothers. During one of my tearful moments, Mom said, "LeeAnn, Carrie is not here to live up to your expectations. She's here to be God's child, the Carrie God wants her to be." And so she is. Carrie (now eighteen) is God's woman, and a sign of hope to her mother.

PRAYER: Gracious God, help me focus on the places in my life where I suffer. (Pause and reflect on your personal grief or loss.) I offer my suffering to you, trusting your grace will sustain me. Amen.

FRIDAY, JUNE 8 • Read Romans 5:1-5

Therefore, since we are justified by faith, we have peace with God through our Lord Jesus Christ.

Those same Presbyterian friends taught me the Westminster Shorter Catechism, which poses this question: "What is the chief end of man?" The catechism, written long before any sensitivity to gender inclusiveness, supplies the answer: "To glorify God and enjoy him forever." And that response presents the final stage of grace according to John Wesley: *glorifying grace.* (At this point, the house image breaks down; but for me, the room of God's grace would be the kitchen.) This grace puts creatures in the heart of the home with the Creator, where we ultimately belong. Homecoming is complete.

The glorious homecoming is only a hope to those of us who are yet alive. *Only* a hope is something like *only* a homemaker, underplaying the importance of what is crucial to life and community. The hope of home keeps us balanced in the midst of all that would pull us away and apart from God's realm.

Wesley's theology also calls us to practical balance. The Wesleyan quadrilateral, an ideal for Christian decision making, has helped me when the way home to God seemed unclear. First in the quadrilateral is *scripture*. How does the biblical witness direct us? Then we consider *tradition*, the history of faithful response—for good and ill. God-given *reason* invites us to use our brains. Does this decision make sense? What are the consequences? Finally, how does this decision play out in our *experience*? This balanced approach to faithful living keeps me engaged with scripture, with other people of faith, and with my own experience. Grandmother Claire used to quote a proverb, "Temperance in all things." I would say, "Temperance in all things, except hope."

PRAYER: God, you created me and your world for shalom, the perfect balance of wholeness, health, and peace. Thank you for the hope that keeps me centered when I feel pulled apart. Amen.

SATURDAY, JUNE 9 • **Read Psalm 8**

O Lord, our Lord, how majestic is your name in all the earth!

I collect hymnbooks. They sit on a shelf of honor in my office, and, next to my Bible, collect the least amount of dust. I read hymn texts the way I read *The Upper Room*—for devotion and inspiration. It's hard to separate the words from the music, and I seldom try. But even if I don't know the tune or flip through an Anglican hymnal with no musical notations, I enjoy the poetry.

A recent archaeological discovery and scholarly investigation have turned up evidence of what was already suspected: that the psalms were sung in Jewish and early Christian worship. Little dots and lines above the letters, once thought to be specks of dust and extraneous marks from a careless scribe, are really musical notations. Such evidence may be the closest we come to knowing how the oldest hymns actually were sung.

I'll bet they were sung with great passion. At one place in the sacrament of Holy Communion, the liturgy goes like this: "And so, with your people on earth and all the company of heaven we praise your name and join their unending hymn." Then in most Protestant worship, the congregation responds in a unison spoken drone: "Holy, holy, holy Lord, God of power and might, heaven and earth are full of your glory. Hosanna in the highest. Blessed is he who comes in the name of the Lord. Hosanna in the highest."

I found new life in worship when, visiting a college chapel, I was invited to sing the Communion liturgy for the first time. There's something about the addition of music to liturgy that lifts the poetry and the singers to heaven. The "mysteries of faith," whether the Creation, the Incarnation, the gifts of the Spirit, or the holy Trinity, are best proclaimed with every creative gift we can bring to them.

PRAYER: (Sing!) Holy, holy, holy! Lord God Almighty! Amen.

SUNDAY, JUNE 10 • Read John 16:12-15

TRINITY SUNDAY

"I have much more to say to you..." (NIV).

In his swan song to the disciples, Jesus says these words, not in defeat but knowing his friends can bear no more. What they don't even know they need is just what Jesus promises: the "Spirit of truth,...[who] will guide you into all truth." On Trinity Sunday, we celebrate the gift of the Spirit, completing the mystery of Creator, Redeemer, Sustainer, the triune God we worship.

Another old hymn, known as St. Patrick's Breastplate, honors the Trinity:

I bind unto myself the Name,
  the strong Name of the Trinity
By invocation of the same,
  the Three in One and One in Three!
Of whom all nature hath creation;
  Eternal Father, Spirit, Word:
Praise to the Lord of my salvation,
  salvation is of Christ the Lord.

At times in my life I address my prayers only to Jesus. Lately the prayers go up consistently to "Gracious God." I direct the prayers that never quite take the form of language to the Spirit. The variety of God's nature engages me in a balance of practical spirituality. I sit on this three-legged prayer stool; if one leg is longer, more prominent than the others, I slide right off.

The doctrine of the Trinity brings balance, expressing God's extravagant generosity to all creation. God wants humanity enough to create us. God loves humanity enough to save us and to give us the gift of God's own Spirit to sustain us in community. This hints at the "more" that Jesus had to say to his disciples. May we be ready to hear.

PRAYER: Mysterious, awesome, powerfully loving God, thank you for the ways you come near to me. Amen.

173

The Hidden Person of the Heart

June 11–17, 2001 • *Eloise George Weatherspoon**

MONDAY, JUNE 11 • **Read 1 Kings 21:1-7**

Reading about King Ahab and his desire for Naboth's vineyard reminds us of another king who looked out over the rooftops, saw a woman bathing, and determined that he must have her. King David had other wives, as King Ahab had other vineyards. We know he had other vineyards because he offers to give Naboth "a better vineyard" in return. When Naboth refuses, he becomes sullen. The greed of both of these kings leads them to covet that which belongs to someone else. Out of their greed arise deception and murder.

In our prosperous society, many of us live in greater comfort and luxury than any king from previous centuries. Yet an affluent society apparently does not produce contented and appreciative people. In fact, almost the opposite appears to be true. We read about pioneer children who woke up Christmas morning, delighted to find a rag doll and an apple or an orange in their stockings, while our own children seem to take for granted the expensive gifts we lavish upon them.

Instead of feeling gratitude for all the wonderful things we have, it is all too easy to wish for that one thing we do not have and to become sullen and ungrateful. We cannot change the century in which we live or the society in which we find ourselves. We can, however, be consciously aware of and grateful for what we have. We are truly rich when we are contented, appreciative, and, most of all, generous.

PRAYER: Lord, help me hold my possessions loosely, remembering that all things are yours. May I be ready to give generously. Amen.

---

*Adjunct instructor of English composition, prayer group leader, and speaker for women's groups; Clarksville, Tennessee.

TUESDAY, JUNE 12 • Read 1 Kings 21:8-21*a*

Jezebel. The name conjures up images of the worst kind of evil. If Ahab was bad—and he was—Jezebel was worse. But what ruling characteristic made Jezebel the queen of evil?

Most of us would never identify ourselves with the kind of evil that Jezebel personifies, but when we look at her defining characteristic, we must admit that we have been guilty of it: Jezebel tried to manipulate in order to get her own way.

Ahab wanted a vineyard, and Naboth refused to sell. As far as Ahab was concerned, that refusal settled the matter—but not for Jezebel. If she could not get what she or Ahab wanted through proper channels, she would figure out a way to control the situation.

I remember as a newly married woman having my life enriched but also complicated by the presence of another person's will. I remember a weekend when I wanted to go home to Birmingham to see my family and that other person was set against the trip on that particular weekend. Whatever I did by means of persuading, whining, complaining, and cajoling, my next memory is of being in the car on the way to Birmingham but not being completely at peace about it. I had won, but there was a hollowness in the victory.

It is a part of human nature to desire to get our own way. One of the greatest miracles in our lives occurs when God helps us to be content with whatever happens, whether we win or lose. Instead of struggling to get things to work out the way we want, we can relax and trust in the will of that One who knows the end from the beginning.

PRAYER: Lord, help me say with the Apostle Paul, "I have learned, in whatever state I am, to be content" (Phil. 4:11*b*, RSV).

WEDNESDAY, JUNE 13 • Read Psalm 5:1-3

I am a night person. If I had my way, I would stay up late every single day. For years I had my devotional at night, at which time I did most of my praying and Bible reading. After all, I reasoned, everyone was in bed. The house was quiet. And I was more alert at that time of day.

A few years ago, however, I heard a teaching that made me change that ingrained habit overnight. The speaker made several persuasive points that I could not refute. For one thing, if God really is first in our lives, God should have our precious time, not our spare time. By meeting with God first thing in the morning, we indicate God's importance in our lives.

Praying at night, after the events of the day, is somewhat like closing the barn door after the animals have escaped. Prayer at the beginning of the day helps us appropriate God's wisdom and direction for whatever that day may bring.

Probably the most persuasive point, and the one that compelled me to change my routine, was that God's perspective differs greatly from the world's perspective. We so easily get caught up in the motives, cares, and distractions of this world that it is vitally important to read God's word, seek God's heart, and be in tune with God's mind-set before the busyness of our hectic day sweeps us away.

I enjoy my morning times with the Lord so much that I have to drag myself away to go to work. I still pray at night quite often, but if I run out of time or energy, I know I have given God the best hour of my day.

PRAYER: "Lord, in the morning thou dost hear my voice" (RSV). Amen.

THURSDAY, JUNE 14 • Read Psalm 5:4-8

One day last semester, one of my students and I were discussing our experiences of answered prayer. I was pleased that she was a person of prayer who was learning more about God. Several days later, she talked enthusiastically about her favorite psychic and her live-in boyfriend, and it became clear to me that we were not on the same wavelength after all.

New Age rhetoric can often sound much like Christianity, but a watershed issue divides the two, an issue that Psalm 5 addresses. God is a holy God, and only those who do evil will not find themselves in the divine presence.

New Age philosophy presents a god who seems to accept whatever we do. The New Age god winks at sin. In fact, there is no real concept of sin, because whatever we do is fine as long as it does not hurt anyone. Conventional standards of morality are passe, and the moralist is viewed as intolerant.

Psalm 5, as well as many other passages in the Bible, presents God as intolerant of sin; we should be holy as God is holy (Lev. 11:44). This is not a popular notion for our early twenty-first century mind-set, but it is clearly what the Bible tells us about God.

The seriousness of sin, and God's inability to tolerate it, finds its culmination in the cross. The huge price God paid there would mean little if sin were a nonissue. However, because our sinfulness and God's holiness are irreconcilable, Christ died so that we may become "the righteousness of God" (2 Cor. 5:21, RSV). Therefore, we can say along with the psalmist, "But I, through the abundance of your steadfast love, will enter your house" (Ps. 5:7).

PRAYER: **Lord, thank you for making a way for me into your presence. Amen.**

FRIDAY, JUNE 15 • Read Galatians 2:15-21

As we saw yesterday, if sin were not such a barrier to our fellowship with God, then the death of Christ would lose its significance. But this passage in Galatians tells us of another misconception that would also minimize the death of Christ: "I do not nullify the grace of God; for if justification were through the law, then Christ died to no purpose" (2:21, RSV). The error Paul addresses here acknowledges the seriousness of sin but assumes that by keeping the law, by means of our own righteousness, we can be reconciled to God and enjoy divine fellowship.

As a Pharisee who had attempted to obey every possible law down to the smallest detail, Paul knew the futility of trying to keep the whole law. And as a Christian who had experienced forgiveness and grace through Jesus Christ, he knew the freedom that the cross had bought for him. Nothing seemed to scare him more than to see Christians who had received the free gift of God's saving grace fall back into legalism and a dependence on their own righteousness.

Paul never got over the difference it made in his life to be "crucified with Christ" (2:20), so that instead of working himself up and struggling to be righteous in his own strength, he could trust the spirit of God to live the godly life of Christ through him. Connected to the vine, Jesus Christ, he experienced change in the inner man rather than imposing an outward law on his behavior. His trust in Christ, not his own goodness, transformed the quality of his life.

PRAYER: Lord, thank you for the freedom I have in Jesus. Amen.

SATURDAY, JUNE 16 • Read Luke 7:36-39

I will never forget a church conference I attended many years ago when an unexpected visitor disrupted the carefully planned ceremony. A pastor from Africa who had received support from this denominational body emerged from the audience and made an emotional speech expressing his gratitude for our help and his love for his Savior.

I sensed a general feeling of awkwardness and discomfort among those distinguished men and women. This kind of deep emotion and profound love was out of place in such a respectable gathering. We did not quite know how to respond.

The woman with the alabaster flask of ointment becomes a disruption to the Pharisee's orderly meal. When the Pharisee notices that this woman's unconventional act of worship does not offend Jesus and that Jesus actually welcomes it; it annoys him. Surely Jesus would not be so receptive of her if he knew what sort of woman she was!

I suspect the Pharisee experienced more discomfort with the woman's emotional show of love and her tears than with her reputation as a sinner. Deep, heartfelt love and emotion based on a relationship with the Savior will always be met with scorn, self-righteousness, and skepticism from those who have substituted religion for relationship.

That day Jesus taught the self-righteous Pharisee a lesson about love—that those who have been forgiven much, love much, and that those who have been forgiven little, love little. Certainly the Pharisee had more to be forgiven for than he realized. Sometimes, like him, we have a veneer of good behavior that blinds us to the depth of our sin and our need. We too need to learn a lesson about love.

PRAYER: Lord, help me be more concerned with the hidden person of the heart than with how I appear to myself and others. Amen.

SUNDAY, JUNE 17 • Read Luke 7:40–8:3

It was time for the yearly stewardship campaign. Each Sunday for several Sundays, a different member of the church got up to tell about his or her own giving and to encourage others to give. Conspicuously absent from this honor roll of givers was anyone resembling the woman who gave the widow's mite. These were prominent people who could afford to give generously.

How different were the people Jesus singled out for special recognition from those we would choose! I can think of three people whom Jesus praised highly. One was the poor widow, unnoticed by anyone but Jesus. Other people noticed the expensive gifts, but Jesus knew who was making the greatest sacrifice, and this woman's generosity deeply touched his heart.

Another person for whom Jesus reserved high praise was an officer in the hated occupying army. This man's compassion for his servant, discernment in coming to Jesus for help, and faith that Jesus had merely to speak a word from a distance and his servant would be healed so impressed Jesus that he shocked the disciples by saying that this man's faith exceeded any he had seen in Israel (Matt.8:5-13).

A third person on the Lord's honor roll was this woman, by all accounts a notorious sinner, who did a seemingly strange thing by anointing Jesus' feet with costly ointment and wiping them with her hair. Her act of humility, love, and worship touched the heart of Jesus so deeply that he foretold that her story would forever be included as part of the gospel—and so it has been. God's perspective differs so greatly from ours, for "the Lord does not see as mortals see; they look on the outward appearance, but the Lord looks on the heart"(1 Sam.16:7).

PRAYER: O God who looks on the heart, help me to please you rather than mortals. Amen.

God Points Us Past Our Troubles

June 18–24, 2001 • Mark A. Pearson*

Monday, June 18 • Read 1 Kings 19:1-10, 15

This week's lessons all focus on various troubles we face. God does not encourage us to deny the reality of our troubles but asks that we focus on God and God's plan for us instead. Many great preachers and evangelists over the centuries have noted that right after great spiritual victories, they go into a spiritual depression. So too with Elijah.

Fresh from God's victory over the priests of Baal on Mount Carmel, Elijah flees from the wrath of King Ahab and Queen Jezebel and indulges in self-pitying introspection. Where was the courage he so recently demonstrated in confronting God's enemies? Where was the faith with which he confidently soaked the wood that was going to burn the sacrifice? In the midst of his crisis God commands Elijah to eat to strengthen himself for the tasks God still has in store for him.

Dropping into spiritual depression, especially after a great spiritual victory, is something over which we have no control. But what we do next *is*. Yes, our problems are real, but we must focus on the size of our God, not on the size of our problem. Yes, we are to acknowledge our unworthiness and inadequacy, but we must not brood on them. Instead, we should confess and then listen for God's next assignment. In other words, don't look down; look up. Don't look back; look ahead.

Suggestion for meditation: Read Hebrews 12:1-2. Remind yourself when you are feeling spiritually alone that, like Elijah, you are in fellowship with many believers; God does provide for you materially and spiritually. Remind yourself also to avoid self-pity; get up and run the race in which God has put you.

---

*Canon Theologian of the Charismatic Episcopal Church; author and leader of healing missions and conferences, Plaistow, New Hampshire.

TUESDAY, JUNE 19 • Read 1 Kings 19:11-15

There has been much talk lately about various dramatic acts God is supposedly performing. Christian magazines contain accounts of instantaneous healings, dental fillings turning to gold, people in worship services spontaneously bursting forth in a laughter that lasts for hours, "words of prophecy" through which God speaks information known only to ourselves.

I find my friends' responses to these stories fascinating. Some friends automatically reject anything dramatic, sudden, miraculous, or loud, as if God couldn't possibly do this sort of thing. Yet doesn't the New Testament describe many such events? Why shouldn't God do Godlike things? On the other hand, I have friends who insist that God works *only* in this manner. All healings must be miraculous and instantaneous. All interventions of God must defy human reason and exclude human effort.

We may forget the many occasions in the New Testament when our Lord combines his own effort with the hard work of people to make something special happen. In 1 Kings 18, God dramatically, miraculously sends fire from heaven to consume the sacrifices offered. In today's passage God is not in the wind, the earthquake, or the fire but in a still small voice. God acts instantaneously and gradually, miraculously and with human cooperation, dramatically and subtly, loudly and softly. The key is not to tell God the style in which God ought to operate but to pray that our eyes may see God at work in whatever way God chooses.

SUGGESTION FOR MEDITATION: Reflect on whether you demand that God work in only one way, not in others. Talk with mature Christian believers whose spiritual "styles" differ from yours to discover that God can work in other ways too. Pray for the discernment to see God at work in various ways.

WEDNESDAY, JUNE 20 • Read Psalm 42

The psalms do not present idealized believers but real believers going through real crises. The author of Psalm 42 is undergoing a spiritual crisis. He is spiritually parched and cannot find God. Compounding this situation are the taunts of people who imply that God has abandoned him. Instead of dwelling in self-pity or passively waiting for something to happen, the psalmist takes action. His heart may not be in it, but he is doing the right thing, knowing that sometimes the head has to lead the heart out of the wilderness.

First (v. 4*a*), he recalls what God did in his life previously. His hope that things will get better is based on the confidence that God who once blessed him will do so again. Second (v. 4*b*), he remembers the blessings received in corporate worship, and, presumably, decides to join in once more. How often does a downcast Christian go to church out of duty, only to find that God honors that obedience and lifts him or her up? Third (v. 6*b*), he meditates on the actions God has done in Israel. God has been at work, so he can confidently believe God will work again—in him. Fourth (v. 8), he sings to the Lord. Fifth (vv. 8*b*-9), he prays. He may not feel anything while praying, and his prayer is one of complaint; but he keeps talking to God. Therefore, he has hope.

The biblical word *hope* differs from the meaning of the word in common parlance, which means "wouldn't it be nice if...but I doubt it'll happen." In scripture *hope* means a certainty that hasn't happened yet...but it will!

PRAYER: O God, when I'm downcast, remind me to hang in there with you; to remember your past mercies to me and to others; and to worship, praise, and pray. Amen.

THURSDAY, JUNE 21 • Read Galatians 3:19-26

I remember the first time my parents went out for the evening and did not leave me with a baby-sitter. They said, "Previously, you were not mature enough to make the right decisions, and you needed someone to keep you in check. Now you're grown up enough not to need a baby-sitter."

The law functioned that way in Israel, as a disciplinarian (baby-sitter) until grace was poured out in Christ. In our previous two meditations, the problems faced were external (Ahab and Jezebel and the taunts of the psalmist's acquaintances) and emotional (a downcast soul). Here the problem derives from being under the Old Testament law. As Paul elsewhere says, the law is good. It is good because it represents the will of God, because it tells us right from wrong, and because eventually it convicts us of sin by showing how far short we fall.

The law is good but it does not bestow the grace to help us obey. Because we can never keep it perfectly, it can never lead us to salvation. But now faith has come. Actually, Israel was a people of faith, so verse 23 means either "the faith" (the content of the gospel) or "faith in what Christ did and does for us." The grace of Christ works in us so that we can become the people God wants us to be, not through a baby-sitter's reining us in but out of God's word deep within us. The grace of Christ who died on the cross makes us children of God through faith.

PRAYER: Thank you, Jesus. My sins are such that I could never be saved by my own accomplishments—only by your grace. Help me grow to become like you. Amen.

FRIDAY, JUNE 22 • Read Galatians 3:27-29

When I was young, I realized that the Protestant churches in our area were stratified socially. Company owners attended the Episcopal church in the next city, middle management attended the Congregational church, and blue-collar workers the Methodist or Baptist churches. It surprised me to learn that at the Roman Catholic church the superintendent of schools sat in the same pew as an assistant janitor at the junior high school. It seemed to me as a ten-year-old that this was right. Yes, of course, rank and position matter, but before God both men were equally important and beloved.

The Galatians had a lot to unlearn. Many Jewish men prayed daily, "Thank God I was not born a woman." Jew and Gentile alike disdained slaves as nonpersons.

No, scripture does not *erase* the distinctions between male and female, boss and worker, parents and children, or even clergy and laity. The New Testament even assigns different roles to each and speaks of various kinds of submission. For example, children are to obey their parents but not vice versa (Eph. 6:1). There are orders of ordained people in the church, and each has a specific role, including a disciplinary one. A Christian worker still has to obey the boss at work!

But in the church no one group is better than another. And, in the economy of God, it may be a car mechanic who ministers most effectively in the nursing home and a lawyer whom God assigns to clean the rest rooms. Whatever our distinctions, we are to be one in Christ.

PRAYER: Lord, forgive me when I've been snobbish, and forgive me when I've been too intimidated by another's rank or position to obey you. Remind me of the unity of all believers in Jesus. Amen.

SATURDAY, JUNE 23 • Read Luke 8:26-37

What do you think about the subject of evil spirits? Today's passage describes a man thus possessed. Just as the citizens of his area feared the deliverance Jesus worked in the man and asked him to leave, the subject of a ministry of exorcism may terrify us or we may banish the subject from consideration.

Perhaps we have seen "deliverance ministries" that harmed people. Perhaps movies such as "The Exorcist" left a bad taste in our mouths. Perhaps we believe the notion of demonic possession is a superstitious relic from the Dark Ages.

Yet demonic possession may require a second look. Both psychiatrist Scott Peck and professor C. S. Lewis have written best-sellers inviting us to take this subject seriously. I work with a team of people in whole-person healing ministry, including physicians and psychotherapists, all of whom acknowledge that sometimes a person's problem stems from the demonic, in whole or part.

The man in today's passage was harming himself and was cast off from society. He needed something far greater than exhortation to better behavior or counseling to resolve emotional distress—helpful as those are in other circumstances. His neighbors' remedy, guarding and chaining him, did not solve his problem. He needed a powerful encounter with God. Jesus came with power and authority to free people from all that harms them, including the demonic.

SUGGESTION FOR MEDITATION: **Read the various New Testament passages that mention deliverance from evil spirits, and notice how they differ from current perceptions of exorcism, particularly as portrayed in the movies.**

Sunday, June 24 • Read Luke 8:26-39

How can we best say thank you to Jesus for all he has done and continues to do for us? One way is to share the good news with those who don't know it. While pointing people who don't know Jesus to the scripture is important, equally important is a firsthand account of what God has done in a person's life. Spreading the good news out of gratitude for what God has done for us is just one source of God's blessing. James K. Wagner puts it this way: "We are blessed to be a blessing."

In my doctoral work on Christian healing, I discovered that most people in the average, mainline Protestant congregations believe that God heals in response to prayer. Many of them shared personal experiences of healing with me, noting that few fellow Christians ever told them of their healing experiences. This lack of sharing and confirmation of experience led them to wonder if their beliefs about healing were odd. They also wondered if they might more readily turn to God for help if regularly encouraged by others' testimony.

Sharing our stories doesn't require a seminary degree. Consider the healed blind man of John 9. All he said was, "I was blind; I now see; and Jesus did it." Not profound, not technical, not "advanced level" but not a bad start either! If that's all you can say, say it! People are waiting to hear.

PRAYER: You have blessed me in so many ways, Lord, and I want similar blessings for others. Help me overcome my shyness and share the good news with all I meet. In Jesus' name. Amen.

Strength for the Long Haul

June 25–July 1, 2001 • Glory E. Dharmaraj*

MONDAY, JUNE 25 • **Read 2 Kings 2:1-2, 6-12**

Let us begin this week with the assurance that God promises us strength for the long haul. Today's scripture reading is about Elisha's receiving additional strength for his spiritual journey and prophetic calling. Elisha witnesses his mentor and guide, Elijah, ascend into heaven in a storm. Elisha takes up his late master's mantle and resumes the work of the Lord.

Most of us may not receive affirmation of our spiritual call by such a dramatic witness. But God gives us power equal to the task ahead. The shoes we have to fill may seem oversized, so also the size of the mantle. Yet the spirit of God that was with our spiritual forebears is with us too. God continues to raise God's people like Elijah and Elisha to fulfill God's mission.

Are there spiritual voids left in you by loss and bereavement of your spiritual mentors? Does your journey seem arduous and purposeless? Does it tend to become a "wandering"?

Today's scripture also directs our attention to an "inheritance." Elisha asks for a double portion of Elijah's spirit, God-given grace, for the long haul ahead. A double portion is usually given to the firstborn in Hebrew tradition. Elisha's plea is like a child's request to his or her parent. Even Jesus encourages such asking. "How much more will your heavenly parent give the Holy Spirit to those who ask God!" (Luke 11:13, AP). Let us fulfill our inherited legacy of Christ's commission by asking for the ever-present spirit of Christ.

PRAYER: O God, grant me your Holy Spirit to show me the way ahead. Amen.

---

*Women's Division staff, General Board of Global Ministries, The United Methodist Church, Church Center for the United Nations, New York, New York.

TUESDAY, JUNE 26 • Read 2 Kings 2:13-18

In today's reading, Elisha watches and experiences an out-of-the-ordinary event. His master, Elijah, is taken to heaven alive. Elisha is the closest eyewitness to this event.

Yet another group of people witnesses the event from a distance: a community of prophets. Soon after Elijah's ascension, the prophets witness Elisha's parting of the river Jordan with the mantle of Elijah. Witnessing this parting of the river convinces the community of believers that Elisha has indeed inherited the power of his master. However, these believers soon lose their focus when they insist that Elisha allow them to search for Elijah. They think God may have caught him up and then thrown him down on some mountain or in a valley. They insist on attempting this dysfunctional search, until Elisha is "ashamed" and gives his assent. A helpful insight for us is that alignment with God's vision comes only when we are attuned to the spirit of God. In this instance, the distant witnesses do not "get it."

This same Elijah, who was taken up alive, reappears thousands of years later with Moses on a mount where Jesus is transfigured before a core group of his disciples: Peter, James, and John. Like the community of prophets in the Old Testament, Peter loses his focus. He insists that they set up tents for Elijah, Moses, and Jesus on the mount (Matt. 17:1-9). Though Peter is a close witness, he does not "get it" either. How can one come so close to the holy of holies and still lose the sense of alignment with the Spirit's moving? The Holy Spirit often decenters and destabilizes us from established norms in order to fit us into new "Gilgals" (2 Kings 2:1), which literally means new "circles."

PRAYER: Jesus, keep me attuned to your spirit's working so that when you lead me into new horizons, I may be a frontier witness. Amen.

WEDNESDAY, JUNE 27 • Read Psalm 77:1-2

Today's reading captures the deep anguish of an individual soul who finds itself in an exiled situation, far removed from a known and rooted community. We can almost hear the anguished human voice that struggles in its human extremity to establish, maintain, and be in a relationship with God.

Most of us can relate to such a dark night of the soul. Certainly I can. As a five-year-old child, I lived in Sri Lanka. My parents wanted me to have a stable and good education, which was not available to immigrants on the tea estate of Hatton, in what was then Ceylon. They sent me to India to live in my paternal aunt's home so I might get a good education. Being a trained teacher, my mother had taught me how to read and write before I was five. She told me that whenever I felt lonely, especially before going to bed, in a faraway land, I should read Psalm 4.

Keeping one eye on God and the other on one's personal journey, however painful it may be, is the relational triumph of Psalm 77:1-2. We are not alone. We are in a relationship. We are in a voice-centered relation. Our cry calls forth God's response. Our human lament brings forth a divine response. God speaks to us as God did to Elijah, in a still small voice. The still small voice literally means a "sound of fine silence" (1 Kings 19:12, AP).

God knows our soul's voiced silence; its burnouts, stress, and numbness. The living Christ knows our voice as a shepherd knows the sheep (John 10:3-4), and he gathers us into his fold. He makes us see that our individual journey is part of a collective journey, a community journey. Hence we are not alone.

PRAYER: God in Christ, thank you for sharing our humanity. When the going gets tough, fill me with your grace and power. Amen.

THURSDAY, JUNE 28 • Read Psalm 77:11-20

Recently I was invited to conduct a workshop on the topic "Too Blessed to Be Stressed" to a group of United Methodist women. The workshop took place on Saturday afternoon immediately after lunch, so I wanted to avoid a lecture.

I had brought with me some broken and bent-over paper cups. I placed them on each of the tables around which the women were seated. I invited the women to reflect in silence on experiences of brokenness in their lives. Then I wrote on the chalkboard a sentence fragment for the participants to complete: "In the sight of God, in the sight of Christ, a broken cup is…." I invited the participants to share their thoughts. Many did. One woman from the last row responded, "In the sight of God, in the sight of Christ, a broken cup is in the company of other broken cups." Her words resonated with the rest of us, a moment of shared heritage of brokenness and "bent-overness."

Today's reading relates to a remembrance of solidarity. The psalmist looks back and recalls that his individual journey is part of a community journey. He connects with events across time; he recounts God's deeds in history. In particular, the psalmist remembers the Exodus event that stands head and shoulders above all the other events in his nation's collective memory. The cry of the psalmist turns into a doxology because he calls to mind God's parting of the mighty waters of the Red Sea and leading God's people like a flock by the hand of Moses and Aaron. This remembrance further connects him to his fellow travelers in life, recipients of God's abundant grace yet in continuous need of God's deliverance. For the psalmist, then, the memory does not retreat into self-pity anymore; rather, his memory becomes the bearer of God's salvation.

PRAYER: **God, my help in ages past, help me not to retreat into anguish and self-pity but to recenter on you. Amen.**

191

Friday, June 29 • Read Galatians 5:1, 13-25

Today's reading offers a checklist of pluses and minuses. Going up and down from the zero space of this list are plus and minus numbers. The top plus numbers are love, joy, peace, patience, kindness, generosity, faithfulness, gentleness, and self-control; they form the Spirit-Meter. Then below the zero space are the minus numbers. They indicate transgressions such as fornication, impurity, licentiousness, idolatry, sorcery, enmities, strife, jealousy, anger, quarrels, dissensions, factions, envy, drunkenness, and carousing, which show up on our Flesh-Meter.

The scripture passage urges us to read our Spirit- and Flesh-Meters: the pluses and minuses that daily form the sum score of our Christian being and witness. Let us look at the qualities on the plus side listed on the Spirit-Meter. Some of these qualities like gentleness (meekness), patience, and peace seem to be passive virtues.

However, Jesus exemplified these in his life and demonstrated that these are hardy virtues. It takes extraordinary courage to repay evil with good, violence with nonviolence, hatred with love. The Christian life is not toll-free living. When we allow the Holy Spirit to invade our lives, we say no to the flesh and don't allow it to use our life as its military base.

In a society that values and rewards aggressiveness over gentleness, militarism over nonviolence, and instant gratification over patience, the Spirit-Meter sets a different standard of witness. It calls us to accountability by its unswerving readings of our spiritual temperature. The power is within each of us to feed either the Spirit- or the Flesh-Meter.

Prayer: Holy Spirit, strengthen my resolve to walk in the Spirit. Amen.

SATURDAY, JUNE 30 • Read Luke 9:51-56

Jesus "set his face to go to Jerusalem." His journey to Jerusalem is about resoluteness. It is about accomplishing his mission. It is the "exodus" that he, Moses, and Elijah talked about on the Mount of Transfiguration. Jesus fulfills his messianic calling as he walks this walk to his cross, death, and resurrection.

In this journey through Samaria, Jesus becomes the object of ethnic prejudice. When the Samaritans do not receive him, his disciples want to bring down fire from heaven to destroy the Samaritan village. Jesus rebukes his fiery disciples, and they learn one more lesson on not repaying evil. This resolute walk of Jesus is a costly walk. It *costs* to lead a life of discipleship, a life dictated by a culture of calling. It is the way of the cross.

Many of the women followers of Jesus also walked this walk. They had followed him all the way from Galilee to Jerusalem (Matt. 27:55). Even when the male disciples fled in fear, some of the women were at the cross as well as the Resurrection site (Matt. 28:1-7).

The fiery disciples and faithful women discover a new and generative experience in their journey to the cross of Jesus and to the site of his Resurrection: transformative solidarity. It is a walk that transforms people.

Today Jesus continues to walk this walk with the poor and the oppressed. That is one of the reasons the poor and the suffering often identify themselves with the Jesus who walked to his cross and resurrection. Ignacio Ellacuria called the poor and oppressed Latin American people "crucified Christs of the Indies." Let us walk the walk of solidarity with the Christ who time and again accompanies the crucified among us.

PRAYER: **Dear God, guide my feet so that my walk is worthy of my calling. Amen.**

SUNDAY, JULY 1 • Read Luke 9:57-62

Discipleship is not a Christian's avocation; it is his or her vocation. Jesus' journey to Jerusalem provides a testing ground for his would-be disciples. No one who puts a hand to the plow and looks back is fit for the kingdom of God. Elisha met with a similar challenge of discipleship when Elijah called him to God's ministry. Elisha too was behind his plow on his large farm. But he left it in order to follow Elijah (1 Kings 19:19-20). Such a discipleship embodies God's strange economy. To be in discipleship is like being a seed dying unto itself but springing forth in an abundant harvest for others (John 12:24). It is also like partaking in the journey of Jesus by living out the mystery of the cross, death as well as resurrection.

The church is about the business of disciple making and the fostering of the culture of calling. Recently I heard an East Coast seminary president appeal to a group of United Methodist Women, asking that they help recruit good candidates for his seminary. He regretted that the "culture of calling" has almost disappeared from the churches, and the community of believers must cultivate this culture in the churches.

I have also come across a memory device used by the poorest of the poor Christians in the ghettoes of Bombay, India, to remind themselves of their daily discipleship. They paste Bible verses like "Take up your cross and follow me" and "Be faithful to the end and you will obtain the crown of righteousness" on their humble dressers, doorposts, and across windowsills.

These verses constantly remind them that the route of Christian mission is through daily discipleship. Discipleship is also the church's caller I.D.; its missionary relationship with the culture outside depends on the culture inside: the culture of calling and disciple making.

PRAYER: God of mission, keep me in your high calling for me. Amen.

Restoring the Fallen

*July 2–8, 2001 • Gregory V. Palmer *

In most respects Naaman, commander of the Aramean army, has it all: position, power, prestige, and recognition. But he is nagged with leprosy. The text does not tell us how long he has had the disease. A young Israelite woman who serves Naaman's wife expresses confidence that "the prophet in Samaria" can cure him. Naaman prepares to go to Samaria in search of the prophet Elisha and a cure for his leprosy. The word of an unnamed "servant girl" opens a new future for Naaman.

Howard Thurman in his autobiography *With Head and Heart* shares a marvelous incident from his early teens when he found himself with his back against the wall. He sat crying on the steps of the train station. He was trying to get to Jacksonville to enroll in school but lacked the funds to ship his trunk. A stranger approached him, inquired about his tears, and ultimately provided the funds needed to ship the trunk. Thurman observes, "Then, without a word, he turned and disappeared down the railroad track. I never saw him again."

So much in our culture makes us leery of strangers, of the unfamiliar, the unknown. We often expect that strangers will do us harm. While this wise strategy may help us prepare our children to leave the safe cloister of home, we must also practice and teach the ways that the unnamed, faceless people we encounter may be channels of blessing. More often than not I have been the recipient of kindness rather than hurtful behavior from even those whose names I may not know.

PRAYER: Dear God, thank you for the nameless people who have opened new futures for me. Amen.

---

*Pastor, The United Methodist Church of Berea, Berea, Ohio.

TUESDAY, JULY 3 • Read 2 Kings 5:5b-14

Naaman proceeds to Samaria with a letter of introduction from the king of Aram, lots of money, and extra clothes—obviously prepared to impress with his position, rank, and prestige. He comes with official credentials and lots of money to spread around if needed. He's prepared to do anything for a cure.

Naaman finally reaches Elisha's house. Through a third-party messenger, Elisha directs Naaman to "go and wash in the Jordan seven times." Elisha promises that such a washing will result in a cure. Naaman is angry, livid.

Naaman's outrage comes on two counts. One, Elisha does not address Naaman personally. No doubt he is offended, having come a great distance. Given Naaman's prestige he surely expects to be treated with more deference. Two, he finds the nonsensical simplicity of the "prescription" insulting.

How often in our lives have we missed a great blessing because it came disguised? We stand ready to entertain the big and the complex as a means to our healing and salvation, and God confounds us with babies and baptism. Naaman indeed is willing to do anything to be cured except take a simple bath in the Jordan River.

Perhaps this story's message to us is not to box God in, not predetermine how God will act. When we box God in through our preconceived notions of how God will act, then God's actions seem ridiculous. We want to bolt in the opposite direction. God welcomes our acknowledgment of our need and rejoices that we seek God's help. God does not need our expertise in determining how God will help us. When help comes, receive it as a gift. The only appropriate response to a gift and its giver is "thank you."

PRAYER: Gracious God, make me open to receive what you offer so I don't miss your blessings. Amen.

WEDNESDAY, JULY 4 • Read Luke 10:1-11

A tone of urgency saturates this text. Jesus is expanding the team and multiplying the ministry. He cannot be everywhere at once. The twelve also have their limitations. Now Jesus broadens the base and appoints seventy (or seventy-two) to serve as a sort of "advance team" for him. I have wondered if he sent these followers out figuring that he might never physically get to all the places he wanted to go. After all, Jerusalem is beckoning.

The tone of urgency is conveyed not only by the need for more help but by the specific instructions Jesus gives the seventy. Jesus urges them to stay focused. He sends them to announce the inbreaking of God's reign and to be gracious guests. But he also instructs the seventy not to tarry where they receive no welcome.

I am persuaded that people in our time, no less than the time of the historical Jesus, hunger for meaning and salvation. The people I encounter yearn for a living relationship with God. They don't always express their hunger and yearning in the vocabulary of Christian faith. But if we engage and probe and live in dialogue with those around us, we often discover that they yearn for the God made known in Jesus the Christ. That yearning may be the sign of a budding harvest.

"The harvest is plentiful, but the laborers are few; therefore, ask the Lord of the harvest to send out laborers into his harvest." With the help of the Holy Spirit, we bring in God's harvest when we help people name their hunger, pointing them to the feast of God, helping them make the vital life-giving connection.

The church must discover anew the capacity to discern the hungers of the heart that surround us. We must be engaged with the cultures where we live, so we can listen deeply to all of God's children. We must be unapologetic in pointing people to the one who is life and who gives life—Jesus Christ our Lord.

PRAYER: God, give me faith and courage to share the gift I have received in Jesus Christ. Amen.

THURSDAY, JULY 5 • Read Luke 10:16-20

The text says, "The seventy returned with joy, saying, 'Lord, ... even the demons submit to us!'" They sound rather impressed with themselves, don't they? Who wouldn't be amazed and astonished that they had cast out and subdued unclean spirits. It's heady, inspiring stuff. We church folk can be like that. In fact, I believe we are going through a period of such powerful spirit work in the Christian church that we sometimes think and act like it's our own doing and not the Spirit's.

We often see this attitude in churches that really take off—either starting from nothing and blowing up to thousands of members in just a few years or a long-standing but stagnant congregation finds itself in the midst of phenomenal growth. I visited such a church recently to discern the key to their phenomenal growth. I left the worship service sorely disappointed; I had heard the pastor and people exalted but not the Savior. The message seemed to celebrate success rather than affirm faithfulness.

What is it about success that makes us want to take center stage? Why is it so hard to remember in plenty or little "that this extraordinary power belongs to God and does not come from us"? (2 Cor. 4:7)

So while the seventy are overjoyed at their apparent success, Jesus helps them refocus by saying, "Nevertheless, do not rejoice at this, that the spirits submit to you, but rejoice that your names are written in heaven." Paul offers a helpful reminder to us also. In 2 Corinthians 4:5 he says, "For we do not proclaim ourselves; we proclaim Jesus Christ as Lord and ourselves as your slaves for Jesus' sake."

PRAYER: Deliver me, O God, from allowing my success to seduce me. Help me keep my eyes on Jesus in whose name I pray. Amen.

FRIDAY, JULY 6 • Read Galatians 6:1-6

In spite of our conviction and preaching of the church as a community of love, redemption, and forgiveness, churches really do not restore the fallen very well. I'm not sure what we fear in reaching out to and working with the fallen. But we often seem comfortable with the philosophy of "out of sight, out of mind."

I believe we fear our own vulnerability and weakness. Addressing others' failings in a straightforward way reminds us that we too have "come short of the glory of God." It also serves to remind us of the ways in which we fear that we might fail.

Paul's counsel to the Galatians was this: "If anyone is detected in a transgression, you who have received the Spirit should restore such a one in a spirit of gentleness." If we accept Paul's counsel as helpful and instructive for the church today, we will have to change the way we support and hold one another accountable.

The church as a community of restoration must practice and encourage the sharing of the journey. Sometimes we fail and fall because we have chosen to or been left to walk alone. I find that I cannot be an effective Christian alone, much less live a life of holiness. Ours is a shared journey. We need one another both for support and accountability.

In such a relational context I can both hear and speak the truth in love. When fellow pilgrims, who I know without a doubt love and value me, speak truth to me (even the truth of my shortcomings), I hear it differently than when it is spoken outside the context of covenant and community.

Perhaps truth can only be spoken and heard in the context of binding relationships. The only reason for speaking painful truth is to seek deeper relationship with God and reconciliation with neighbor, a truth speaking that seeks only to heal and restore that which is lost and broken.

PRAYER: **Deliver us, O God, from cheap grace. Rescue us from no grace at all. Amen.**

SATURDAY, JULY 7 • Read Galatians 6:7-16

Context is everything; knowing the context in which someone said something delivers his or her words from becoming gossipy tools of destruction. Knowing the context of many a beloved, oft-quoted saying may enrich its meaning even more.

Like many persons, I grew up hearing snippets of Bible all the time. Some phrases or sayings from the Bible I heard outside the walls of organized religion. Some were harmless; some even proved helpful in their witness.

If you think context is important, I assure you that tone carries equal weight. I remember as a child hearing Paul's words to the Galatians, "Do not be deceived; God is not mocked, for you reap whatever you sow." I often heard these words as chiding and chastising, or I received them as a negative warning.

Granted Paul is discouraging the saints from "sowing to the flesh"; but he presents a balanced picture, reminding them that in sowing to the Spirit "you will reap eternal life from the Spirit." Paul builds his words, moving to what I think is a great crescendo of hope and encouragement: "So let us not grow weary in doing what is right, for we will reap at harvest-time, if we do not give up." These are not the words of someone shaking a finger in another's face as if expecting him or her to do the wrong thing. These are words of encouragement cheering the saints on as they persist in doing the right thing. Context is everything.

PRAYER: Dear God, help me know your word and proclaim it. By the power of your word give me life. Amen.

SUNDAY, JULY 8 • Read Psalm 30

I am a wimp. I don't like pain. I avoid pain, whether physical, emotional, or spiritual. But none of us gets through this life without it. No matter how great life has been to us, we have all faced pain. If you haven't yet, it's just a matter of time.

That is what I find so inspiring about the psalms: They talk about life as it is. The psalmists do not view life through rose-colored glasses. They don't gloss over the painful and unpleasant. Life, according to the psalmists, is filled with great joy, high inspiration, and many reasons to praise God. Life is also touched by disappointment, loss, grief, and many things that drive us to despair.

But these seasons of life are not to be avoided. They are to be acknowledged and even embraced. We embrace them not because they are good in and of themselves, but because even in seasons of "distress and grief" we discover the never-failing presence of God.

When I run from my pain, I also deny myself the assurance that God remains steadfast and faithful even in tough times. When I avoid my pain, I live in an artificial zone of comfort that cannot be sustained, let alone be sustaining.

When I embrace my pain, I experience more fully the God who gives "joy in the morning," who turns "mourning into dancing." God can do that because God journeys with us all the way—not just part of the way. In so doing, God transforms even the most discouraging seasons of life into new seasons of opportunity.

PRAYER: O God, it seems easier to hide, to cut and run. Reassure me that you are ever with me, in joy and sorrow even "to the close of the age." Amen.

No Other Gods

July 9–15, 2001 • Patricia Cruser*

MONDAY, JULY 9 • Read Amos 7:7-10

God is holding a plumb line. When the people of Israel, led by the king, worship Baal and Ashtaroth and do not take care of their own people, they are not standing erect. The king has abused his authority; the high places of idol worship must come down. God says, "I will never again pass [my people Israel] by." God will not overlook Israel's transgressions again.

Most of us have areas of authority, if only in our own families. Sometimes we build idols to worship in place of God. We may let a game or sport consume us. Maybe our golden calf comes in a bottle. Maybe we belong to an organization that helps us feel superior to others.

An African American friend tells of being at a full-service gas station and asking the attendant to clean his windshield. The response: "Clean it yourself."

My friend, attempting to stand erect in his convictions, repeated the request somewhat more firmly. (His wife was patting his leg to calm him.) This time the attendant understood the request and cleaned the windshield. He put down his racist idol momentarily, not out of respect for God but for fear of the consequences of not doing his job. My friend's insistence on what he believed to be right brought about change.

To stand erect means to put God above personal indulgence and to put our God-given relationships above all others. If we stand erect, we have the time and energy to do God's work.

PRAYER: Lord, help me remember that you alone are God. Teach me to love you with all my heart and to love my neighbor as myself. Amen.

---

*Teacher, Texas School for the Blind; poet/author, member of Bethany United Methodist Church, Austin, Texas.

TUESDAY, JULY 10 • Read Amos 7:10-17

"She told me not to tell, but I told anyway."

Amaziah warns Amos to stop prophesying at Bethel, the king's sanctuary. Amos is not disheartened. Prophets are not known for lack of assertiveness. The authority of humans holds little sway over them. The authority of the Almighty demands their respect and reverence.

A ten-year-old boy is called to be a prophet, a truth-teller. He tells the truth at his own peril. Because he reports physical abuse as a result of alcohol abuse in his home, he may be sent to a foster family—again. The social workers will try to make the wisest decision for the boy's health and well-being, while attempting to encourage health among the other family members.

Sometimes telling the truth means going from a familiar but hopeless situation to an unfamiliar place that offers a glimmer of hope. Another student speaks up: "You're not the only one. It happened with my mother and her boyfriend. He had her down on the floor, hitting her."

"Does your mother still have the same boyfriend?"

"Yes, but he doesn't do that anymore."

"Did they get counseling?"

"No, they just both stopped drinking."

At times each of us is called to be a prophet—times when, even though we are not in a position of worldly power, we must assume the power that God gives and speak the truth. Speaking the truth can be hazardous to our health; yet if we align ourselves with God, we can do nothing less. Our physical beings, our jobs, our households may suffer, but to withhold the truth in the presence of obvious lies would be abominable to a person who worships the one true God.

SUGGESTION FOR MEDITATION: **Consider your home, your workplace, your community. What would be the risks for the person who speaks truth in these places? Could you be that person? Ask God for courage to find and speak the truth.**

WEDNESDAY, JULY 11 • Read Psalm 82

The psalmist, Asaph, a priest, envisions the one true God as sitting in judgment among other gods. In the psalm God admonishes the others, telling them they do not judge fairly. The poor and downtrodden do not receive justice. God warns these lesser gods that they may be gods, but they will die like humans.

The psalmist's yearning is clear, as is the anger. Baal and all other gods worshiped by the surrounding tribes must fall. The God of the Jews will reign supreme, and the poor and downtrodden will receive justice. Those who practice idolatry will no longer prosper.

Sometimes it seems that there is no justice, that politicians are corrupt, lawyers despicable, and lobbyists less than honest. The rich are powerful and seem able to buy their way out of trouble. Perhaps our fascination with wealth and power is a form of idolatry.

I recently attended a production of *Jesus Christ Superstar*. The director, through clever use of props and costumes, mixed elements of the present with the past. In the scene where Jesus overturns the money changers' tables, posters of Marilyn Monroe and James Dean are displayed in the foreground. When we idolize other people for their physical beauty or abilities, we set ourselves up to be cheated.

Just as the psalmist longs for justice, we may find ourselves longing for fame, wealth, and power. Instead of justice, personal glory is often our goal. When all our golden calves fall down, when we long to stand in the presence of God instead of our public, our mirror, or our accumulations, then there will be enough justice for everyone—not just for those who can pay for it in cash.

PRAYER: **Lord, remind me of your priorities. Help me see past my personal wishes to a vision of universal peace and justice. Amen.**

THURSDAY, JULY 12 • Read Luke 10:25-28

A lawyer questions Jesus: "What shall I do to inherit eternal life?" (RSV). Jesus, as he often does when put to the test, returns the question to the lawyer and then agrees with his response.

"Yes, if you love God with all that is within you, and your neighbor as yourself, you will live."

Love God and neighbor. Scholars agree that to love God is to love one's neighbor. First John says, "Those who say, 'I love God,' and hate their brothers or sisters, are liars" (4:20). Without love for neighbor, love for God cannot exist.

A friend told me that the three most important things in his life were sex, alcohol, and music of the sixties. Enjoyment of life is healthy when we recognize that what we have comes from God. In the context of celebrating our God-given gifts and relationships, we may partake of any of these things. When sex, alcohol, music, work, acquisition, food, drugs, gambling are the most important things in our lives, they have become our gods. We no longer serve God; we serve that which we most value. Ultimately we worship ourselves. Addictions keep us from paying attention and close us off from relationships with God and our neighbors.

When we accept and love God above all else, we must remember God's commandment to value our neighbor as we do ourselves. How simple it seems to put God above everything else. How simple it seems to love our neighbor. How simple it is to forget both God and neighbor.

PRAYER: Lord, help me remember that you are the source of my life. Help me remember that love for you and love for neighbors are more important than any thing or pastime I may be tempted to idolize. Amen.

FRIDAY, JULY 13 • Read Luke 10:29-37

The lawyer who has answered his own question goes a step further in his conversation with Jesus. "Who is my neighbor?" he asks.

Jesus takes this opportunity to set a Samaritan as the example of a person who does God's will. The Samaritans have been despised by the Jews for hundreds of years. They don't worship correctly. They have intermarried with Gentiles.

Yet Jesus upholds a Samaritan as the neighbor to emulate. "Go and do likewise," he says.

At the school for handicapped individuals where I teach, the range of handicapping conditions goes from severe to mild. The range of people who work at the school is also wide. Some teacher aides are trying to finish their university work; other administrators have doctorates. Some people wear crosses; some wear yin and yang symbols. Some wear jewelry in unconventional places. Many different lifestyles are represented.

If I were to meet some of these people on the street, I might make a judgment based on their appearance or on the people with whom they associate. At work I see them gently and patiently encouraging deaf-blind students, pushing the wheelchairs of disfigured students, reasoning with emotionally disturbed students.

Who is my neighbor? My neighbor is my coworker who lives in a different part of town and dresses differently. My neighbor is the student who needs extra help to get an education. My neighbor is anyone with whom I come in contact.

SUGGESTION FOR MEDITATION: Think of the kind of person you are most tempted to judge. Consider how she or he dresses. Listen to the accents in the voice, the type of speech used. Then imagine yourself being rescued by that person from a building toppled by a hurricane, earthquake, or flood. Thank God for that person and ask for the courage to become the kind of neighbor you have imagined.

SATURDAY, JULY 14 • Read Colossians 1:1-14

"Would you give these to Heather?" asked Mary as she held out a bag of candy. Mary wanted to share something with Heather, who had been awaiting the birth of a baby sister. But the sister arrived much too early and did not survive. Mary, though living with a mentally handicapping condition, understood the pain of loss. Just two years before, her mother had been killed while crossing a busy street. Shared joys and sorrows tend to draw people together in love, especially when they have experienced God's love in their lives.

Think of Paul, a former Pharisee, writing to former pagans and thanking God for them. These people may not have even at one time been aware of the Lord, the one true God. Imagine Paul before his experience on the road to Damascus. Could he have dreamed that he would be writing to ungodly Greeks and praising them for their love of God and neighbor?

Yet Paul has something in common with the Colossians. Paul has experienced the redemptive love of Christ, the same love that the Colossians must have experienced when they heard the stories of Jesus. Paul, a devout Jew, has loved the law while hating those who seemed to despise the law. After seeing and hearing Jesus Christ, after being blinded by the light of love, Paul is filled with love instead of hate, with acceptance instead of rejection.

How wonderful it must be for a church or even a small prayer group to hear these opening words from Colossians. When we work together to do God's will, when we actively show love for our neighbors, we can read these words as though they were written specifically for us.

SUGGESTION FOR MEDITATION: **Read today's passage as though it were a personal letter to you. Remember the people who have shared the words of Christ with you. Think of them as saints; then think of yourself as a fellow saint.**

SUNDAY, JULY 15 • **Read Colossians 1:9-14**

Paul tells the Colossians that he and the other apostles are praying for them. He has heard of their love in the Spirit and now prays that they may be strengthened. Paul has had an encounter with Jesus Christ. He knows that his prayers will be answered. He also knows that all the new believers will need strength to endure present and future hardships.

Prayer is an essential ingredient for maintaining loving relationships. Even when our work is in the field of service, and we have beautiful, loving coworkers; even when our families are loving, caring, and nurturing; even when our church members are driven by compassion for others, we are not immune to dissension, loss, and temporary or permanent estrangements. We may never have to endure trials or persecution comparable to those of the early Christians, but we need strength beyond our own to maintain our walk with God in an ungodly world.

Two of the most love-filled experiences I can recall are the Walk to Emmaus and the week I spent at Mountain T.O.P. The Walk to Emmaus is a three-day retreat infused with discipline in doctrine and personal examination of our walk with God. Mountain T.O.P. provides an opportunity to help rebuild or restore homes of people whose rural lifestyle and livelihood have been jeopardized by an industrialized society. Both of these experiences involve a sacrifice of time and money. Neither of these intense activities would be as successful without the bi-daily gatherings for worship and prayer.

Paul has given us direction by praying unceasingly for the early Christians and by reminding them and us that strength comes from Christ, God's beloved Son. If we pray fervently and sincerely that we and our neighbors can continue to work together for the good of all, then justice and mercy will become a reality for all God's people.

PRAYER: **Read Colossians 1:11-14 as a prayer for yourself and your neighbor.**

Welcoming God

July 16–22, 2001 • *Mickey Bergeron**

MONDAY, JULY 16 • **Read Luke 10:38-42**

Because my personality has strong elements both of Martha the industrious and Mary the contemplative, I find that this story gives me fits. The Martha side of me wants to ask, "If everyone chooses the Mary role, sitting at Jesus' feet, who will feed the hungry, give water to the thirsty? Who will visit the sick and imprisoned, who will clothe the naked, who will welcome the stranger?" (Matt. 25:37-40) And the Mary side responds, "If you Martha types don't take time to listen to the Savior, to sit at Jesus' feet in preparation for welcoming God into your lives, then all your work will be useless."

The Bible is so incomplete! Where are the details that would flesh out the stories? What did Martha do (or stop doing) when Jesus told her that Mary had chosen the better part? Did she drop her dishtowel immediately and sit down? If so, did the dinner burn?

Only Luke tells this story; it seems almost an aside after the parable of the Good Samaritan. So what is the lesson here? Perhaps it is as simple as realizing there are different ways to welcome God; we are not limited to one. Sometimes we will actively serve "the least of these" made in Christ's image. Sometimes we will greet the Spirit as we search the scriptures in silence and solitude.

Whoever we are and whatever our strongest personality traits, let us resolve to open our hearts wide in work and in worship.

PRAYER: Welcoming God, teach me when to be a doer of your word and when to be still and know you. Amen.

---

*Diaconal minister in The United Methodist Church; mother of four, grandmother of four; living in Nashville, Tennessee.

TUESDAY, JULY 17 • Read Amos 8:1-12

Why is God so angry with the covenant people? Why does God show Amos a vision of summer fruit as a symbol of imminent, destructive judgment? At this time in Israel's history, the nation is at relative peace with its neighbors; there is great prosperity; there are many priests and places of worship. Surely these are signs of God's blessing!

Yet through the prophet God says, "I won't overlook my people's sins any longer. Their songs of praise will turn to dirges of mourning. So many people will die that all who survive will be stunned into silence. I will remember their evil deeds." What have the people done? Why has God's welcome for the covenant people gone?

They have perverted the worship of their just God. They attend every service, observe the rites of new moons and Sabbaths. But they get drunk on the sacramental wine, then lie down at the very altar of God on cloaks taken as collateral for loans to the poor. Or they chafe until the rituals are done, so they can get back to work.

I'm not always clear about the right mixture of worship and Sabbath rest relative to work. Yet seeing people rush out of worship to engage in business or to patronize business the way they did in Amos' time troubles me. Why are we so anxious to buy and sell? Is it because being successful in commerce and acquiring material goods are our criteria for measuring merit in others and ourselves?

God's kingdom has room for all kinds of persons, but this passage clearly indicates God's displeasure with those who "trample on the needy, and bring to ruin the poor of the land."

SUGGESTION FOR MEDITATION: **How does worship transform what I do afterward? How long does the effect last?**

WEDNESDAY, JULY 18 • Read Amos 8:4-8

This book from Hebrew Scriptures is one of those upon which social justice advocates have always relied. These verses are just one of several passages in Amos that describe the disconnect between worship and everyday living. The ancient shepherd's message is as relevant in the early twenty-first century as it was eight hundred years before Christ.

The nation of Israel delights to hear Amos preach God's condemnation against their enemies; their delight increases when Amos denounces Judah, Israel's kinfolk and also a nation of chosen people. But then the prophet attacks Israel itself. God has indicted Israel's enemies for war crimes and atrocities, actions almost expected of these heathen nations. But God's anger with Israel, the covenant people, is directed at their vain, corrupt worship and their trampling of human rights.

We are created to worship, but worship isn't just attending services on Sunday. Nor is it giving time and talents to the church, important as these things are. Real worship allows God to change us! We are also created to work, but we must ask, "Does the work honor God?" In the case of these merchants of Israel, the answer is no. These tradesmen get their wealth by cheating their neighbors, by using false weights, and by selling shoddy goods.

What about our work today? Does it benefit our community? Does it improve the lives of the weak and helpless? Does it provide a welcome for the poor, the outcasts?

PRAYER: God, help me remember that your welcome includes integrity, fairness, and justice for my community. Remind me that when our worship is honest, our everyday lives will be as well. Amen.

THURSDAY, JULY 19 • Read Amos 8:11-12

When I was a child, sometimes food was rather scarce; but I have never been near starvation. Therefore, I cannot comprehend what food famine is. It is almost as hard to understand a famine for the word of God. I have read that Christians in some nations are nearly starved for the scriptures; they have been without Bibles for so long. Some even risk their lives to smuggle the written word of God into their countries. But in the United States, food is abundant for most; Bibles are readily available. Many homes have several versions, large volumes and small. Does this mean that we are well fed in scripture? Do we have plenty of vital knowledge of the word? Do our lives reflect a close relationship with the living Word? Perhaps not always, but we see some encouraging signs.

For example, in recent years some high commitment Bible study series have led thousands of seekers deep into both the Hebrew and Christian scriptures. I spent years in a denomination that places notable emphasis on Bible knowledge, and I learned a great deal that supports me daily. But only after I participated in one of those in-depth study series did I come to view the Bible as a whole, all parts telling the story of God in relationship with God's people.

Dick Murray says that in deep Bible study, he "came to know God in a very personal fashion through encounter and dialogue with the text of the scripture, the life and teaching of Jesus Christ, and the enlivening of the Spirit." He wishes the same for his readers. Reflect on Isaiah 55:2.

PRAYER: O God, let me never mistake the appetite for bread and meat for hunger for your word, your word that truly satisfies. Amen.

FRIDAY, JULY 20 • Read Psalm 52

First the psalmist, possibly David, describes his enemy. The enemy is strong and boastful, inflicts mischief, is sharp-tongued, loves evil, loves lying, and loves hateful speech. The psalmist only implies that the enemy is subtle. David's enemy and ours today are one and the same. In the face of such a strong adversary, how can we keep our spirits and hopes high?

We can take heart because the psalmist then describes God's punishment for the enemy: the destruction of everything this enemy has desired and obtained for self-abundance of riches and a prominent position. Moreover, the enemy faces what is perhaps worse to this prideful spirit: ridicule from the righteous. Finally, the enemy faces the loss of life.

The psalmist concludes by describing those who make God their refuge, who trust God, who give thanks to God. The righteous thrive in their spiritual lives, regardless of what is going on around them. No matter what we suffer—poverty, depression, illness—we do not give up. Indeed, we cannot give up; we wait to welcome God once more. We will be like green olive trees, flourishing and contributing to our faith community.

PRAYER: **God of righteousness, grant me a thriving life. Even when evil seems to be on the rise, let me remain confident that if I have enlightened eyes, I too can laugh at the evil all around. You make me grow in joy, and I thank you. Amen.**

SATURDAY, JULY 21 • **Read Colossians 1:15-23**

What a glorious hymn! These verses give us a magnificent view of the incomparable Christ. He is the express image of the invisible God. He is cocreator of the universe and the one who even now holds all things together. He is the head of the church. This holy One, this Christ who is very God, nevertheless welcomes us to God. Jesus is himself the open door. In *The Message*, verse 17 reads, "So spacious is he, so roomy, that everything of God finds its proper place in him without crowding." There's room for all of us, misshapen, curious, odd, twisted though we may seem to the world. We fit into God's kingdom. What a joyous thought!

When we worship this awesome God, there is a place for us whether we have an affinity for lofty Bach fugues or for toe-tapping gospel songs. We can fit into a faith community whether we need ornate vestments and grand liturgy or Quaker simplicity. We are welcome wherever our faith journey takes us, anywhere along the theological and doctrinal spectrum.

The concept of the general ministry of all Christians reminds us that in our daily work, whether we are custodial staff or CEOs, professors or secretaries, we are ministers of the gospel of Jesus Christ. Furthermore, if we're called to specialized ministry, we still can find our niche in the infinite varieties of service: preaching, teaching, nursing, or administering church agencies. There's room for us, plenty of room!

SUGGESTION FOR MEDITATION: **Where in this wondrous, complex body of Christ do I fit? Am I trying to conform to the world, or am I part of the work of transformation by a welcoming God?**

SUNDAY, JULY 22 • Read Colossians 1: 24-29

The words from the Communion service reverberate in my mind, "That we may be for the world the body of Christ, redeemed by the blood of Christ." What is this body of Christ? Paul replies that it is the church. He writes of becoming the servant of the body of Christ, the church.

What does he mean? Paul's commission is "to make the word of God fully known," to reveal the mystery, "this mystery …of Christ in [us], the hope of glory." Is this not also our task, to illustrate God's astonishing welcome by proclaiming that our God comes to dwell in each of us uniquely?

When we share the mystery of Christ in us, we participate in bringing the kingdom into being; we let God's will be done on earth as it is in heaven. The Gospel lesson for the Sunday on which I write these lines concerns John the Baptist's role in the life of Christ. "Get ready," he says. "Get ready!" So whether we do it with the hustle and bustle of Martha or with the placid contemplation of Mary, let's get ready to welcome one another into Christ's body, the church.

PRAYER: **Loving God, mold me so that I fit into your body just where you want me to be, and let me rejoice in that. Remind me often that it's not my task to make anyone else fit into the same mold. Keep me welcoming your image in everyone who wants to be part of the kingdom. Amen.**

The Faithfulness of God

*July 23–29, 2001 • Richard V. Shriver ***

MONDAY, JULY 23 • Read Hosea 1:2-5

The story of Hosea is one of the most beautiful in all literature. A stern and righteous prophet, Hosea preaches against the faithlessness of the people of Israel. After the death of Solomon, the Jewish nation had been divided—Judah in the south and Israel in the north. Hosea uses the naming of his children as a means of pronouncing the wrath of an unbending God against the faithless people.

There is no compassion in Hosea's life, and there is no compassion in Hosea's message, because in his mind he perceives no compassion in God. We tend to become like our perception of God. Hosea feels so sure of the wrath and righteousness of God that there is no room for mercy.

King Jehu and his descendants had ruled Israel for a hundred years. Jehu, a general in the army, had become king by murdering King Joram and the other sons of King Ahab in the valley of Jezreel. Hosea names his first son "Jezreel" to pronounce God's wrath against the house of Jehu and the slaughter that Jehu had committed at Jezreel.

Jezreel, in Hebrew, means "God sows." It names a town and a fertile valley in Israel. Hosea warns of God's sowing destruction against a sinful people.

We will continue Hosea's story in our devotionals for the next two days, but it seems that Hosea's stern preaching is too much for his wife, Gomer. She eventually leaves him and sells herself into a house of prostitution.

SUGGESTION FOR MEDITATION: How does your faith withstand the tragedies of life?

---

*United Methodist minister; Professor of Philosophy and Religion at Cumberland University, Lebanon, Tennessee.

TUESDAY, JULY 24 • Read Hosea 1:6-7

Before Gomer leaves Hosea, they have a second child, a daughter. Hosea's concern for the sins of his nation, Israel, have increased, as has the sternness of his preaching. He names the daughter Lo-ruhamah, which in Hebrew means "not pitied" or "not loved." Hosea conveys God's message related to Israel's faithlessness—God will not again show the Israelites pity.

The people of Israel are forsaking their God, Yahweh, and worshiping the pagan gods of the Canaanites and Phoenicians, especially the Baals. Baal heads up a whole pantheon of gods of the sun and of fertility. They are the gods of the people who inhabited the Promised Land before the time of Moses and Joshua. How distressing it was to the Hebrew prophets to see such faithlessness! It was a return to idolatry. This faithlessness brought to mind a faithless husband or wife. Hosea predicts that it will bring destruction to Israel.

A storm brews in the northeast. The nation of Assyria is becoming the most powerful and aggressive nation in the world, and it hungers for conquest. Hosea seems to sense the danger. Hosea's message continues to be void of compassion and mercy. God has stopped loving Israel, the children of Abraham, the chosen people.

Trouble brews at home for Hosea too. One must assume that the preacher has lost his compassion, even for his wife and family, so obsessed has he become with a pronouncement of righteousness.

SUGGESTION FOR MEDITATION: **When have I become so sure of my sense of "rightness" that I have lost my ability to love?**

WEDNESDAY, JULY 25 • Read Hosea 1:8-10

Today we conclude the beautiful story of Hosea. As months pass by, the people of Israel do not return to God. A third child, a son, is born to Hosea and Gomer. Hosea names the boy Lo-ammi, the name of ultimate wrath. The meaning of the name is "not my people." God has disinherited the people of Israel.

Soon Hosea's world falls apart. The armies of Assyria are on the move, and they march across the land of Israel. They destroy the nation, slaughter much of the population, and take many more as slaves to Assyria where the terrible King Sennacherib is building the greatest and most terrible city of the ancient world: Nineveh. Israel is laid waste.

At the same time, Gomer, Hosea's wife, has deserted him and the children to become a prostitute. How Hosea must have hated her—or did he?

No, Hosea discovers that he still loves her. For the first time in his life, Hosea discovers the divine quality of love. He does not want to hate Gomer; he does not want her punished. He wants her well again. She is sick with sin—the same sin as Israel's! She has been unfaithful and played the harlot. But Hosea's heart fills with compassion and mercy. Hosea loves Gomer and does not wish her harm.

Hosea's heart has become bigger than his mind's idea of God! Hosea's heart causes him to learn of God's heart. He learns that forgiveness is greater than retribution. His idea of God has grown. Hosea buys Gomer back, and his preaching changes, becoming a message of peace and hope.

PRAYER: O God, show me your heart that I may learn, as did Hosea, the magnificence of your love. Amen.

THURSDAY, JULY 26 • Read Psalm 85

In the year 1741, in a matter of only twenty-four days, the great composer George Frideric Handel wrote the oratorio, *Messiah*. For those of us who have sung, listened to, and grown to love this marvelous music, the level of inspiration involved in such composing is awesome! From verses of scripture, Handel with his music tells the story of the prophecy, the coming, the life, the death, and the victory of Christ.

In Part XVIII, Handel sets the music to a text from the King James Version of the prophet Zechariah, "Rejoice greatly, O daughter of Zion," and includes the promise, "And he shall speak peace unto the heathen" (Zech. 9:10). Zechariah speaks a message of hope to the Jewish people soon after their return from their years as slaves in Babylon. Life is hard; the people need such hope.

Clearly Psalm 85 inspired Zechariah: "He will speak peace unto his people, and to his saints" (v. 8, KJV). Zechariah expands God's message to include even the enemies of the Jews.

Psalm 85 contains beautiful words of forgiveness and peace. The eloquence of the King James Version is hard to surpass: "Lord, thou hast been favourable unto thy land," and "thou hast forgiven the iniquity of thy people, thou hast covered all their sin," and "mercy and truth are met together," and "righteousness and peace have kissed each other," and "truth shall spring out of the earth; and righteousness shall look down from heaven."

Indeed, God does speak peace to the people.

PRAYER: O God, I pray for peace. Grant me your ways. Amen.

FRIDAY, JULY 27 • **Read Colossians 2:6-19**

I teach philosophy at the university. Ideas sometimes greatly challenge students brought up in the narrow "Bible belt" of conservative Christianity. One day a young woman stood up in class and shouted at me, "You're going to hell, and you're trying to take us with you!" Another morning I came into the room to find written on the chalkboard, "See to it that no one makes a prey of you by philosophy and empty deceit" (Col. 2:8, RSV).

Many of us have favorite "proof texts" from the Bible that we use to defend our smallness. The Bible, like all of God's great gifts, can so easily be twisted and used as an instrument of division—enmity instead of peace.

In a logic class I teach, I require my students to write their own philosophies of life based on a central theme that they believe so strongly that they would stake their lives on it. Then each student is required to apply his or her philosophy to ten issues or problems. The assignment is an exercise in logical consistency.

The students do not always agree with my example, but I suggest as a central theme a definition of God, rooted in the life and teachings of Jesus: "God is self-sacrificing, parentlike, eternal love."

I believe that the author of Colossians does not attack the study of philosophy or question the value of academic inquiry. The point in the Colossians passage is that we substitute nothing for the centrality of Christ—that in Christ we have knowledge of the true God and that only God should be worshiped.

SUGGESTION FOR MEDITATION: Contemplate the nature of God as you have discovered it in Christ.

SATURDAY, JULY 28 • Read Luke 11:1-4

Today we contemplate the great prayer called the Lord's Prayer. It is significant that Roman Catholics call it the "Our Father," for those two opening words in Matthew's version (6:9-13) make the prayer so unique and useable. After nearly two thousand years of use, we take for granted the suggestion of addressing God as a familiar parent. Jesus used the Aramaic word *Abba*. An argument could be made that it should be translated "Daddy" or "Papa." When we consider also Jesus' prodigal son story (Luke 15:11-32), where Jesus paints a picture of God as a loving father who never gives up on his children, it would appear that Jesus intends that we perceive God as the perfect parent.

I had wonderful parents. I am not so sure that I have been one. But whether our experience of parents and parenting has been good or bad, we have no trouble knowing the qualities of the ideal parent. Jesus has given us a marvelous way to think about God's nature.

Paul took the suggestion of God as parent and added other dimensions. If God is parent and we are God's children, then we are all brothers and sisters (Gal. 3:28); we are to grow up to be like God; and we inherit all that is God's (Rom. 5:2; 8:14-17).

Maybe the best part of all is the realization of how much God loves us. When we contemplate God as parent, we realize that God can never forsake us—that whatever comes in life is for us, never against us—and that God wants our mistakes, our sins, our evil changed. God wants selfish and sinful people to become good people. With this change comes the understanding of forgiveness.

PRAYER: **Our Father, thank you so much for loving us. Amen.**

SUNDAY, JULY 29 • Read Luke 11:5-13

In today's text, Jesus continues to compare God's way to that of a good human parent. I'm not sure that we believe Jesus! We act as if we think that good religion is a set of rules. We must belong to the right church, or we must be baptized a certain way and at the right time in life. We must take Communion so often and in the pew or at the altar. Or we do not have altars, only Communion tables. We use instrumental music in worship—or we do not. Some of us take our greatest pride in accepting all ways as valid—and condemn those who are less tolerant!

Of course, our doing good pleases God. Similarly, when our children do well, we are pleased. But God loves us regardless. I believe that the word is *unconditional*. Our salvation is the aim of God's love for us, which makes sense when we think of God as parent. Of course we would not give our children serpents or scorpions. We want good for our children, as God wants good for us.

Yesterday's meditation mentioned forgiveness. Many times in life we want an eye for an eye. John Doe did this to me, and he is going to pay! Society cries out for punishment for criminals, the tougher the better. Jesus tells us that God is not interested in revenge. God wants our evil changed. When an evil person becomes good, that is all God wants—like a parent who watches a child doing evil, selfish things. We parents grieve. We wonder what to do. How much punishment should we use?

What we know is that we want our children to be happy, creative, useful people with a sense of purpose. Whatever we can do to achieve that happiness, that is what we want for them. "'How much more will the heavenly Father give...?'"

PRAYER: Heavenly Father, thy will be done on earth. Amen.

God's Steadfast Love

July 30–August 5, 2001 • *Richard Corson**

MONDAY, JULY 30 • **Read Psalm 107:1-9**

As we hear the words of this psalm today, it helps if we can picture in our mind's eye the radiant, tear-streaked yet joyous faces of people utterly amazed and filled with wonder at having survived their terrifying ordeals.

As we learn in the day's text, some of the people have been lost in the wilderness, hungry and thirsty, ready to give up. If we read on, we discover that some of them have been through defeat in battle. Some of them have been imprisoned in dark dungeons. Some of them have experienced violent storms at sea. Others have been so ill that all hope of recovery seems to have vanished. Yet each has made it through.

And now they gather as survivors to share stories and memories of their amazing deliverance from hopeless situations, which fills them with awe, gratitude, and wonder. Out of the sharing they come to one great overwhelming desire—to praise and give thanks to God: "O give thanks to the Lord, for he is good, for his steadfast love endures forever."

That is the way Psalm 107 begins. It is the way our week begins, our Sabbath time—with an invitation to offer words of praise and thanksgiving to our faithful, saving God: "Let the redeemed of the Lord say so, those he redeemed from trouble and gathered in."

PRAYER: Eternal, ever-faithful God, when I am in life's tough places, help me remember that I am not alone, that you are with me always, seeking to lead, heal, save, and make me whole. Amen.

---

*Senior pastor, First United Methodist Church, Campbell, California; former missionary to Peru.

TUESDAY, JULY 31 • **Read Hosea 11:1-11**

In dark and difficult times, when I have strayed from God and from my own best self, I've been humbled and blessed by my experience of the *faithfulness* of God who seems never to give up on me. In fact, through the years of my wandering, I have concluded that the central, unwavering message of the Bible is this: God never gives up on us. God gave a promise, made a covenant, and will be faithful.

No one makes this any clearer than Hosea who in today's text imagines God as a parent torn between the behavior of the child and the feelings only a parent can have. In an exquisite soliloquy, God, as parent—mother or father—says, "When Israel was a child, I loved him....I taught him to walk....I bent down and took him in my arms and healed him. But he has gone away. He has broken my heart....Nevertheless, I will not abandon him, or destroy him in my anger. Rather my compassion grows warm and tender. I will continue to love my child, Israel, for I am God, the Holy One."

Trusting that God will keep the promise is the essence of biblical faith. Knowing that it doesn't always look as if God keeps the promise is what makes life difficult for a person of faith. That's why faith is more about having courage than answers; it is trusting, in spite of the evidence, that someday the absurd will make sense, the lost will be found, the crooked made straight, the innocent justified. We may not see it now, but we will. Yes! For God's steadfast love endures forever!

PRAYER: Merciful God, warm and tender in your compassion, help me this day and always to trust that you will keep your promise even when I break mine. Help me, like the prodigal, come home to your waiting embrace. Amen.

WEDNESDAY, AUGUST 1 • Read Hosea 11:8-11

For all our differences, what we believe as Christians resembles the beliefs of our Jewish cousin Hosea; namely that God always keeps God's promises, because God loves with a love that is determined not to let us go. This love will pursue us like a hound of heaven, as the poet Francis Thompson put it in his famous autobiographical poem.

A number of years ago, a good friend and colleague of mine looked up at the end of a worship service to see a man, the husband of one of his congregation, walking slowly down the aisle. Surprised and not knowing what to expect, he waited. The man drew near, stopped, and said quietly, "Pastor, I want to be baptized." An audible gasp arose from this normally undemonstrative church.

Knowing that this man had for years refused to have anything to do with the spiritual side of church, showing up only for social events or work parties, my friend's initial response was speechlessness. Finally he asked the question in everyone's mind: "Joe, what happened? Why now?"

Joe replied with a smile of resignation, "Pastor, God outlasted me."

Later it came out that this man's wife, through the fifty-two years of their marriage, had been quietly praying for her husband that one day he would draw near to God, accept Christ, and be baptized. She never told him of her prayers, nor did she ever nag him about it. She just trusted that God, with unhurried pace, would pursue her husband in life, in death, and beyond if need be. She believed that with all her heart; he experienced it with all his heart.

"Joe, what happened?"

"Pastor, God outlasted me!"

PRAYER: I pause today, dear God, grateful for the gift of your patient, searching, steadfast love. May it never let me go. Amen.

THURSDAY, AUGUST 2 • Read Luke 12:13-21

A recent trip to Bolivia and Peru forcibly reminded me that we in the United States cannot begin to compare our possessions with those of others in this world. I literally had as much in my suitcase as some of the people I lived and worked with. I came back to a house, if not a barn, full of things—clothes, computers, telephones, books, appliances, gadgets and doodads that do for me practically everything that I can't or don't want to do for myself. And I'm not alone.

Living squarely in the heart of Silicon Valley, a part of the world noted for its technological brilliance as well as its conspicuous consumption, I rub shoulders with people who have so much grain and so many goods that their barns burst at the seams, and still they are tempted to build newer, larger barns to hold the extra stuff.

Perhaps that's why I find the parable of the rich fool so timely and compelling. Not as a condemnation of success—that's not the point of the parable. The point, the challenge of it, is to find some balance between a world that seduces with great wealth and a God who calls to great compassion.

The rich man had been seduced into building larger barns instead of considering other options. He used up his life amassing wealth in the apparent hope that he could *then* "relax, eat, drink, be merry," only to discover what we all will discover: that no *then* is guaranteed. *This* is the day we have. *This* is the place we live. *These* are the people with whom we can share the abundance of God's blessings.

PRAYER: **Lord Jesus Christ, when my days are done help me leave an inheritance rich in goodness, rich in God. Amen.**

FRIDAY, AUGUST 3 • Read Luke 12:21

Affluenza is a disease, and it's fatal. Its symptoms include measuring worth by what we own or what owns us, whether it's the latest pair of sneakers or the newest lineup of cars. Wealth, and the accumulation it affords, becomes the standard for talent, intelligence, and success.

That's the nature of affluenza, and it's everywhere, threatening to infect everyone. So be careful. That's the message of the parable. Be careful; wise up. What good is all this wealth that you have stored in all these barns in the face of your mortality?

Somewhere I read of a young man, a lawyer, father of four young children, who one day woke up with a headache. Unable to escape the pain he reluctantly went to his doctor and learned that he had a brain tumor. His only choice was risky surgery. Months of pain and rehabilitation followed, but he survived and now lives a normal life.

"Did you learn anything from the experience?" someone asked.

"I did," came the reply. "I learned that your life is on loan. Use it well."

Jesus left us this parable. Nobody else is going to pay much attention to it, but we might because we have some sense of what it means to be rich toward God. That richness implies a trust in God, a faith in God—not in things. That richness comes when we invest in the kingdom by doing justice, loving kindness, walking humbly and gratefully with a God whose steadfast love endures forever.

PRAYER: Generous God, be patient with me as I learn to savor you and your kingdom more than all the time-bound treasures on earth. Amen.

SATURDAY, AUGUST 4 • Read Colossians 3:1-11

In today's text Paul assumes that Jesus came to call and encourage us to become the persons God created us to be, to do the right thing and the important thing by responding to the highest and best that is in us. This is how the apostle puts it: "If you have been raised with Christ, seek the things that are above."

"If you have been raised with Christ," Paul says, start living the life that Christ lived. Start living according to the highest and best that is in you. Get rid of the old stuff, he says, the earthly stuff like fornication, impurity, greed, anger, wrath, malice, slander, and abusive language. Get rid of that stuff because it's going to hold you back and keep you from rising with Christ.

That's where you must begin, Paul writes, because no one can do it for you. You are responsible. You have choices to make: choices between good and evil, life and death, right and wrong. Others can help you with those choices. Pastors, therapists, and friends can help you. God will help you. The Holy Spirit will help you. But finally it's up to you to desire a new self so desperately that you say to the old stuff: Be gone!

Do that patiently, prayerfully, consistently, even though you slip back and fall short of your intent; and you will one day discover that you've changed, that you're different, that you are more like you were meant to be in the first place, more like your original image-of-God self than ever before.

What a beautiful, encouraging assurance, that Jesus the Christ is waiting for you to follow him into the kingdom in which he is all and in all! That's a promise!

PRAYER: Lord Jesus Christ, son of God, lead me through my misery, guilt, and despair to that place where all things exist in the harmony of your love. Amen.

SUNDAY, AUGUST 5 • Read Psalm 107:1-3

Following one final debilitating stroke, our mother was left virtually speechless. Only two words remained of her once literate and compelling vocabulary: *All right.*

Most often using them appropriately to indicate an affirmative response, Mother would respond selectively to our greetings and small talk with those two gentle words: *All right.*

Eventually my brother, John, arranged those words into a kind of litany, an affirmation of faith, in which Mother joined the psalmist in "[giving] thanks to the Lord, for he is good; for his steadfast love endures forever." Her litany went like this:

Life has been good to me—
All right!
My family and friends have been kind and caring—
All right!
Though the way is hard, God still loves me—
All right!
I'm ready to begin my heavenly journey
whenever God calls—
All right!
For I know that nothing can separate me from God's love—
All right!

Throughout her life, Mother was confident in God, just as you can be confident in God. Trust the promise that God "is good...his steadfast love endures forever."

PRAYER: Lord God, even when it's tough, even when time passes slowly and relief seems far away, may I find within my soul the grace to trust that I am never alone, that you are with me, now and forevermore. All right!

Our Covenant with God

August 6–12, 2001 • *Jane Ellen Nickell**

MONDAY, AUGUST 6 • **Read Psalm 50:1-8**

Modern life is defined by contracts. We want agreements spelled out in detail, and we want assurance that the other party will adhere to the terms. At the least sign of a breach of contract, we drag the other party into court. If our coffee is too hot, we not only want back the seventy-nine cents we paid for it but millions of dollars for the mental and physical anguish we suffered when we spilled it. We base our contracts on distrust and greed. We assume everyone is out to get what we have, and we want protection. Prenuptial agreements often accompany marriage—we don't even trust our life partners.

God draws us into a covenant based on an entirely different proposition, an agreement based not on distrust but on the depth of God's love. God, who has authority over all creation, willingly binds Godself to us by covenant promises. Some scholars see Psalm 50 as liturgy for a covenant renewal ceremony. God summons us to court, and the heavens and earth serve as witnesses, judging our faithfulness to that covenant. Yet this court is like no other: The judge is our covenant partner, as well as the great asset we seek to protect. God testifies against us (v. 7) yet is not our opponent but our advocate. God helps us maintain our end of the covenant to assure us of divine love.

PRAYER: Loving God, I thank you for drawing me into a covenant of love and showing me how to be faithful to it. Keep me ever mindful of your promises. Amen.

---

*Associate pastor, First United Methodist Church, Huntington, West Virginia.

TUESDAY, AUGUST 7 • Read Isaiah 1:1, 10-17

God has harsh words for the warring people of Judah. Although they follow the rites of sacrifice laid out in the covenant with Moses, their hearts are not right with God. God judges them and finds them wanting. They do evil, not good. They stretch out their hands to God for mercy, while showing no mercy to the oppressed. And yet they continue to bring prayers and burnt offerings before God, believing that ritual will make everything right.

We often find ourselves guilty of the same thing. An hour in church on Sunday and hasty meditations each day will surely take care of any misdeeds. One woman I know speaks of writing "conscience-salving checks." When we have no time to perform personal acts of compassion, we at least can contribute to those who do. We take comfort in thinking that we do not engage in overt acts of evil, but our very participation in a consumer culture oppresses people in developing countries—people who work for pennies a day so we can buy cheap clothing, who have little to eat so we can have plenty, and who live among the waste that we don't want dumped in our land.

Our covenant with God requires not just empty ritual but truly devout hearts. God wants us to do more than give mental and financial assent to justice and mercy. God wants us to embody these qualities in our lives. God re-calls us to our covenant, urging us to cleanse ourselves so that our covenant relationship can be put right.

PRAYER: Merciful God, forgive me for my often unwitting participation in the evils of this world. Cleanse my heart and show me how to live out your compassion and justice in every aspect of my life. Amen.

WEDNESDAY, AUGUST 8 • **Read Isaiah 1:18-20; Psalm 50:22-23**

During the impeachment proceedings against American President Bill Clinton, someone commented on the striking difference between that process and the one employed by the Truth and Reconciliation Commission in South Africa. Where Americans will turn anything into an adversarial situation, South Africa is attempting to dissolve years of hatred and division by confronting the truth and seeking reconciliation. Where America makes a federal case out of sexual indiscretion, South Africa is responding to murder and gross injustice with gestures of healing.

"Come now, let us reason together" (NIV), says God to the people of Judah. God brings judgment, but also reconciliation. Bound by covenant, God does not make us adversaries but works to restore the divine-human relationship. Humanity on its own is powerless to repair the breach we create by our sin. Our sinfulness only drives us farther from God. Still God holds out salvation.

Through the prophet and the psalmist, God spells out the terms of our covenant. In these passages, God asks for obedience and thanksgiving. God reminds us of the promises that await if we succeed—but also the dangers if we fail. If we obey, we will enjoy the goodness of the land; if we rebel, we will be abandoned to the conquering foe. If we bring God thanksgiving, we will find salvation; if we forget God, we will be torn apart. Obedience and gratitude will earn God's favor and cement our covenant. God will work with us, but only through God can we be made right.

PRAYER: God of grace, help me find those places of division or discord in my life; show me how obedience to your covenant can bring about reconciliation and healing. Amen.

THURSDAY, AUGUST 9 • Read Hebrews 11:1-3

I marvel at the way illusionists can make large objects disappear before our very eyes: people, train cars, even the Statue of Liberty. The magician shows us the object and convinces us of its reality. Then after a few dramatic gestures and some tension-building music—voilà!—the object vanishes. We know the trick is an illusion; we know the object is still there, but we cannot see it. This is how the writer of Hebrews describes faith. Faith is the assurance of God's presence and all that God is, even though not visible to us. We cannot see God, yet we know God is there.

Our covenant with God requires such faith—to believe in something we cannot see. Thus faith involves an apparent contradiction: having a steadfast certainty about something we cannot prove in any empirical way. Hebrews 6:19 uses the image of an anchor hidden behind the Temple veil: firm and unwavering but invisible to us. Faith accompanies hope as we become certain of what we long for.

Yet God remains shrouded in mystery. Hebrews 11:3 tells us that creation itself is a mystery. From nothing, an invisible deity created the universe and all of its wonders. Rather than increasing our doubt, however, such mystery only fuels our faith, for all of creation stands as witness to a divine Creator. The Book of Hebrews as a whole describes the strongest witness to God: the life, death, and resurrection of Jesus Christ, a sacrifice that mediates a renewal of the promises God made to Israel and that calls us to new faith.

PRAYER: God of mystery, even though I cannot see you, I witness your work in creation and your revelation in Jesus Christ. Thus assured of your presence, I answer your promise of salvation with my own promise of faithfulness. Amen.

FRIDAY, AUGUST 10 • Read Hebrews 11:8-16

Our covenant with God sometimes requires that we enter strange, new places. Looking beyond our situation in this world, we see God's final reign of love; and, as Jesus taught us, we pray for that reign to come on earth. Faith enables us to follow God's call, knowing that finally we will arrive at home with God.

The writer of Hebrews describes Abraham as a model of such faithfulness to the extent that he willingly became a stranger in this world. Because of his faith, Abraham left home not knowing his destination but trusting in God's promise of land. Resisting the temptation to return to the safe and familiar, he lived as a stranger in this new land, sure of God's promise that it would one day belong to his heirs. Finally, ignoring their biological clocks, he and Sarah entered the strange new territory of parenthood in their old age, as God had promised they would. Even in death Abraham and Sarah looked forward, knowing that God's promise had not yet been fulfilled. A familiar spiritual describes how God's promise sustains us, especially as we face trials in this life:

> I am a poor wayfaring stranger,
> traveling through this world of woe;
> Yet there's no sickness, toil or danger
> in that bright world to which I go.
> I'm goin' there to see my father.
> I'm goin' there no more to roam,
> I'm just a-goin' over Jordan,
> I'm just a-goin' over home.

PRAYER: Source of life, guide me safely through this world, giving me courage to follow when you call me to strange new places and sustaining me with the assurance that I will rest finally at home with you. Amen.

SATURDAY, AUGUST 11 • Read Luke 12:32-34

As I prepared to enter seminary midlife, I found myself grieving the home I had to sell as much as I grieved any other part of this transition. A sense of home is important to me; I would be leaving a charming bungalow for apartment life. Around that time I dreamed that I had won the lottery, but I picked up my winnings from my church, not the state. I used that money to buy a spectacular mansion. As I walked through this mansion, I saw spacious bedrooms and baths, my mother baking bread in the kitchen, a wedding celebration in the ballroom, and an African American man who had lived through the civil rights era presiding in a court chamber. My dream depicted the home I longed for: a place of rest, cleansing, nourishment, joy, and justice. To this end, I realized that I should abandon my misguided search for security in this world and focus on my home with God.

Part of our covenant with God is relinquishing our attachment to worldly wealth, going against the very heart of our consumer society. Money brings possessions, prestige, power, and security; but in the end these things are fleeting. God, not the bank, serves as our trustee. Don't worry about material wealth, Jesus says; in fact, give it all away. Put your heart in God's care, for only there will it be safe. If we don't entrust our lives to God's care, they will be as empty as the religious rituals we read about in Isaiah (1:10-17). Money and possessions eventually fall away, but God's love endures.

PRAYER: Giver of all gifts, I thank you for the blessings of this life and your promise of greater riches beyond. Pry my hands loose from the treasures of this world, as I put my life in your gracious and abiding care. Amen.

SUNDAY, AUGUST 12 • Read Luke 12:35-40

"Be prepared!" says the scout motto. Be prepared with pocketknife, canteen, mess kit, and matches. Be ready for any emergencies that might befall you in the woods. Our covenant with God also requires that we be prepared. Luke describes the importance of readiness in two different situations: the return of the master and the intrusion of a thief.

The first occasion is one of joy. The master returns from a banquet and rewards his alert servants by serving them himself. God in human form served us by feeding thousands and washing disciples' dusty feet. Jesus' example calls us to serve with a readiness to do God's work in the world. God calls us to help bring about the glorious new age, the fulfillment of God's ultimate promise. Finding us ready, God invites us to the banquet.

What are we to make of the second warning? Are we to compare Christ to a thief in the night? Perhaps this warning reminds us of how easily the world can snatch our attention away from God's purposes. In grasping for money and possessions, we may lose our hold on the wealth of grace that God promises. Not knowing when Christ will return, we keep a firm grip on God's treasures, not those of the world.

We can test our alertness by asking ourselves, "If I die today, will my life have furthered God's kingdom?" We always have plans and goals for ourselves, but those should not distract us from striving to live out God's covenant each day. In so doing, we fulfill our promise of faith, obedience, gratitude, and service and learn to treasure the riches God freely gives us.

PRAYER: Covenant God, with humility I thank you for the promise of your gracious love. Help me live each day in the fullness of that promise until I join you in glory. Amen.

The Fire of Christ

August 13–19, 2001 • Charles F. "Skip" Armistead*

MONDAY, AUGUST 13 • Read Luke 12:49-50

It was the state tournament semifinal basketball game. Our entire county's six-thousand residents were at the game. Our team was behind the whole game as much as ten points. The opposing team thwarted every effort to rally.

Our players on the bench lowered their heads. Tears flowed as our supporters lost hope. With two minutes to go, the coach called "time out" for some last-minute strategy. His brother, the most valuable player in the tournament, interrupted and pleaded, "Just give me the ball!"

They gave him the ball; he drove the length of the court, scored, and was fouled. He sank the free throw. He intercepted a pass, scored, was fouled, and hit the free throw. One of our players intercepted the next pass and threw it to our star. He scored. As our star led the onslaught, the entire gym became energized! When the team went ahead, the crowd erupted in uncontained celebration! Our star scored twenty-six points during that last two minutes of the win. The team went on to win the state championship.

Jesus says, "I came to bring fire to the earth, and how I wish it were already kindled!" Many need a "Monday jump start" to get through the week. Many face debilitating stress before the week begins. Fire energizes! The fire of Christ's spirit says, "Give the week to me! Give your tasks to me! Let me energize your life. Let me transform this week into a win!"

PRAYER: Loving God, let your fire burn within me! Please energize me, and help me transform this week into a win! Amen.

---

*Senior pastor, McKendree United Methodist Church, Nashville, Tennessee.

TUESDAY, AUGUST 14 • Read Luke 12:51

When out of control, fire can be dangerous. The fire of Christ, when misunderstood or wrongly used, can be volatile. It troubles us to hear Jesus say that he came to bring division. Matthew records Jesus' saying that he brings a sword instead of peace. If Jesus is the Prince of Peace, why a sword?

Jesus brings peace and reconciliation. Jesus wants the end of wars, crime, and poverty. Division is not of God. So why does Jesus say he brings division instead of peace? I believe Jesus is stating a fact: Division will occur because some people will accept Jesus as Christ, and others will not. He wants peace, but his presence will create friction because there will be those who reject Christ's followers. Also, some people will misuse the name of Jesus, resulting in religious wars, church fights, and even hate groups.

A college student from India grew up in a Hindu family. Eventually he became a Christian. The reaction of his family was painful! While most treated him as dead, some acted as if he had never lived.

When others treat us badly, should we say, "Well, Jesus told us this might happen. My family has turned against me. So, I'll forget them." No! Jesus still seeks peace and reconciliation even though the world rejects him. The Prince of Peace is working through this student seeking reconciliation with his family. Despite the volatility among religions, hate groups burning crosses in the name of Jesus, and fiery hot debates within denominations, Jesus still seeks to help us be peacemakers, bringing the kingdom of God to earth as it is in heaven.

PRAYER: Lord Jesus, may the fire of your presence burn in my life so that people will come to you today. And Lord, if some choose to reject you or even reject me because of you, please help me love them in a way that will overcome division. Amen.

WEDNESDAY, AUGUST 15 • Read Luke 12:53

I thought God gave the fire of love to unite families, not divide them. If the "family that prays together, stays together," why does Jesus speak of division? Is Jesus saying here that he is against "family values"? I can understand a mother-in-law and a daughter-in-law being at odds with each other, but is he encouraging this tension?

In the same passage in Matthew, Jesus adds, "Whoever loves father or mother more than me is not worthy of me; and whoever loves son or daughter more than me is not worthy of me; and whoever does not take up the cross and follow me is not worthy of me. Those who find their life will lose it, and those who lose their life for my sake will find it" (10:37-39).

I love my parents, my wife, my children, and my in-laws. I can already see that I will especially love grandchildren. I don't believe that Jesus says not to love them. Instead, as some Bible scholars tell me, he employs a teaching technique to shock us into an understanding of our relationship with Jesus Christ. I believe he says, "Look how much you love your family. Please love them, but love me more! Don't elevate the love of anyone or anything greater than your love for me!"

My friend could hardly talk when he discovered his two-hour-old son had to have surgery. While sitting in the hospital cafeteria crying, he wrote out what his emotions blocked his speech from saying, "I wish I could take his place." That's a passionate fire of love willing to suffer for another. Likewise Jesus says, "If you love your children this much, love me more."

PRAYER: Lord, thank you for the people I love. Help me follow you and love you even more. In Jesus' name I pray. Amen.

THURSDAY, AUGUST 16 • Read Luke 12:54-56

The weather is integral to news programming. Severe weather is headline news. The "weather channel" reports that one in five persons watch this channel an average of three hours a day!

How can people see the weather and understand its implications in a three-minute segment of news, yet not see the implications of crime, poverty, and injustice in the rest of the "news"? Persons cheer or agonize over sports scores and understand the implications of wins and losses when they watch the news; but the other social issues reported seldom get a comment.

Revelation 1:14 says Jesus' "eyes were like a flame of fire." Fire enables persons to see. Jesus wants us to see the world situation through his eyes. One theologian says that we are to hold the Bible in one hand and a newspaper in the other. When I've done this, I can better see that much of the "good news" being reported is empty. I can better see that a lot of the bad news being reported really is a cry from God for help.

This may sound trite, but when I prayerfully seek God's guidance in meetings, in family dialogues, in conflicts, in social gatherings, and in one-on-one conversations, I can better see God's evaluation of a situation. I can also better see God's guidance as to my role in the situation. I am usually more at peace.

Why is this? When I truly seek God's presence, I can better see the face of God in the people around me. Thus, I am more sensitive to God's guidance.

PRAYER: Lord, let your fire provide the light that will enable me to discern the situations I encounter, to follow your guidance, and to see you. Amen.

FRIDAY, AUGUST 17 • Read Isaiah 5:1-7

Just as an owner of a vineyard expects the vineyard to produce good grapes, God expected Judah to produce people of faith who would build a kingdom of justice and righteousness. God expects the same today of our congregations. As with failed vineyards and Israel of old, when churches today fail, God either transforms or replaces them.

A friend tells of his disappointment in his congregation. The bishop appointed him to this church because he thought its needs and his gifts were a perfect match. Yet, as the months went by, his frustration grew.

The members appeared to care only about Sunday worship. My friend sensed that a major void existed between their faith and the rest of their lives. The church's status, tradition, and standing were obstacles of faith instead of assets. My friend met with the bishop and begged to be appointed to another congregation as soon as possible. The bishop told my friend that he wanted him to lead the congregation prayerfully to receive the fire of Pentecost. My friend replied, "I hope that church burns to the ground!" After the conversation, my friend drove the hour's distance back to his office. When he arrived, he discovered the church had burned to the ground. He immediately called the bishop and told him that he didn't do it.

The members of the congregation then realized that all they had left was Jesus Christ. No one in the congregation believed that God caused the fire. Today they all believe that God transformed the fire from a tragedy to a cleansing and purifying of their faith. The congregation rebuilt its facility, but its new cornerstone of faith was Jesus Christ. Today the congregation wins people for Christ, disciples them in faith, and works to transform its community.

PRAYER: Lord, Jesus Christ, please use your fire to cleanse my life of useless chaff. Amen!

SATURDAY, AUGUST 18 • Read Hebrews 11:29–12:2

As the event was ending, the leader asked us to imagine that we in small groups were the disciples in the boat when Jesus walked on the water. Jesus invites us to take a step of faith from our boats of security. The leader then inquired, "What is your next step of faith?" Each person took a cross from the cup sitting in the center of our circle and told the group of his or her next step of faith. The group then gave encouraging and affirming words to each, followed by a commissioning prayer.

One man's step was reconciliation with his wife. One woman gave up her cigarettes. One student decided to become the A student she knew she could be. As the other eight made their steps of faith, I began asking, "What is my next step?"

When the others finished and looked at me, I took a step of faith by retrieving a cross. As I did, my next step crystallized in my mind. I felt I was already walking on faith; so my next step was to get into the boat, find others who were not walking on faith, and help them take steps of faith out of their boats of security. I still wear that cross to remind me of my step of faith.

As I help others with faith, I know I'm doing the impossible because I can't change another person's life. Only the Holy Spirit can do that. But as I persevere, I feel the Holy Spirit's fire energize and encourage me with a fiery faith to take more steps.

PRAYER: Lord Jesus, please fill me again with the fire of your faith to help me dare to accomplish only those things that can be accomplished with your power. In Jesus' name I pray. Amen.

SUNDAY, AUGUST 19 • **Read Psalm 80:1-2, 8-19**

A childhood friend told me that God sat on a throne writing down every bad thing I did. He said if I wasn't good, God would send me to hell. So during many worship services, I silently pleaded for forgiveness. I experienced an unhealthy fear of God. Later I realized that God could be forgiving, but as in today's scripture, God could be extremely harsh.

Eventually I experienced another kind of reverent fear. It came when a friend asked, "How can I be sure God forgives me?" At that moment, his two-year-old was being very two-ish. I asked if he loved her before she was born and before he knew how she was going to turn out. He said, "Yes." I asked if his love intensified at her birth. "Yes!" I asked if he still loved her in spite of her crying and keeping him up at night, in spite of her doing what she knew was wrong, and in spite of the tantrums she was having at that moment. "Yes!" We then talked about the grace of God loving us no matter what.

We both got the message. What I knew in my head became part of my heart. I had a new loving awe of God. I felt the radiant warmth of God's love, grace, and forgiveness. While God's fire could consume me, God's radiant face shines lovingly upon me. I have a healthier reverence, worship, respect, and awe of God. My relationship is no longer that of God watching and judging. It is now one of God's living within and through me.

PRAYER: Lord, as I worship you this morning, help me transform any unhealthy fear I may have of you into reverent rejoicing. Let your face shine upon me, that I may be saved. Amen.

Taken to the Next Level

August 20–26, 2001 • Valerie L. Runyan*

MONDAY, AUGUST 20 • Read Jeremiah 1:4-10

Jeremiah, a gentle and timid poet by nature, struggled intently with God's call. He tried to argue with God, but the word of God was unwavering. He finally relented, knowing God would not leave him alone. Later he was forced to leave his native city in order to escape persecution from family and friends. He had to give up everything and everyone he had grown to value. He argued with God at different times only to bend once again to God's will. These conflicts ultimately brought Jeremiah into a uniquely intimate relationship with God.

I believe there is a mistaken sense that when we finally relinquish something or someone of personal value in order to become a more committed Christian, we become stronger. This is deceptive.

While we open ourselves up to a more profound and intimate relationship with God, we can expect even more intense struggles with the personal giants of doubt, discouragement, self-pity, and numerous others. Every step we take toward God requires more assiduous reading of God's word, more cultivation of a constant and consistent prayer life. We cannot relax our guard, lower our shield, or drop our sword.

Jeremiah's life was not an easy one. Neither is the life of a cross bearer. But we can be assured as Jeremiah was, "Do not be afraid…for I am with you and will rescue you" (NIV).

PRAYER: As I journey toward you, God, all that is within me warms at the thought of drawing closer to you. Amen.

---

*Laywoman, First Presbyterian Church, Silver City, New Mexico; elder, writer, worship leader, full-time volunteer at local gospel mission.

TUESDAY, AUGUST 21 • Read Luke 13:10-13

I would love to know more about the woman in today's reading. After eighteen years of not being able to straighten up, she curiously draws me into the scene. I picture her on the outside of the crowd trying to get just a glimpse of this young man so many have sought out and spoken about. I imagine because of her infirmity, her feeble attempts fail. Going unnoticed, others taller and stronger push her aside and to the back.

I wonder why she is there. After all those years bent over is she possibly seeking, hoping for healing? The scripture records no clues that perhaps she prayed he would come close enough for her to touch his robe or to hear his voice. I can pose many questions about the text, but the answers are not there—only the facts that Luke believes are important.

Jesus treats the woman with dignity. He doesn't ask one of his disciples to bring her to him. He can see she has learned to manage her disability with dignity. Instead, he calls out to her, "Woman" (a term of great respect), and I believe he speaks in a tone that doesn't command but lovingly beckons. She responds. All eyes must have been on her, then back on Jesus.

I imagine that those assembled quiet to a whisper. I like to picture Jesus smiling as she comes before him. Nervously she smiles back, then her eyes fall downward. He knows before he speaks how she will respond. "Woman, you are set free from your infirmity" (NIV).

When Jesus lays his hands upon her, "immediately she straightened up and praised God" (NIV). Then those around them join in. What a scene that had to have been!

SUGGESTION FOR MEDITATION: **Who needs your help this week? Call a lonely individual, send a card, offer a ride, or take someone to lunch. Honor him or her.**

WEDNESDAY, AUGUST 22 • Read Luke 13:14-17

I think it's interesting in today's reading that the Pharisee sees and concedes that a miracle has taken place. A crippled woman who has been bent over for eighteen years has received Jesus' healing touch. The teacher for the people then steps on center stage and invites all to "come and be healed." But he cries out in rage that *no* one should come for healing on the *Sabbath*!

The Pharisee fails to see that the woman deserved at least as much compassion as the Jewish law extended to lowly oxen and donkeys. He fails to see that he too is bent over, crippled by the numerous Jewish laws.

He has taken on the role of a Pharisee. All dressed up in the righteous garb, I imagine he enjoys playing the part of an indignant man who loves the laws both of God and Jews. But Jesus nails the pious authorities: "Hypocrites!" (Greek for "play actor"—someone who puts on a false face.)

Jesus' words, "This woman [is] a daughter of Abraham," clearly indicate that the woman is, in essence, their sister. Now is the time to release her from the eighteen long years of bondage—and not a moment too soon. Jesus humiliates his opponents and brings joy to the people. Finally someone has stood up to the authorities! The people delight in all the wonderful things that Jesus says and does.

After the first century, the meaning of the word *hypocrite* took on its present meaning: a two-faced individual. But play acting still exists. As we take on new jobs, face new responsibilities, develop new relationships, let us strive to be true to the role of a disciple of Jesus.

PRAYER: Lord, what I continually need today and always is to take on true humility found only in you. Amen.

THURSDAY, AUGUST 23 • Read Luke 13:17

I enjoy my work at our local gospel mission. I deal with the poor, the unbelieving, the thieves, and those entangled in the power of alcohol and drugs. I see our mission as the world in miniature. It's the same world with the same human conditions, suffering, and issues that Jesus dealt with over two thousand years ago.

Where some see a locale of losers, God would have us gaze upon an oasis of care. While some see only the drunks and users, others envision dozens of lives they have the privilege to touch with a word of hope, a hug, a smile. Many needs for food, a warm wool blanket, a winter coat are met here. The Spirit has shown me and others the face of Jesus shining through the homeless as they respond with a "thank you." As volunteers tending to these endless needs, we are not offended by another's dress, odor, or language. God's astonishing grace enables us to understand and love each of them.

I have personally been drawn into a depth of compassion that enabled me to hug a stranger who discovered she had cancer. Christ empowered me to clutch the not-so-clean hand of a grandmother who lost her five-year-old grandchild during "routine" surgery and to pray with her. We have all been blessed to experience Jesus in the least likeliest place—not in an exquisitely ornate sanctuary but in a refuge for the poor and the needy.

Oswald Chambers wrote in *My Utmost for His Highest*, "To turn head faith into a personal possession is a fight always, not sometimes. God brings us into circumstances in order to educate our faith, because the nature of faith is to make its object real."

PRAYER: Wherever you call me, wherever you are, here I am, Lord. Send me. Amen.

FRIDAY, AUGUST 24 • Read Psalm 71:1-6

Reading the scriptures may bring several levels of appreciation and understanding. Reading today's psalm, for example, simply as historical literature, we appreciate how well the writer of several thousand years ago has expressed his fears, pleadings, and praises. Psalm 71 was written by an elderly person. Some believe David wrote it, but the writer remains unknown. Even so, we can also appreciate learning this bit of trivia.

On another level we can delight in the familiar phrases and beautiful poetry we may have heard all of our lives. Like favorite symphonies we enjoy repeatedly, the word of God continually brings us pleasure. We can admire and love the writer's style of presenting a number of requests before God. If we believe the writer to be David, we gain a sense of why he was "a man after God's own heart."

On the deepest level, scripture becomes a part of us. Having been written by the One who indwells us, scripture brings us those moments of grace when we find ourselves moved by a new insight so profoundly personal and intimate that we can scarcely speak. God's word then becomes a precious tool we use in times of tribulation and trial. When we experience a need to hide from horrendous and overwhelming pain, we learn, like the psalmist, what a refuge God is! When we undergo an excruciating loss, our own inexpressible words stifled in sorrow, the psalms give comfort. When we no longer know how to pray, we have the assurance that God's Spirit intercedes for us (Rom. 8:26).

SUGGESTION FOR MEDITATION: A Chinese proverb states, "Tell me and I will forget. Show me and I will remember. Involve me and I will understand." Take time to pray quietly through Psalm 71. Prayerfully think about each level.

SATURDAY, AUGUST 25 • Read Hebrews 12:18-24

"Jesus…[whose] sprinkled blood…speaks a better word than the blood of Abel" (Heb. 12:24). This verse refers to the murder of Abel by his brother, Cain (Gen. 4:10). Numerous commentaries and some biblical footnotes believe Abel's blood cried out to God for vengeance. But after studying a number of translations, I find that none uses the word *vengeance*.

Reading what little has been written about Abel, I know he was the second son of Adam and Eve, Cain's little brother. Abel kept flocks, brought his offering to God, and was looked on "with favor." He was a good obedient son, pleasing to God and his parents. If I were to speculate, maybe Abel's blood cried out for mercy on his brother's behalf. It would seem to be far more suited to his character.

But whatever the cry, it matters not. Even if Abel was a good person of high moral character, it doesn't matter. Even if he did all things pleasing in God's sight and in the sight of his family and friends, it falls short. Even if his blood did plead for God to spare his brother and to let his own blood cover Cain's sin, to let his personal death end the matter, it did not, could not, affect our compassionate and merciful God. Because Abel was still only human. He had the same heritage we have in Adam and Eve. He had (and we have) no atoning power to cover his own sin, let alone Cain's.

Hebrews continually makes one point clear: Jesus Christ is better in every way! Jesus' blood alone can make the sacrifice complete.

SUGGESTION FOR MEDITATION: **Take time to study what the scriptures say. Pray about it; be open to another approach; take the scriptures' words to the next level!**

Sunday, August 26 • Read Hebrews 12:25-29

If the Book of Hebrews were a song, the melody throughout would be uplifting and joyful! We would hear the repeated choruses of "Jesus is better than…" and "Jesus is superior to…" and "Jesus is the perfect.…" We would also hear discord, tension, a harsh mingling of sounds: a distinct warning for those who will not listen.

In today's reading the writer repeats the discord, the warning he presented in chapter 2:2-3: "For if the message spoken by angels was binding, and every violation and disobedience received its just punishment, how shall we escape if we ignore such a great salvation?" (NIV). The "message" refers to the law given to Moses on top of Mount Sinai. The mount was wrapped in smoke, for God had descended on it in a fire, and its foundations "quaked greatly."

Today's verses contrast the two messengers. Moses was merely a man from earth whose voice was used by God. Jesus *was* the very voice of God who had descended from heaven. The discord heard in the chorus would be, "Jesus' warning is better than the warning spoken by Moses!"

The writer picks up the tension again: "Once more there will be a shaking of the earth! Created things will not remain! But that which cannot be shaken will remain!"

Chapter 12 ends on a high note: "Let us be thankful, and so worship God acceptably with reverence and awe, for our 'God is a consuming fire'" (NIV).

PRAYER: Dear Jesus Christ, may my unbelieving loved ones hear the music I hold so dear in my heart. Amen.

Open Your Heart and Be Filled

August 27–September 2, 2001 • Vicki and Bo Gordy-Stith*

MONDAY, AUGUST 27 • Read Hebrews 13:1-8, 15-16

It happened so suddenly we were not prepared to respond. While sharing prayer joys and concerns during worship, one member began telling a story about a friend who was pregnant with her first baby. I glanced at the clock as she went on about her friend and her husband's excitement: They couldn't wait to hold this child. I was already forming the "praise summary" in my mind when the woman who was sharing told us that the child had been stillborn the night before.

Something gripped me inside when the news took this dreadful turn. The pain and sorrow of that young mother struck me all at once, and tears flowed from my broken heart. The Holy Spirit called every member of the body that Sunday morning to share this couple's heavy burden. I felt their sorrow in my own body, if only for a moment.

Could this be the "mutual love" to which the writer of Hebrews calls God's people? We cannot simply manufacture love that showers strangers with hospitality. We cannot pretend to love and remember those in prison, sharing in their sufferings. That special kind of enabling love comes from God.

Everything hinges on the simple promise in verse 15, that "through Jesus" (NIV) we will continually offer our sacrifice of praise to God. Sometimes, quite by surprise, the love of Christ flows powerfully through us. And for a moment we are one in the bond of true Christian love.

PRAYER: Lord, make me a vessel of your love for your people. I pour out my selfish concerns at your feet. Fill me with your love for the stranger, the neighbor. Amen.

---

* Copastors, Skyline United Methodist Church, Wilmington, Delaware; parents of Joy and Eli; singers, writers, runners.

TUESDAY, AUGUST 28 • Read Jeremiah 2:4-13

Our two-year-old son, Eli, likes to drink warm milk. We warm the milk in the microwave, carefully stirring it before he drinks. Eli wants to do everything himself. Unfortunately, our microwave is located above our stove; the resulting safety concern prevents us from letting him have this freedom. He cannot accomplish this task at his age, and he gets so frustrated when we prevent him from trying to do the job himself.

The alternative we gave him, of lifting him in our arms to reach the microwave, just does not satisfy him. When I watch Eli's struggle, God reminds me of myself. I get frustrated with myself for not being able to accomplish some task, while God patiently waits to lift me with tender arms. The passage from Jeremiah demonstrates how rejected God feels when we continue to try to do things our own way. Jeremiah speaks these words to the people of Judah, who continue to put their trust in things other than the covenant God: "My people have committed two sins: They have forsaken me, the spring of living water, and have dug their own cisterns, broken cisterns that cannot hold water" (Jer. 2:13).

What the people want and what God wants to provide are the same—the life-giving water. We try to provide it for ourselves in cracked pots that can hold no water, when God alone is the true source of the life we seek.

SUGGESTION FOR MEDITATION: **Where in my life (both in big ways and small) do I insist on doing things my way, instead of trusting God to provide?**

PRAYER: **Lord, I have heard your promise today that you want to provide the life-giving water. Open my heart to you so that I may be filled. Amen.**

WEDNESDAY, AUGUST 29 • Read Luke 14:1, 7-14

We both were attending a week-long retreat on "Spirituality and the Active Life," but I was feeling anything but refreshed. One of the participants had stolen my laptop computer, and with it my journals, letters, notes, and diaries. When I had confronted him that morning, he had angrily driven out of the parking lot. As the morning session began, I felt hurt because of my personal loss. Yet I was also ashamed of how angry I felt over losing a material thing.

As we stood together in a circle and sang "Spirit of the Living God," tears gently flowed down my face. We sat down, and the leader began the session. Then someone across the room interrupted him and said, "I believe Bo is hurting." From that lowest place of conflicting emotions, Jesus took my arm and said to me, "Friend, move up higher."

Bless the members of the group that day who willingly and gently listened to my story. Bless the leader of our group, who patiently laid aside his planned material to attend to my immediate need. And thanks to our wonderful and awesome God for filling my empty soul that day with generous and loving friends and giving me the highest place.

Living with the strong memory of that Wednesday morning six years ago, we both hear Jesus' gentle urging to make way for God to move in the lives of those who desperately need Christ's healing touch. Mindful of how blessed it was for others to make room for me to "move up higher," I try to let the Holy Spirit make the seating arrangements for God's people.

SUGGESTION FOR MEDITATION: **Recall and give thanks for a time when someone made room for your healing and escorted you to the Master.**

PRAYER: **God, thank you for lifting me higher when I need it most. Attune me to others' needs this day, so that I lift them into your gracious presence. Amen.**

THURSDAY, AUGUST 30 • Read Psalm 81:1, 10-16

Several years ago, we both served as division officers aboard different Navy ships. Part of our job involved accompanying sailors accused of misconduct in our divisions to Captain's Mast. The solemn proceeding, where the ship's captain serves as judge and jury, always seemed graceless to us.

One day, however, I stood at Captain's Mast with a sailor in my division who had heavily abused alcohol, resulting in several incidents off the ship. I vouched for the man's performance and potential in answer to the captain's query, a standard part of the procedure. Then the captain turned to the accused sailor and spoke. "Young man, you obviously have a problem with alcohol. We stand ready to help you in every way we can to combat and overcome this problem in your life. If you are willing to undergo treatment, your division officer will arrange everything necessary for your counseling and rehabilitation. But only you can decide if you want this treatment." Then the captain looked sternly at the man who stood before him. "If you do not undergo this treatment, son, you will be discharged from the Navy before the sun goes down."

Reading again these precious scripture promises from Psalm 81, I remember the grace that filled that room of judgment aboard a Navy warship. How quickly God stands ready to subdue our enemies, if only we would listen! The sailor that day refused the captain's offer of restoration and chose a path of destruction, just as God's people often do. Yet God continues to place redemptive power in our grasp whenever we are ready to walk in God's paths. "Open your mouth wide," God calls to you this new day, "and I will fill it with good things" (AP).

PRAYER: God of good things, I open my mouth in praise and confession to you this day and stand ready to receive all the good things you are waiting to give me. Amen.

FRIDAY, AUGUST 31 • Read Jeremiah 2:4-13

Why do we continue to do things our way? Have we forgotten God's provision for us in the past? God reminds the people of Judah, "Your ancestors refused to ask for my help, though I had rescued them from Egypt.…I brought you here to my land, where food is abundant" (Jer. 2:6, 7, CEV). We often live our lives as if we were alone on a boat in the water, trying to row to our destination. Although rowing makes us feel that we are in control, we have to work extra hard to provide both power and direction for the boat. We tire and wonder why God does not help us.

But God gives us a motorboat, not a rowboat. God provides the power through the Holy Spirit; we participate by choosing our direction in life. Asking for God's help feels like we're giving up control; but when God provides the power, we can respond more readily to new directions in our lives.

Yet the hectic pace of our lives tempts us to react without reflecting. We do what comes naturally, which is to trust in ourselves. But when we take time to reflect, we remember what God has done for us, just as Jeremiah calls the people of Judah to remember.

As part of the bedtime prayer routine, we ask our children, "What was your favorite part of the day? What was your least favorite part of the day?" We thank God for our favorite parts, and we give God our least favorite parts. The first time we tried this, when our daughter was three, she asked us, "What was your favorite part?" By sending the question back to us, she reminded us of the importance of reflecting on the abundance of God's provision. If God keeps reminding us, we will not forget that we travel in a motorboat, not a rowboat.

PRAYER: God of abundance, you have provided for me time and time again. Remind me of your love and care, and open my heart to be filled. Amen.

SATURDAY, SEPTEMBER 1 • Read Hebrews 13:1-8, 15-16

"Who are the saints in our congregation? Who are the leaders in this body of believers who have taught us the word of God with their lives?" I asked the church one Sunday during a sermon series on passing the mantle from Elijah to Elisha. It was my first summer serving as their associate pastor.

Later, as I sifted through the notes people had placed into the offering plates that Sunday, I was amazed at how many people lifted up the names of an older couple, Helen and Kemp Malone. Over the years I spent with the congregation, I came to love Helen and Kemp as their graceful, faithful lives taught me the word of God. I remember them now and the good that has come from their lives as this New Testament letter encourages me to do. Their lives fragranced the air with grace and praise to God whom they trusted never to fail or forsake them.

When Kemp lay on his deathbed, stricken with pancreatic cancer, I watched them both trust God through the pain. We sang praises around that bed and talked about a time when we would sing again around a feasting table prepared and hosted by Jesus Christ, the same yesterday, today, and forever.

This scripture calls to my mind all the good that has come from their graceful lives. It also calls me to join them in continually offering my sacrifice of praise to God who will never fail or forsake me, in good times or bad. Perhaps my life can also fragrance this new day for strangers, prisoners, people who need care, and my wonderful mate.

PRAYER: Sweet Jesus, you are the same yesterday, today, and tomorrow. Thank you for the saints who have taught me your word through their fragrant lives. Help me this day to offer my sacrifice of praise to God by proclaiming your glory in all that I say and do. Help me entertain strangers and angels. Amen.

SUNDAY, SEPTEMBER 2 • Read Luke 14:1, 7-14

As one of our ongoing missions, our church members volunteer at a downtown men's shelter, preparing food at home and serving it at the shelter. After volunteers serve the meal, they sit and eat with the men, sharing in fellowship. Last spring, our church's turn fell on Easter Sunday—a nice volunteer opportunity for our family and a good example for our children.

Easter Sunday afternoon we piled the food into the back of our Blazer, and the four of us followed the other volunteers out of the church parking lot. On the way to the shelter, we talked with our kids about this passage from Luke, especially where Jesus says, "But when you give a banquet, invite the poor, the crippled, the lame, and the blind. And you will be blessed, because they cannot repay you" (Luke 14:13-14). Although we felt we understood the blessing we receive through serving others, we weren't sure our children would understand.

When we arrived at the shelter, our toddler son, Eli, began to play, lighting up the whole room with smiles. Our daughter, Joy, helped serve the food and then sat down to eat beside several of the men at one of the tables. We were amazed at how much she paid attention to them and how much attention they paid to her. At the close of the evening, we shared a song and then invited all the men to sing hymns with us. Our children joined in the singing. Then one of the men shared some jokes with our daughter. The laughter and smiles spread throughout the room again. As we got into our truck to return home, Joy said, "Wow! That was fun! When can we come back?"

Though we had enjoyed Easter worship earlier that day, we truly experienced Christ's resurrection at the shelter. When we feasted with the poor who could not repay us, God opened our hearts and filled us with love and joy.

PRAYER: Lord, teach me your love. Open my heart to love those who cannot repay me, and fill me with the joy of serving them in your name. Amen.

The Spiritual Life—Living a Life with God

September 3–9, 2001 • Marilyn J. Littlejohn*

MONDAY, SEPTEMBER 3 • Read Psalm 139:1-6, 13-15

The psalmist reminds us of two truths: (1) that each of our lives with God began while still in our mother's womb and (2) that the work of God there was wonderful. Think of the profundity of this reality of God's creative presence. No matter the physical, social, or familial conditions of our lives, God has been with each of us from the beginning. And as the psalmist affirms, no matter the conditions of our birth—and perhaps through the conditions—wonderful are the works of God.

"But wait!" you exclaim. "This child's body is deformed. That child's mind is impaired. These children are imperfect. God cannot be the creator of the imperfect."

Who among us is perfect? And whose life is without hardship? Beauty is in the eye of the beholder, so maybe there is another way to see. When we judge people or ourselves, are we seeing as God sees? We may choose one of two ways of seeing: Either we can marvel at the astonishing reality of a unique human life, or we can focus on the imperfections of a life. While both perspectives reflect truth, only one is life affirming.

One challenge of the spiritual life comes in being attuned or reconnected with the fundamental reality of created goodness that transcends imperfections. Sometimes we forget the truth; we lose sight of God's creation as something wonderfully made. But we who are children of God can continue to remember and proclaim that each of God's creations is wonderful.

PRAYER: Thank you, God, for creation and my life. Help me focus on and celebrate the wonder of being alive and of life itself. Amen.

---

*Clergy member, Pacific Northwest Annual Conference of The United Methodist Church; consultant, Tacoma, Washington.

TUESDAY, SEPTEMBER 4 • Read Jeremiah 18:1-6

Despite our wonderful beginning, some people do lose their way in life. Failure, oppression, pain, fear, ignorance, and arrogance—any one of these experiences can lead us to lose sight of God. And while in this state of estrangement, we can cause great harm to ourselves or to others.

Sometimes the lost are easy to spot. We think readily of the spouse batterer, the child molester, the thief, the addict, and the alcoholic. But those who feel trapped in an unhappy marriage, who suffer through an unfulfilling job, who believe that life is without meaning, or who live without compassion for others are just as lost. The hope for each lost one, no matter the form of lostness, comes in remembering God. God alone has the power and the compassion to rework our lives into another vessel.

One such lost person was John Newton, the self-described wretch, who wrote the beloved hymn "Amazing Grace." Newton, as a slave trader, made his living in the sale of human beings. But on March 10, 1748, his life changed. In the midst of a violent storm that could have sunk his ship, he surrendered his life to the will of God. God heard his cry and began reshaping his life. Newton's life changed slowly. It took him several years to get out of the slave trade business, but in time he became a minister and shared with others the grace of God.

God can change lives. Today's drug addict could be the head of a community drug treatment program in the future. Today's disillusioned corporate executive could be your church's minister in a few years. Today's successful attorney or paralegal could have been a single parent with no marketable skills a few years ago. With God there is hope, and God's hope can become a reality.

SUGGESTION FOR MEDITATION AND PRAYER: **Consider those areas in your life where you feel lost or broken. Surrender these areas, indeed, your life itself to almighty God, the merciful and compassionate one. Pray for healing and guidance.**

WEDNESDAY, SEPTEMBER 5 • Read Jeremiah 18:7-10

Children have fresh eyes through which they view the world. They have a natural curiosity. They laugh and love easily. But at some point in their young lives they stop listening; ask any elementary school teacher. This may occur for several reasons:

- a preoccupation with making friends, keeping friends, and avoiding bullies;
- worrying about what's happening at home;
- believing they are going to fail anyway;
- not believing the teacher really cares about them.

Adults stop listening to God for similar reasons. Some put their spiritual lives on the back burner because of their preoccupation with work, their love lives, or families. Others forego life with God because they believe God doesn't really care about them. Those of us who believe these things may never realize our error unless we stop to listen.

This listening to God in the language of the spiritual disciplines is called meditation. In his *Study Guide for Celebration of Discipline*, Richard J. Foster says that this discipline "is characterized more by reflecting than by studying, more by listening than by thinking, more by releasing than by grabbing. In...meditation we are not so much acting as we are opening ourselves to be acted upon. We invite the Holy Spirit to come and work within us—teaching, cleansing, comforting, rebuking. We also surround ourselves with the strong light of Christ to protect us from any influence not of God."

Through meditation upon the scripture, for example, we hear the voice of God. As we attune ourselves to this voice, we receive guidance for our lives.

SUGGESTION FOR MEDITATION: **Meditate on one of your favorite Bible stories by placing yourself in the scene: identify with one of the characters; imagine what that person felt, thought, or did even after the story as written ends.**

THURSDAY, SEPTEMBER 6 • Read Luke 14:25-27

Who and what are the important people and things in your life?
- Your love life?
- Your relationships with parents or children?
- Financial security?
- Being recognized in some field of your choosing?
- Sustaining the natural beauty of the earth?
- Golf, fly fishing, football, gardening, music?
- Having a lot of friends and acquaintances?
- Life itself?

The initial question has as many answers as individuals who respond. But the more significant question is this: Are any of your important things or people more important than your relationship with God? This may be a hard question to answer. One's love, passion, or need may be so great that to let go of some relationship, goal, or object would be like submitting to death.

Remember Christ's struggle in the Garden of Gethsemane, where his sweat became like great drops of blood as he prayed that God "remove this cup from me." Yet his prayer concludes with words of surrender, "Not my will but yours be done."

To surrender all to God, including renouncing the life and things of life one desires, is the sacrifice of self that an individual makes to be a true disciple. In doing so, he or she experiences the truth captured in the words of Saint Augustine, "Our hearts are restless, Lord, until they find rest in Thee."

SUGGESTION FOR MEDITATION: Have you surrendered your whole life to God? What parts of your life are you still trying to control?

FRIDAY, SEPTEMBER 7 • Read Luke 14:28-33

In 1927 a sculptor began a work that would take him fourteen years to complete. What enabled him to complete this work? A few examples:

• Resourcefulness—Having enough money was a constant stumbling block, particularly during the Great Depression. But he lobbied extensively and constantly during the project. In the end, he secured from the federal government $836,000 of the $1 million the project cost.

• Ingenuity—The scale of his project was so big he had to create new tools and methods to produce his work.

• Courage—The material with which he worked, granite, was so strong, he had to risk using the powerful and potentially destructive tool of dynamite to shape his work.

• Flexibility—In the course of creating the monument, he had to make a make a major change in his original plan. The head of Jefferson had to be moved from Washington's right to Washington's left.

The sculptor's name is Gutzon Borglum. His work is the memorial of the four presidents atop Mount Rushmore. Borglum was the kind of person to whom Jesus alludes in today's lesson. He was a man who did not give up. He did what he needed to do to finish the work and avoid ridicule.

Did he know ahead of time all the work would require of him? Probably not. But he remained committed and persevered during the difficult times. Resourcefulness, ingenuity, courage, and flexibility—qualities needed by anyone who would surrender his or her life to God.

PRAYER: Gracious Lord, I pray for resourcefulness, ingenuity, courage, flexibility, and any other quality of spirit that will enable me stay the course. May I receive or uncover the tools required to live faithfully in this world and fulfill my responsibilities as your disciple. Amen.

SATURDAY, SEPTEMBER 8 • Read Philemon

According to biblical scholars, an epistle of Ignatius written soon after the beginning of the second century reveals that the bishop of the church at Ephesus was a man called Onesimus. Was he Paul's beloved Onesimus? Perhaps. If so, how ironic. Paul in his letter to Philemon says of Onesimus, "Formerly he was useless to you, but now he is indeed useful both to you and to me." Can there be any greater understatement if Onesimus the slave became Onesimus the bishop? Onesimus became useful to the whole church!

Life with God is not just an individual experience. The experience has some manifestation in the Christian community itself, if not the world. Saul/Paul, a persecutor of the early Christians, spread the Christian gospel to the Gentiles. Saint Augustine, a Roman rhetorician, became a Christian preacher. And just maybe Onesimus, a slave, became a church leader.

In each case the person chose to nurture some natural talent and dedicate it to the service of God and humanity. The gifts and talents reflected in the aforementioned persons include persuasion, leadership, and oratory.

Each of us has gifts: the gift of music, the gift of storytelling, the gift of teaching, the gift of organization, the gift of healing, the gift of languages, the gift of design, the gift of tact and diplomacy, the gift of.... You get the picture. God has bestowed upon each of us and all of us an abundance of gifts. Our challenge comes in making them useful in a manner that glorifies God and serves humanity.

SUGGESTION FOR MEDITATION: Contemplate one of God's gifts manifested in your life. How useful has this gift been? How useful can it be?

PRAYER: Eternal God, I offer myself as an instrument of your peace, your loving-kindness, your mercy, and your compassion. May my life glorify you in all I do, say, and think. This I pray in Jesus' name. Amen.

SUNDAY, SEPTEMBER 9 • Read Psalm 139:16-18

"I come to the end—I am still with you."

Life contains many points of transition, during which one thing ends as another begins. We let go of one reality to grasp another. One of the first transitions for many of us occurs as we learn to walk. Remember how that transition happens? The infant who has explored her world as a crawler is encouraged to stand upright. Perhaps her parent lifts her by her arms and holds her upright so she can begin to get used to standing on her own two legs. Another time, the parent might hold the child and walk with the child, slowly and gently guiding her through her first steps. Next the parent may help the child stand supported by a sofa or a sturdy coffee table. Soon the child, with the parent watching nearby, may shuffle along the sofa. Eventually, the child will let go of the sofa and take a few unassisted, wobbly steps into the open, safe arms of mom or dad. Everyone erupts with joy. The child has entered a new world of experience and exploration.

Through the course of this transition, the parent is ever present—coaxing, holding, guiding, watching, and waiting. I imagine that the child is aware of the presence of the parent throughout. The child's awareness of parent is like the awareness of God that those of us who endeavor to live a spiritual life desire. We desire to be awake to the omnipresent, gracious, living God. This is the ultimate transition in life. It is the transition in which we loosen our grasp on all that is material, all that makes us secure in the world, and take the plunge of faith. We will then discover a living God and a new, richer life, a life Christ described best: "Seek ye first the kingdom of God…and all things shall be added unto you."

PRAYER: Give me the courage, O Lord, to loosen my grip on one more attachment in the world today. Open my heart that I might experience your presence in my life more deeply and know with assurance that I am still with you. Amen.

Hope and Joy

September 10–16, 2001 • *Patricia Walworth Wood**

MONDAY, SEPTEMBER 10 • **Read Psalm 14:7**

A friend once told me, "Don't let yourself give up hope, and don't let John give up hope." My husband had worked for the same law firm thirty years; it was the oldest law firm in the city. This firm had closed its doors, leaving John without work.

In Romans 8:25 Paul counsels, "If we hope for what we do not yet have, we wait for it patiently" (NIV). In Lamentations 3:24 we read, "'The Lord is my portion,' says my soul, / 'therefore I will hope in him'" (RSV). The importance of hope became clearer to me during this period of my husband's unemployment than any previous time.

Many passages throughout scripture speak of hope, referring to having hope even when there is no visible source for that hope. The bulk of Psalm 14, which we will look at on Wednesday, appears to be all gloom and doom for the Israelites. But the last sentence says *when*, not *if* "the Lord restores the fortunes of his people."

Though none of this week's passages uses the word *hope*, I see in them the promise of something better to come and I know joy.

SUGGESTION FOR MEDITATION: **Consider hope and the role it plays in your life. Where do you need hope? Who do you know who needs hope? What might you have to offer?**

---

*Free-lance writer and speaker, active layperson, forty-year member, Fairview Presbyterian Church, Indianapolis, Indiana.

TUESDAY, SEPTEMBER 11 • Read Jeremiah 4:11-12, 22-28

When I read today's scripture I wondered what Jeremiah's prophecy of doom had to do with me. How could I relate to it? What did it mean?

As I thought about prophecies I realized that I think of two kinds: the pleasant and the unpleasant. The former speaks positively, such as the prophecy found in Isaiah 11:1-2: "There shall come forth a shoot from the stump of Jesse, / and a branch shall grow out of his roots. / And the Spirit of the Lord shall rest upon him" (RSV).

The passage in Jeremiah is an unpleasant prophecy. If I had lived during that time, I either would have ridiculed Jeremiah or lived in fear. Jeremiah prophesied the destruction of Judah, the southern kingdom. Since the northern kingdom of Israel had already fallen to the Assyrians, his message would have seemed plausible.

But even with the threat of destruction, God's people seem unable to change from going their own way to relying on God. According to Jeremiah, the Israelites knew how to do evil but not good. I believe the same phenomenon holds true today for myself and for our society as we struggle with what to do in a variety of social and civil situations. Could our fruitful land become a desert? Sometimes I worry about what will be here for my grandchildren, their children, and their children's children.

The hope comes for me in Jeremiah 4:27 where it is written, "Yet I will not make a full end." Scholars indicate that this sentence was a later addition to the text. Whenever it was included, I thank God for this hope.

SUGGESTION FOR MEDITATION: Do you respond to God's direction? On whom do you depend—yourself, others, or God?

WEDNESDAY, SEPTEMBER 12 • Read Psalm 14

Let us now consider the bulk of Psalm 14. This psalm offers no prayer or praise. Like Jeremiah's words, it seems to be a prophetic exhortation. The psalmist looks at society as a whole and sees foolish people who reject the reality of God. Their leadership is corrupt. God looks for the wise ones who seek God, but finds none.

This is a pretty depressing psalm—far less joyous than many. Paul, however, wasn't put off by words I'd just as soon forget or ignore. He used these dismal words for a positive redirection of thought. He quoted the first three verses of Psalm 14 in Romans 3:10-12 to make the point that all of us are sinners. From that point he proceeded to grace.

The psalmist acknowledges this grace of God when he refers to the Lord as a refuge: "For God is with the generation of the righteous" (RSV). And the generation of the righteous encompasses those people who acknowledge God in trustful obedience.

Compare Psalm 14 with Psalm 53. They are almost identical, but I much prefer Psalm 14 for the hope I see reflected in it. Psalm 53 does not refer to the "generation of the righteous" or to the Lord's being the refuge for the poor whom the evildoers would overthrow. The good news of Psalm 14 is that God is able to gather sinners into the "generation of the righteous." It is that hope to which we cling.

PRAYER: Lord, thank you for the hope that has reigned throughout the generations. Amen.

THURSDAY, SEPTEMBER 13 • Read Luke 15:1-3

In Luke 14, Jesus told the parable of the householder who had prepared a great banquet, but when it came time for the guests to come to the banquet they all made excuses. The householder then had his servants invite all who were on the streets.

In today's reading we learn the tax collectors listened to Jesus and ate with him, along with the sinners. Tax collectors are invariably spoken of in the New Testament in the same breath with sinners and are generally hated as representatives of the Roman rulers. But these people responded to Jesus: "Now all the tax collectors and sinners were coming near to listen to him."

The Pharisees and the scribes must have felt uncomfortable in such a crowd. Yet they stand near enough to hear what Jesus has to say, all the while grumbling about his spending time with low-life sinners. What might generate such grumbling? Perhaps they're jealous; perhaps they're indignant. Maybe in the Pharisees' opinion, Jesus should have been seeking them out to learn from them. They are, after all, quite pious. But whatever the cause, when Jesus eats with sinners the Pharisees and scribes just don't understand. Why doesn't Jesus see things the way they do?

I'm glad Jesus didn't and doesn't. I rejoice that Jesus' perspective is God's perspective. Because Jesus broke bread with the tax collectors and sinners, I know he breaks bread with me.

SUGGESTION FOR MEDITATION: **Would I, do I, eat with the people Christ sits with and makes welcome? From what perspective do I view others? Does it come from within me or from God? How does that perspective guide me?**

FRIDAY, SEPTEMBER 14 • Read 1 Timothy 1:15-17

Who are sinners? You and I. We don't intentionally become sinners, but we have periods of inaction, action, or harmful attitudes that create a wedge between ourselves and God.

Adam and Eve created a wedge when they ignored God's direction not to eat the fruit of one particular tree. Eve claimed to have been tempted by the serpent, and Adam claimed to have been tempted by Eve. Blaming another compounds the sin of ignoring God's direction.

Some people consider alcoholism a sin; others believe it to be a disease to which people are predisposed. As far as I'm concerned both of these views are true. I didn't set out to abuse alcohol and cause my family worry, but it happened. The problem, though not caused by anyone, separated me from the power of the Lord. And that separation, in and of itself, was a sin. Once I made a conscious decision to make myself available to God's power, the wedge of separation was removed. As I came to rely on God's power one day at a time, I came to know a closeness to the Lord that I had never experienced—I received mercy.

Other behavior also separates me from God and thus is a sin. Hatred, compromising of beliefs, and not forgiving others create a distance between God and me. But Paul experienced mercy, and he considered himself the foremost of sinners. Since he received mercy, we too have hope of receiving mercy.

PRAYER: Dear Lord, show me what problem you would have me turn over to you for removal so I can walk more closely with you. Amen.

SATURDAY, SEPTEMBER 15 • Read 1 Timothy 1:12-14

Paul's blasphemy of God and persecution of the Christians were well known to all. He was a man to be feared. Acts 7:58 tells us of Paul's presence, although nonparticipatory, at Stephen's stoning: "And the witnesses laid their coats at the feet of a young man named Saul." And in 8:1 we read, "And Saul was consenting to [Stephen's] death" (RSV). Saul, convinced he is in the right in his determination to revere and follow Jewish law, doesn't care who is hurt or how. Paul in today's passage confesses his past as "a blasphemer, a persecutor, and a man of violence."

I'm not Paul; I haven't consciously or actively persecuted others. As I proclaim my innocence of any persecution, I hear in my mind a variation of, "Lord, when did we see thee hungry or thirsty or a stranger or naked or sick or in prison, and did not minister to thee?" (Matthew 25:44, RSV).

I ask the Lord, "When did I persecute you?" The response includes the way I sometimes treat other people, family members, friends. I often want strangers to remain strangers. I avoid, as much as possible, persons with handicapping conditions. Too frequently I become irritable or impatient with those I love.

No, I don't persecute Christians in the way Saul did, but I fall far short of the way I believe Jesus would have me be. I read of Paul's experience and rejoice because God called him into service despite his sordid past; Paul finds himself the recipient of God's grace, and I can too.

PRAYER: Lord, may I continue to strive toward changing my responses to others. I thank you for your mercy and grace, which are freely given to me even as I continue to fall short in my relationships. Amen.

SUNDAY, SEPTEMBER 16 • Read Luke 15:3-10

Jesus often told parables in response both to criticism and questions. The Pharisees and the scribes have been complaining about Jesus' being with the tax collectors and sinners. Jesus reminds them of the importance of the lost by telling two stories.

The shepherd loses one sheep out of one hundred. Does that really matter? The shepherd thinks so, even though it means leaving the ninety-nine in the wilderness while he seeks the lost one. Once he finds the sheep, he doesn't just prod the lamb home. He picks it up, lays it across his shoulders, and carries it home.

The woman uses every means available to find the lost coin. She lights a lamp to see better; she sweeps the house and searches diligently until she finds it.

The woman calls in her friends and neighbors for a celebration. Likewise the shepherd invites his friends and neighbors to rejoice with him. And there is joy in heaven. One sinner has repented.

What might the Pharisees and scribes hear in these stories? Are they the ninety-nine over whom there is no rejoicing? The parable of the lost coin, unlike the parable of the lost sheep, does not close by mentioning the other nine coins—but again rejoicing takes place over the finding of the lost. Rejoicing initiates celebration. Who's invited to the party? Everyone. Who will come? Those who can celebrate with the angels when one sinner repents.

PRAYER: God, I rejoice and thank you for carrying me home when I am lost. Encourage my willingness to join the party. Amen.

2002

Now is the time to order your copy of
THE UPPER ROOM DISCIPLINES 2002

Published for over 40 years, *Disciplines* is one of
the most popular daily devotional books available.
Year after year, *Disciplines* continues to appeal to
more and more Christians who, like you, desire
a more disciplined spiritual life based on scripture.
Order your copy today, while the 2002 edition
is still available.

THE UPPER ROOM DISCIPLINES 2002
$10.00 each — 10 or more copies $8.50 each
Ask for product number #930
Large-print edition available—$14.00

Shipping Charges:

Actual shipping charges will
be added to your invoice.

We accept Visa and
Mastercard, checks and
money orders.

Visit our Web site at
www.upperroom.org.

To Order Your Copies, Call:
1-800-972-0433.
Tell the customer service
representative your
source code is 2002D.

Or Write:
Customer Service Department
The Upper Room
P.O. Box 340004
Nashville, TN 37203-0004

THE UPPER ROOM DISCIPLINES 2002
is also available at most bookstores.

What Christians Do

September 17–23, 2001 • Martin Thielen*

MONDAY, SEPTEMBER 17 • Read Jeremiah 8:18–9:1

Tony, a young man in my congregation, visited me the day after his baptism. He said, "Pastor, now that I'm a Christian, what am I supposed to do?" Answering that question is a lifelong journey. However, this week's lectionary readings provide numerous answers to the question, "What do Christians do?"

In today's reading we learn that Christians *ask hard questions*. Jeremiah, heartsick over the destruction of Israel, asks, "Is the Lord not in Zion?…Is there no balm in Gilead? Is there no physician there? Why then has the health of my poor people not been restored?" Like Jeremiah, we sometimes ask, "Where is God in the midst of suffering? Why doesn't God heal God's people?" Although no simple answers exist for these questions, God's people dare to ask them. Even Jesus, during his crucifixion, asked, "My God, my God, why have you forsaken me?"

During the Holocaust, Jewish prisoners were forced to witness the execution of a teenager. Elie Wiesel relates the following story in his book *Night*: One man, overcome with despair asked, "Where is God now? Where is He?" Another witness responded, "Where is He? Here He is—He is hanging here on the gallows."

Although God does not answer all our questions about suffering, God does not leave us alone in our pain. Even when no simple answers exist, the crucified God is with us; and that is enough.

PRAYER: Like Jeremiah, Lord, I have hard questions. Thank you for your presence even when answers are not forthcoming. Amen.

---

*Pastor of Monterey United Methodist Church, Monterey, Tennessee; author of four books and numerous articles.

TUESDAY, SEPTEMBER 18 • Read Jeremiah 8:18–9:1

This week we're asking the question, "What do Christians do?" In today's reading we learn that Christians *openly acknowledge their doubts and struggles.*

Jeremiah doesn't pretend to be strong when he feels weak. Instead, he says, "I am hurt, I mourn, and dismay has taken hold of me." Jeremiah asks the hard questions such as, "Where is God in our suffering?" Although some Christians think it's sinful to express doubts and struggles, Jeremiah teaches us that faith and doubt go together; authentic believers can freely express their deepest despair to God.

Robert Veninga in his book *A Gift of Hope: How We Survive Our Tragedies* relates the following story. A boy's mother had just died. Hospital personnel took him to see the chaplain. On the wall in the chaplain's office hung a wooden crucifix, and attached to the cross was a ceramic figure of Jesus. The boy's eyes focused on the crucifix. The chaplain, sensitive to the boy's hostility, said, "Do whatever you need to do."

The boy reached for the crucifix, removed it from the wall, raised it over his head, and smashed it against the floor over and over again until the ceramic figure of Jesus was broken into bits. After his destructive deed the boy collapsed on the couch next to the minister. The chaplain held the boy tightly as he poured out his grief in deep, powerful, and unrestrained sobs.

That boy in the hospital didn't hate God. But at that moment he needed to express his anger, doubts, and struggles freely. Just like Jeremiah. Just like you and me. God can take it!

PRAYER: Thank you Lord, for allowing me to express myself to you freely, even my confusion, anger, doubts and struggles. Amen.

WEDNESDAY, SEPTEMBER 19 • Read Psalm 79:1-9

This week we're asking the question, "What do Christians do?" In today's reading we learn that Christians *accept God's forgiveness*. Although the author of Psalm 79 wanted God to punish the nations for their desecration of Israel, the psalmist also admitted that God's people had sinned and that they needed God's forgiveness.

In 1972, during the Vietnam war, John Plummer set up an air strike on the village of Trang Bang after being assured there were no civilians in the area. Shortly after the strike, John saw the Pulitzer Prize-winning photo of nine-year-old Kim Phuc running naked and horribly burned by napalm from the village of Trang Bang. The graphic depiction of the results of his act devastated John, who had a nine-year-old child of his own. John's guilt produced sad consequences in his life.

Years later, John saw a news story that updated the life of Kim Phuc. John learned that she was alive and that she was coming to the Vietnam Veterans Memorial in Washington for a Veteran's Day observance. Arrangements were made for them to meet each other.

When Kim Phuc spoke at the Vietnam Memorial, she said she had forgiven the people who bombed her and that instead of dwelling on past wrongdoing, people needed to work together to build a better future. After Kim Phuc finished speaking, she was escorted toward John, who was overcome with emotion. In a later interview John said, "She saw my grief, my pain, my sorrow. She held out her arms to me and embraced me. All I could say was 'I'm sorry; I'm so sorry; I'm sorry,' over and over again. At the same time she was saying, 'It's all right, it's all right; I forgive, I forgive.'"

PRAYER: Thank you, Lord, for forgiving my sins and failures. Amen.

THURSDAY, SEPTEMBER 20 • **Read Psalm 79:1-9**

This week we're asking the question, "What do Christians do?" In today's reading we learn that Christians *affirm faith even when God seems silent.*

The writer of Psalm 79 expresses disappointment in God: disappointment that God has not punished Israel's enemies, disappointment that God has not forgiven God's people, disappointment at God's silence in the midst of suffering. Yet despite these disappointments and doubts, the psalmist continues to affirm faith in God. Despite God's silence, the psalmist believes.

Several years ago, Elie Wiesel, a survivor of the Holocaust, was interviewed on television. During the interview Wiesel recalled a specific experience he had at a Nazi concentration camp. A group of Jewish men decided to have a trial, one unlike any trial you've ever heard of before. These men decided to try God for the horrors of the holocaust. They had been men of faith, but their faith had profoundly disappointed them. So they decided to put God on trial for abandoning the Jewish people.

They asked young Wiesel, only fourteen years old at the time, to witness the proceedings. The charges were brought; the prosecutor listed them one by one. God's people had been torn from their homes, separated from their families, imprisoned, beaten, murdered, and incinerated. A defense was attempted, but in the end God was found guilty of abandoning God's people.

At the trial's conclusion, a profound silence fell upon the room. Moments later the men realized that it was time for the sacred ritual of evening prayer. At this point in the story, Wiesel recounts a remarkable fact: These men who had just found God guilty of abandoning them began to pray their evening prayers.

PRAYER: Lord, I believe; help my unbelief. Amen.

Friday, September 21 • Read 1 Timothy 2:1-7

This week we're asking the question, "What do Christians do?" In today's reading we learn that Christians *make prayer a priority*. In verse one of today's text Paul says, "First of all, then, I urge that supplications, prayers, intercessions, and thanksgivings be made for everyone." There is no doubt that Paul made prayer a priority, and he expected all Christians to do the same.

Making prayer a priority isn't easy. Many obstacles stand in the way. Perhaps the biggest obstacle is our busy schedules. Many of us think we're too busy to pray.

Years ago, before telephones were invented, a top executive with a telegraph company went on a train trip. It was extremely cold when he arrived at the train station. Since his train would not arrive for an hour, he walked next door to the local telegraph station to get warmed up. When he went inside, however, he noticed there was no fire in the fireplace. He said to the young telegraph operator, "Why don't you build a fire in this place?" The young man said, "Listen, mister, I'm too busy sending telegrams to build fires!"

The executive informed the young operator that he was vice president of the company, and he ordered him to send a telegram to the home office. The message read, "Fire this man immediately." Moments later the young telegraph operator brought a load of firewood into the office and began to build a fire. The executive asked him, "Young man, have you sent that telegram yet?" The operator replied, "Listen, mister, I'm too busy building fires to send telegrams!"

If we are too busy to pray—then we are too busy. As one wise pastor said, "I'm too busy *not* to pray."

Prayer: Lord, help me make prayer a priority in my life, starting today. Amen.

SATURDAY, SEPTEMBER 22 • Read Luke 16:1-13

This week we're asking the question, "What do Christians do?" In today's reading we learn that Christians *act as faithful servants, even in small matters.*

Today's passage is difficult to interpret. As one commentator noted, "Uncertainties abound." Many theories exist about the meaning of this strange parable. Therefore, instead of adding to the uncertainty, we'll focus on verse 10, "Whoever is faithful in a very little is faithful also in much." In this verse, Jesus calls us to be faithful in all our responsibilities, even in—especially in—small matters.

Few of us do great things for God. Instead, we do many small things. We serve as an usher or sing in the choir or volunteer in the nursery or serve meals in a soup kitchen or give a donation to the United Way or write a letter to our senator concerning world hunger or environmental stewardship. Although these are simple acts of service, Jesus teaches that small acts of faithfulness are very important in the kingdom of God.

Novelist Walker Percy wrote a book entitled *The Thanatos Syndrome*. In it, Dr. Tom Moore, a psychiatrist, serves a two-year prison term on a drug charge. His prison job entails responsibility for keeping up a golf course. After his release from prison, Dr. Moore reflects on his experience. He says, "Living a small life gave me leave to notice things—like certain off-color spots in the St. Augustine grass which I correctly diagnosed as an early sign of chinch-bug infestation." Then he goes on to say, "Instead of saving the world, I saved the eighteen holes at Fort Pelham and felt surprisingly good about it."

PRAYER: Lord, help me be faithful in all my responsibilities, great or small. Amen.

SUNDAY, SEPTEMBER 23 • **Read Luke 16:13**

This week we've asked the question, "What do Christians do?" In today's reading we learn that Christians *love God and neighbor more than money.*

In a culture that worships money, it's easy to get caught up in materialism. Most Americans can relate to the story of a guru who had a promising disciple. Pleased with his disciple's spiritual progress, the guru left him on his own. The disciple lived in a mud hut and begged for his food. Each morning he washed his loincloth and hung it out to dry. One day, he came back to discover the loincloth torn and eaten by rats. The villagers gave him another loincloth, but the rats ate that one too. So he got a cat. That took care of the rats, but now when he begged for food he also had to beg for milk. So he decided to get a cow. He got the cow, but now he had to beg for hay as well. So he decided to farm the land around his hut. Soon he found no time for contemplation, so he hired servants to tend his farm. Overseeing the laborers became a chore, so he married a wife to help out. In time, the disciple became the wealthiest man in the village. Years later this man's guru returned for a visit. He was shocked to see a palace, a farm, and many servants where previously there had been only a mud hut.

"What is the meaning of this?" the guru demanded.

"You won't believe this, sir," the disciple replied, "but there was no other way I could keep my loincloth."

True disciples resist materialism. Instead of loving money, they seek to love God and neighbor.

PRAYER: Help me, Lord, love God and neighbor more than wealth. Amen.

Responding to Uncertainty

September 24–30, 2001 • Marilyn Dickson*

MONDAY, SEPTEMBER 24 • Read Jeremiah 32:1-3a

Zedekiah, king of Judah, is scared. Jeremiah has predicted not only the fall of Jerusalem but also the capture and exile of the king himself. Like anyone facing the prospect of impending doom, the king reacts by placing Jeremiah under house arrest to squelch the prophetic preaching. His rationale seems to be based on the idea that "if no one knows, then it won't happen." Stifle Jeremiah and the prophecy fails.

So often we receive unpleasant news. Our first reaction, like Zedekiah's, is to deny its reality. We look for ways to forestall impending doom. We try to escape by telling ourselves it can't happen. *Divorce. Cancer. Death. Bankruptcy.* No one wants to hear these words. Like Zedekiah, we react to the messenger instead of taking action to deal with the new and uncertain message of future reality. We prefer to control outcomes but still receive the benefits of resurrection and "new life in Christ" without any trials. To ignore the reality—those tough times of crucifixion filled with waiting—we choose to deny or avoid suffering and pain that are part of life's patterns.

What allows you to check on life's realities? Who celebrates or cheers and encourages you? Who serves as hope-filled guide for detours and potholes that suddenly appear on your path of life? Who are the prophets who call you to listen?

PRAYER: Lord of life, help me identify people who will serve as guides for my daily life, mentors who will face life's burdens and joys and decorate my soul with your hope. Amen.

---

*Senior Associate Minister, Northway Christian Church (Disciples of Christ); Director of Grief/Divorce Recovery; seminar and workshop leader; participant in the two-year Academy for Spiritual Formation; living in Dallas, Texas.

TUESDAY, SEPTEMBER 25 • **Read Jeremiah 32:6-15**

Is Jeremiah the doom-and-gloom prophet for you? If so, consider two pivotal insights that may change your perspective. This man of God has a solid vision of the new covenant. He has a future orientation. His purchase of land is an act of faith dedicated to that vision. His people face exile yet he buys land destined for foreign troop occupation. He believes that his people will someday return home and when they do they'll need land. He willingly invests his cash even though he himself will not benefit, and he makes the purchase at the very time every woe he has predicted is taking place. He believes in God's plan for God's people. He trusts God's vision.

A man called Hubert exemplified a future-oriented faith. Even when dying of bone cancer, he held to God's vision for living. He spoke glowingly of kind and good people he had met during cancer treatments. "Their medical training," he said, "helps me face the present so God can lead me into the future." As a schoolteacher and educational administrator, a teacher of teachers, he directed the lives of many. He chose his profession to make a difference for others. His career, like all of his life choices, was based on his faith as a Christian. His leadership impacted styles of teaching and content, and they were not always popular. But he had an educational vision of possibilities for the future of his students. He also faced his own mortality with a firmly held vision of faith. He left a legacy of living from a Christ-centered soul. Like Jeremiah, he was used by God to make a difference for future generations.

SUGGESTION FOR MEDITATION: **Reflect on your personal vision that you claim as one who can be used by God.**

PRAYER: **Use me, O God, for your sake and for the sake of your future for all. Amen.**

WEDNESDAY, SEPTEMBER 26 • **Read Psalm 91:1-6**

Life circumstances may overwhelm us. We feel as if we are drowning. All that is familiar or stable is collapsing. Where is our lifeline? From whom can we seek help? Where might we find a stronghold, a place of sanctuary of protecting presence? Can all be well even when the externals of life point otherwise?

This psalmist too has experienced fear and uncertainty. But the psalmist also knows that recalling one's source of strength and reaffirming God's everlasting love are fundamental to the steadying of our very self in the face of life's storms. Scripture reading, meditating, giving thanks to God for our daily blessings are all small steps in our regular routines that build the foundation of our faith a bit at a time. Faith doesn't just happen. Faith needs to be molded and remembered. Spiritual footings are poured and solidified through circumstances, traditions, and an understanding of who God is and what God does. When life does collapse, the fundamental foundation of our being is recalled. We rebuild.

There is no circumstance, no danger, and no difficulty beyond God's protecting ability. God is with us; God is for us. God can be trusted in the worst of imaginable circumstances. We have the absolute assurance that we can always seek sanctuary in God's love under the wings of the Holy. This form of divine protection probably referred to the practice of seeking sanctuary in the Temple from persecutors. We repeatedly recall, "God is our refuge and our fortress; our God, in whom we trust." Do we believe it?

SUGGESTION FOR MEDITATION: **What uncertain or difficult circumstances do you face? Do you believe God is working to help you discern direction and attitudes? Pour out your concerns and circumstances in prayer. Seek to trust, even in your doubt.**

THURSDAY, SEPTEMBER 27 • Read Psalm 91:14-16

What a surprise. What a switch. Now we hear the words of Yahweh coming back to us. Instead of the psalmist's repeating our human dilemma regarding life's uncertainties, we hear words of loving intimacy: "I will deliver; I will protect....I will answer....I will rescue...and honor." All are promises made by Yahweh to those who trust. These verses are an incredible treasure of God's assurances and promises. We are to cherish and recall them in our times of wondering who this God is who created us. This God who seeks us out awes us. Just as we develop lasting friendship and move to levels of intimacy with our friends and lovers, we now have God speaking to us in the most endearing terms.

We are told that deep spiritual relationship is the intimacy that humankind has difficulty developing because of our reluctance to give over control or trust to that which can neither be proven nor seen. But our psalmist discounts such tendencies. This redactor places the future in God's tender embrace and simply trusts. These verses speak again of God's loving protection, the confident words of one who trusts and knows the intimate relationship of being loved by one's Creator. These verses emphasize the fact that the last words are spoken not *by* us but *to* us! What a gift.

SUGGESTION FOR MEDITATION: What is your image of God? How does it make you feel to know that God will answer, protect, rescue, honor you if you trust? Reflect on this psalm by using your own name instead of the impersonal second person. Example: "I will rescue (your name here), who loves me." After you have prayerfully considered these verses, write down what they mean to you.

FRIDAY, SEPTEMBER 28 • Read Luke 16:19-31

The rich man and Lazarus live in the same neighborhood but are worlds apart, extreme opposites. Each day that Lazarus lies at the rich man's door the distance between them grows. One dines in luxury; the other depends on scraps. The rich man operates as if Lazarus were invisible. He isn't mean, but neither is he hospitable or compassionate. He lets Lazarus lie at his door day and night, yet he does nothing for him. Would I do even this? Would you? Why then is this man of wealth doomed to an eternity separated from God? Why does Jesus use this indifferent individual as an example?

Could it be that Jesus chooses him because the rich man played it safe? Getting involved with Lazarus was an unknown. Having compassion for others usually means involvement. Ultimately even God's mercy could not bridge the compassion gap when the rich man sought it for his family. The rich man's mistake is an easy one to make. Don't get involved. Play it safe. Don't care. The rich man took no action even when he had resources to spare.

None of us alone can fix the world's ills, but we all have spheres of influence. We choose to enter into community or remain in isolation. Jesus' hands-on, gospel ministry involved living deeds, not passive observation.

Who could benefit from your phone call or encouraging note? Look around. Do you see invisible people? Will you get involved? Opening to brokenness, ours as well as others, allows God's grace to enter. We are forever changed. God's mercy is our reality. The good news means involvement not distance. The rich man didn't know it. We do.

PRAYER: God, who anoints with the balm of grace, enter my circles of brokenness. Let me be a healing presence to another person today. Use me to act on your behalf. Amen.

SATURDAY, SEPTEMBER 29 • Read 1 Timothy 6:6-10

Timothy, the young pastor in a new congregation, receives the charge of managing the church's internal affairs—a church combating external persecution and embroiled in accusations of false teachings. He has to keep the gospel of Jesus Christ fresh and fervent for people who are discouraged. If that isn't enough, he also has to preach about money! In verse 10 we read, "The love of money is a root of all kinds of evil."

We know that money in and of itself is neither good nor evil. One's ethical judgment determines its use. Our personal use of money quickly reflects our understanding of Christian stewardship. Money provides goods and services. We decide what we keep for our own use and what we will give to others, including the work of the church. Newspaper articles recently stated that charitable giving is down even though prosperity is evident. Many church budgets are squeezed.

But we who know the love of Christ—who have been the recipients of his ongoing gift of grace, who have experienced the freeing presence of the Holy Spirit empowering our lives and loving us through all kinds of crazy times—deliberately choose to use our resources of time, talent and, yes, even money, for God's purposes. We give to the church because we acknowledge our blessings. We bring nothing into this world and take nothing out of it, but we have a lot of in-between time to contemplate where our money will serve God's purposes best. Designate money gifts to make a difference. Keep that which is useful, beautiful, or meaningful for yourself and clear out the clutter of stuff. Rethink the use of money. I'm working at that too.

SUGGESTION FOR MEDITATION: **Make a list of blessings this day. Thank God for each.**

PRAYER: **God, there are many demands. Help me discern needs from wants so I may share with a grateful heart. Amen.**

SUNDAY, SEPTEMBER 30 • Read 1 Timothy 6:11-19

The epistles, written to the first Christians, encouraged them to stand fast in the face of mounting suspicion and persecution. Paul writes to his friend Timothy to "fight the good fight of the faith." Living in a hostile environment and facing growing doctrinal tensions, this little band of believers is a group of spiritually needy individuals. Does this sound familiar to you? We too have heard the call to "fight the good fight of the faith," but we burn out and mumble because the load is not equally shared. Our bodies and spirits tire; our prayer life slows down; and our souls become parched. Divisive and petty issues become tiresome. We get discouraged or want to quit. Juggling church, family, and business responsibilities overwhelms us. We want out.

It's easy to feel alienated from God's vision when God's people give us heartburn. But small signs of encouragement will touch our wounded souls and give new life. I can see Paul almost two thousand years ago, writing by candlelight, imagining his friend Timothy and knowing the uphill battle he faces but writing always to remind him again of God's incredible vision, to give him hope. Hang in there, he says to Timothy. Paul the apostle, evangelist, new church planter, and proclaimer is an encourager. Who does this for you? Whom do you encourage?

Good times as well as bad teach us lessons in trust. We learn that God will guide us into the future. Like Timothy and his church we know the source of our strength and the rock of our hope, the great I AM who whispers hope and encouragement into our thirsty souls. Read Paul's encouraging words again.

SUGGESTION FOR MEDITATION: What refreshes your spirit? Who gives you the gift of encouragement? Phone or write and tell them what a gift they are. Thank God for your encouragers.

A Difficult Faith

October 1–7, 2001 • Craig Gallaway*

MONDAY, OCTOBER 1 • Read Lamentations 1:1-6

Jerusalem is forsaken.

When my wife and I returned to the United States after living abroad as students for several years, we were struck by how the landscape was littered with trash, beer cans, and general neglect. One day in Dallas, Texas, waiting in traffic to enter a busy freeway, we saw a large grocery sack of empty cans fly from the window of the car in front of us. The sack hit the ground. The cans scattered in the grass on the side of the road, finding their stations amidst all the other garbage.

Jeremiah's Jerusalem was a forsaken place because its people had given themselves to destructive appetites—lust, gluttony, greed. As a result the city of peace became desolate. This is the story of the modern city as well—not only in the United States but increasingly throughout the world, wherever the culture of consumption has become dominant. Having turned from the things that matter most—community, compassion, generosity, sacrificial love, God—we have become a wasteland of urban blight, suburban sprawl, and inner-city anger.

As the prophet Jeremiah shows, our healing depends initially on our capacity to lament, our ability to recognize and weep for the things that are lost. Before there can be an exorcism, we must "name the demons."

PRAYER: Creator of heaven and earth, I hear voices all the time that teach me to say "peace, peace" when no genuine peace exists. Give me courage to face the desolation of my own life and culture, courage like Jeremiah's to lament, so that I might turn to you and be healed. Amen.

---

*Associate Professor of Divinity, Chair of Methodist Studies, Beeson Divinity School, Samford University, Birmingham, Alabama.

TUESDAY, OCTOBER 2 • **Read Psalm 137:1-4**

How can we sing in a foreign land?

A major sign of the desolation of our technological culture is the loss of personal creativity, of individual skill in artistic endeavors such as drawing, poetry (both writing poetry and listening to it), and other folk traditions and crafts. Ask an average room full of college-educated adults to draw something, and the response is predictable: Ninety percent will begin eyeing the door for a way to escape.

This artistic desolation is no accident. Having given ourselves to the promises of industrial culture—more products made by machines at less cost—we have become a culture of general merchandise outlets, smiley-face cash registers, acres of concrete floor, and flashing-light specials. The throwaway packaging of our consumption litters our roadsides and our lives. Our educational system trains us in the values of this economy, but by about third or fourth grade it quits teaching us to draw or to use the visual side of our imaginations. How indeed can we be expected to sing?

The psalmist cannot imagine singing a song of joy to God so long as he and his people remain captive in Babylon. Creative work and artistic expression—just as much as spotted owls and old-growth forests—are matters of "ecological" balance and rhythm. We cannot expect to find peace or song unless we do the things that make for peace and song.

PRAYER: Creator of Sabbath—of desert wilderness and the unfathomable expanses of space—draw my heart toward its rest in you. Help me resist the workaholism of my culture and to commit myself daily to rhythms of time, space, solitude, and silence that I might rediscover your creative image in me, write poems, dance, and sing the songs barely remembered yet hidden in my heart. Amen.

WEDNESDAY, OCTOBER 3 • Read Psalm 137:1-6

Honesty and hope

The psalmist grieves at being unable to sing the Lord's song. He and his people are in exile, far from home, held captive and made to serve the desires of an alien place. Nevertheless, this grief is itself a kind of song. One might say, without facetiousness, it is a song of the blues. It is a protest of actual conditions even as it remembers the possibility of joy.

Too often, Christian music, art, and spirituality seem bent on avoiding this kind of honesty mingled with hope. Honesty mingled with hope: the recipe for faithful vision in a fallen world. This is not the shallow optimism of wishful thinking such as one hears in the constant sales talk of our media-culture —and all too often in our churches: "Buy this, travel there, eat that and you'll be happy." Nor is it a "cool" critique of culture, standing aloof with no real commitment to change something, anything, for the better.

The psalmist faces honestly the cultural conditions in which he lives—a culture that would willingly trade an appearance of joy ("sing us a song!") for the true and deep joy that the singer longs to remember in his heart. "If I forget you, O Jerusalem, let my right hand wither!" Only in this way can the singer escape the sentimentality of false optimism and reach toward a hope with substance. In his song he must be willing to lament, to long for the recovery of his land, to sing the blues.

PRAYER: Lord, help me be both honest and hopeful in my faith, my living, and my prayer. Help me see the world as it is and as it can be in you. Amen.

THURSDAY, OCTOBER 4 • Read Psalm 137:7-9

Dash their infants against the rocks!

We were out jogging when I heard the harsh voice coming up from behind. "Get out of my way," it bellowed. I thought it must be one of our friends from the neighborhood playing a joke. As I turned I saw Ray—a small, balding man in late middle-age who had once been in the Marines and now seemed to wear his ego and his anger on his sleeve. His eyes were full of hate. Ray and I almost fought before my wife and I managed to jog on by and leave Ray to his bitterness.

I didn't really leave Ray behind. That night and for many days and nights after, Ray haunted my dreams and waking thoughts. Why had he been so mean? What could I do to get back or to teach him a lesson?

As I lay awake one night, wishing I could get Ray out of my head so I could sleep or pray or do something more positive, a thought struck that was new to me. "Don't look for something else to do or to pray; this is it. Pray about your own anger and your inability to forgive Ray. Pray for Ray if you can."

Though the psalmist could not sing the Lord's song of joy and peace in a foreign land, he did open his heart to God. He even let his anger against enemies enter the prayer. Thus, as the ancient Christians explained this psalm, God was able to cut off the "offspring" of bitterness, to kill the "children" of injury before they could grow up, lash back, and continue the cycle of violence.

PRAYER: Lord, when others hurt and harm me out of their anger and injury, help me to pray and forgive so that anger and bitterness will not grow up in my own life. Amen.

FRIDAY, OCTOBER 5 • Read 2 Timothy 1:1-7

The faith that first lived in your grandmother

I remember my grandmother, "Mama" Gallaway. She would rise in the morning before dawn and begin her daily round of preparations—gathering eggs, baking bread, cooking breakfast—while the members of her family (sons, daughters-in-law, grandkids) slept away on pallets spread wall to wall on the floors in the small rooms of her and Papa's old farmhouse in west Texas.

I knew even as a child that Mama's life was not easy. I knew there was tension at times and that there had been bigger trouble in the past between her and Papa. I knew she was poor. I knew she had to work hard to give us the gifts that she gave daily with a sense of steady joy and peace. I also knew from her prayers, her regular presence at the little Methodist church in the country, and the pictures of Jesus on the walls (Jesus praying in the garden, Jesus and the lost lamb) that Mama was a person of faith.

I didn't know until years later—after I had wandered away from my family to the streets of San Francisco, after Mama had died and was buried while I was in the "far country"—just how deeply the grace of God at work in her life had left its imprint on the possibilities of mine. In time, as I began to return to faith, I also began to sing and write songs. The first song that came to me was about Mama and the hills of West Texas.

PRAYER: Father God, giver of every good gift, thank you for those you have placed in my life as embodiments of your grace. Thank you that even now I can rejoice in their memory and find my own faith strengthened by their hope. Amen.

SATURDAY, OCTOBER 6 • Read 2 Timothy 1:8-14

Join me in suffering for the gospel.

Paul is in prison, which is something we easily overlook not only about Paul but about the other leading figures of the New Testament. Peter also went to jail. Jesus died as a common criminal. All of them suffered in this way for the sake of the gospel—that is, the message they proclaimed and embraced in their lives led them inevitably into conflict with the powers that dominate in fallen human culture.

In his letter to Timothy Paul identifies this conflict between powers as a conflict between death and darkness on the one hand, and life and light on the other. Christ Jesus "has destroyed death and has brought life and immortality to light through the gospel" (NIV). But why would anyone suffer or be put in jail, then or now, for proclaiming life and light?

What we must learn to recognize again and again in a culture like ours, which numbs us with constant advertising and with its own vision of the "good life," is that the good news of new life in Christ is inherently countercultural in the fallen world. In this light we must learn again and again to debunk the sales talk that jams our airwaves and fills our minds with lies. But this response, this way of life, will not make us popular with the powers that be in our culture. Indeed, it could land us in jail like Paul and like others who, despite their own failings, have resisted the darkness of their own cultures.

PRAYER: **Lord of creation and redemption, give me courage to stand for the power of your life in my life, even though this requires that I suffer and sometimes be branded as an enemy of what my culture calls good. Amen.**

The mountain moved.

"Have you ever really seen a mountain move as the result of faith?" That's the question I asked the guest preacher after his fine and moving sermon. I knew this preacher could move me, but I was also learned in the ways of skepticism.

My skepticism had grown from years of experience inside a pastor's family. Pastors' families have a tough calling in some ways. Inside, they are like every other family—struggling with their own histories of pain, fear, abuse, and hopes of trying to be better. Outside they represent the pastor, and the pastor represents the expectations of the congregation. Many pastors' kids become desperate to break away from the tension that results between realities inside the home and the public religious appearances. This tension can become a mountain, blocking the way to genuine faith for some members of a pastor's family.

My own mountain grew so large that it led me in 1968 to follow my older brother to the Haight-Ashbury district of San Francisco. There, in the midst of a thousand other young people, our lives fell apart; like prodigals in the far country we were desperate and hungry on the street. Still, coming home was not an easy choice. It meant coming back to the mountain, the massive barrier between the way things had been, the way they were supposed to appear, and the way they might become in faith.

Somehow, despite the mountain, faith had been growing in my life. The guest preacher's only response to my question was this: "Craig, have you really never seen a mountain move?" I knew that a mountain was indeed moving in my own life.

PRAYER: **Lord, help me see your work of faith as it is taking place in my life. Amen.**

Make a Joyful Noise!

October 8–14, 2001 • Karen M. Ward*

MONDAY, OCTOBER 8 • Read Jeremiah 29:1, 4-7

The prophet Jeremiah sends a letter to the "remaining elders among the exiles, and to the priests, the prophets, and all the people, whom Nebuchadnezzar had taken into exile from Jerusalem to Babylon."

Dictionaries define the word *exile* in terms of being banished or removed from one's country or home. Suffice it to say, exile is not a desirable state. Popular culture often treats exiles as tragic figures who somehow survive their banishment or isolation but remain in a state of perpetual melancholia. Many of us have never experienced exile in its extreme form, but we may have experienced various "exiles in miniature" within our daily lives. Exile-like experiences can be physical or spatial (away from home or familiar settings) or emotional (alienated or distanced from persons or things we care about).

In our lives, we must weather many instances of separation or alienation. Though our culture portrays exiles largely as victims of circumstance, the prophet Jeremiah has another view. Rather than being paralyzed by circumstance, the exiles are called by Jeremiah to be people of faith, people of God's promise who bloom where they are planted. He instructs them to set up shop, to plant, eat, build, marry, wherever God has placed them and to pray for and seek the welfare of all people, which is the will of the Lord, the God of Israel, who is the abba (Father) of Jesus Christ our Lord.

SUGGESTION FOR MEDITATION: Pray for vision and courage to do God's will and to reach out to others wherever you are planted.

---

*Associate Director for Worship, Evangelical Lutheran Church in America, Chicago, Illinois.

TUESDAY, OCTOBER 9 • Read Psalm 66:1-7

"Make a joyful noise to God, all the earth," writes the psalmist. The opening verses of Psalm 66 call us to worship God by making noise and singing praises for all the awesome things that God has done.

Once when I visited a small, rural church in the Midwest, a woman felt the need to apologize to me for the fact that the parish choir was small and "did not sing in parts well." The woman went on to say that the choir did "make a joyful noise unto the Lord, the emphasis being on the noise!"

People of faith need not apologize for making joyful noises before God, for that is exactly what God intends that we do. In fact not just humans but all "all the earth," that is, all of creation are called upon to sing or "noise" the praises of God. Birds chirp, cats meow, dogs bark, the wind whistles, and the oceans roar: God hears all these things, and all contribute to creation's praise.

Our society has become one of listeners rather than singers. People listen to music constantly, mostly to the music made by professional singers either in concert, on audiotapes, or CDs. With schools slashing music budgets, one of the few places left for people to sing is the church. The psalms, hymns, and spiritual songs we sing are not just for God's sake but for our own, as music gives voice to the praise within us in a unique and lasting way.

Long after our physical strength departs and our short-term memories fade, songs of faith we have learned and sung throughout our lives will linger with us, bringing us strength and joy.

SUGGESTION FOR MEDITATION: **Choose a favorite hymn verse and sing it throughout the day as your prayer.**

WEDNESDAY, OCTOBER 10 • Read Psalm 66:8-12

Verses 8-12 of Psalm 66 call us to bless God even as we experience trials and tribulations. The psalmist frankly mentions all the things people have to suffer on a daily basis. People feel caught in nets and overlaid with burdens. They feel as if they have been singed in fires and drowned in floods. And to top it all off, God allows people to "ride over our heads"! If the psalmist had known about sport-utility vehicles he might have stated, "tracks are made over our faces, and we have been mowed over by the forces of life." Yet the words of verse 12 echo the exodus theme from verse 6, and the sense of a new exodus comes to the fore.

All of the trying things that happen in life are not God's will. God does not delight as we travel in harm's way, because God is gracious and merciful, slow to anger and full of steadfast love for God's children.

However, our trials can test us as fire tests silver, showing us that indeed God "has kept us among the living." Only those who live have trials to overcome, unlike the blessed dead. To live means we will encounter hardships; yet through them all, as we bless God for what God has done, God will not let our feet slip out from under us and will keep us in God's care. We emerge from the fire and the water into a spacious place.

PRAYER: Blessed are you, O Lord our God, Creator of the universe, for awesome are your deeds among mortals. In your wisdom you have tested me like silver. In times of trial, keep me among the living and do not let my feet slip. Hold me steadfast in your service and bring me to the spacious place you have prepared for all who love you, through Jesus Christ the Lord. Amen.

THURSDAY, OCTOBER 11 • Read 2 Timothy 2:8-13

THANKSGIVING DAY, CANADA

Jesus Christ is raised from the dead. This is the gospel; this is the good news that all Christians have to share. The resurrection of Jesus means that life, not death, is the final word for those who trust in God's promise. This message of life has inspired countless martyrs. The word *martyr* actually means "witness." Thus resurrection has inspired many witnesses to the faith who willingly suffered hardship to share the gospel with others.

In many places throughout the world, people of faith continue to suffer for the sake of the good news. Christians face persecution and find themselves chained in jails, but as Paul writes, "the word of God is not chained," though the messengers may be chained temporarily. Indeed, the messengers may be chained in more ways than one. Often the chains we bear are not metal but mental, making us afraid to share the good news and reluctant to invite others to church.

For many, faithfulness will not involve the risk of death or years behind bars. Many of us may not experience the larger-than-life faith drama Paul describes or that the big-*S* saints and martyrs experience; yet the same call to faithfulness applies to all, those both great and small, who name the name of Christ.

For many of us small-*S* saints, faithfulness involves three parts reluctance and one part courage—and having just enough trust to reach out to others with the good news of Jesus in ordinary ways with the simple words and deeds, rooted in Christ, that form the life of faith.

SUGGESTION FOR MEDITATION: Meditate on the call to be a witness for Christ. What does being faithful to Christ mean in your daily life: at home, at work, and among friends or family?

Friday, October 12 • Read 2 Timothy 2:14-15

In 2 Timothy 2:14-15, Paul warns those who labor for the Lord against "wrangling over words." He states that such wrangling accomplishes no good but only does harm to those we seek to reach. As we work on behalf of God, we need have no shame in what we do in sharing the way of Christ.

It seems that in biblical times, as in our own, people used words to baffle as well as illuminate, to confuse as well as clarify. Each day stories about politicians, government officials, and ordinary citizens who use words to evade, avoid, and cloud the truth bombard us. Sins become "tactical errors"; deaths become "collateral damage"; firings become "staff adjustments"; lies become "misleading statements."

The use of words to support the gospel message is necessary, but we are called to "walk the walk" as well as "talk the talk" of faith. Both to talk and walk are the essence of incarnational theology, faith taking flesh.

In the scriptures the disciples tried to walk the walk, even when they fumbled in talking the talk. The sign of faithfulness is not making eloquent speeches about Christ but joining in the journey of faith with Christ. Joining with Jesus in feeding the hungry, healing the sick, comforting the sorrowing, lifting up the downtrodden—these things, unlike misleading words, become a source of good that all can understand, things about which workers for the kingdom need never be ashamed.

PRAYER: Gracious God, in Jesus your Word became flesh and dwelt among us, full of grace and truth. By your spirit help me make the Word flesh in my daily life as I work for your kingdom, reaching out in loving service to all in need. Amen.

SATURDAY, OCTOBER 13 • Read Luke 17:11-14

As Jesus makes his way from Samaria to Galilee, ten lepers who cry out for mercy and healing approach him. Upon seeing them Jesus instructs them saying, "'Go and show yourselves to the priests.' And as they went, they were made clean."

The message from these verses is quite clear: faith and healing are linked. The lepers on the road do not receive healing because they hightail it to the priests; they experience healing as they place their trust in God.

In our modern world, lepers and temple priests are no longer common sights, yet many people search for healing by turning to faddish drinks, herbs and diets. They seek the wisdom of best-selling gurus and Internet shamans. Yet today's scripture implies a link between healing and faith. The lepers are healed, not because they follow a rigorous ritual prescription but because they trust Jesus.

The good news, which the lepers experience and which is available to all who search for healing, is that those who trust in Jesus will experience healing in their lives. Healing at its core means a restoration to wholeness and well-being in life. Well-being may not always mean "being well," as in having perfect health. Healing may or may not mean physical cure, but it certainly means having the healing power of God's love brought to bear on each and every diseased situation where the name of Christ is proclaimed.

PRAYER: Jesus, Master, have mercy on me. You have only to say the word, and I shall be healed. Cleanse me from fear, and give me faith to go where you send me. Jesus, Master, have mercy in my daily life; bring your healing power to bear all that is diseased within, whether in body, mind, or spirit. Amen.

SUNDAY, OCTOBER 14 • Read Luke 17:15-19

After Jesus heals the ten lepers, one of them, realizing that he has been healed, turns back to give thanks. That one, joy-filled leper (a Samaritan) kneels at the feet of Jesus in gratitude and thanksgiving. The other nine, however, are nowhere to be found.

One amazing thing about this account is that God shows no partiality. Just as the sun rises and sets on good and evil alike, and the gentle rain washes over the righteous and unrighteous, God's healing rests upon the grateful and ungrateful alike!

The love of God falls upon the faithful and the faithless, the churchgoer and nonchurchgoer alike. Knowing that God shows no partiality and that God brings wholeness even to the ungrateful, we might be tempted to wonder, *Hey, what's going on here God? Why should we faithful bother to do this thanksgiving thing, when nine out of ten often don't?*

In the story all ten receive healing, but we don't know what became of the other nine. We do know what became of the one who returned. We can see (at least for that time) that although all ten were healed, only one was saved.

To be saved is to experience God's grace and to turn back to God with joy and thanksgiving. Salvation thus defined is not so much about fleeing hell in death as it is about embracing heaven in life. The grateful leper embraces heaven as he kneels at Jesus' feet. All the thanks-givers who have turned back to God over the ages share in the wonderful knowledge that true joy and peace belong to those with thankful hearts.

SUGGESTION FOR MEDITATION: Give thanks to God, for God is good; God's steadfast mercy endures forever.

A New People

October 15–21, 2001 • Cristian De La Rosa*

MONDAY, OCTOBER 15 • Read Jeremiah 31:27-34

"We are God's people! What seems impossible for us is possible in God," recently proclaimed an immigrant woman, a single mother of three and congregant of a small, storefront church in an inner-city neighborhood where violence, drugs, and poverty are the way of life.

In all my questions and concern for this particular congregation, she caught my attention. In her affirmation of faith and the prayer that followed, she called us to remember—just like the prophet Jeremiah. She called us to remember that as God's people we are to hope for a new reality in the midst of despair. We are to build as others destroy. We are to plant even if the land is not ours.

In light of the new millennium, a new covenant means that life finds a way even in the most difficult circumstances. As part of a new covenant, life continues in the most creative ways in particular contexts. In a small, storefront church of a large metropolis, the word of life makes its way through the least expected—in a different language—for those in desperate need of hope and new life.

The Jeremiahs of our day call us to remember that as life finds a way in the most difficult situations, as God works with us and through us, we become a new people, God's people.

SUGGESTION FOR MEDITATION: Where do I find the word of life for my own situation? Am I so busy in my own understanding of ministry and covenant that I cannot experience or speak as a new person in a new time in history or in new and different contexts for ministry?

---

*Doctoral student of sociology and religion; ordained member of the Nebraska Conference of The United Methodist Church; Lincoln, Nebraska.

TUESDAY, OCTOBER 16 • Read Psalm 119:97-104

It is said that wisdom is the greatest gift one can receive or find for oneself. In a time in history when ethical values seem scarce or confused, when life is not appreciated or respected, when faith is abandoned for the sake of technology and materialism, wisdom becomes a key element in our experience as people of God.

Advanced technology and vast amounts of information and knowledge continue to change our way of life, creating wider chasms among neighbors; and we realize that religion is no longer the center of our culture nor is faith the reason for our existence. Appropriating the wisdom to see and discern the signs of the times becomes our prophetic task as new people of faith. In the experience of God's wisdom we are called to denounce what is false and destructive among us. As new people of faith we are to identify the negative forces that hide and steal life.

The psalmist speaks about law, commandments, testimonies, precepts, the word, and ordinances. All of these complement God's greatest gift of life. A life nurtured, strengthened, and renewed by God's law becomes God's grace through Jesus the Christ, and we share our testimonies to a living God. May we fully appreciate the gift of life, accept the gift of God's wisdom, and be a new people for our time.

SUGGESTION FOR MEDITATION: In your quiet time today give thanks to God for the gift of life and the opportunity to participate in the renewal of creation. Ask God to strengthen you as you become part of a new people.

WEDNESDAY, OCTOBER 17 • Read 2 Timothy 3:14-17

Teachers and parents greatly impact children's learning experiences. Teaching holy scriptures not only as a collection of writings but as God's word inspired through individuals of faith makes for new life.

Timothy, a second-generation Christian, learned about scriptures from his parents and grandparents as a small child. It becomes important for him to remember the faith of those who came before and to remember the credibility of the teachings because of the importance his family gave them. The scriptures are part of his heritage and tradition, his foundation for the present and the future.

I cannot forget that tradition and communal experience of faith bring the scriptures to life. We can find God's words, as we read with the eyes of faith and experience, in our own situation and language. Through our desire to know about God, to experience God's love and care, we establish and strengthen our own relationship with God. That relationship is nurtured in the midst of community as part of God's people.

PRAYER: Creator God, reveal your word to me in the teachings and examples of those who came before me and of those who accompany my journey today. Make me an instrument for those who will come after me. Amen.

Thursday, October 18 • Read 2 Timothy 4:1-5

We find in our reading today an urgent request to "do the work of an evangelist" and to fulfill our ministry. This call for a ministry of teaching and preaching can address the spiritual concerns of our time.

A main concern of our time is that we find it difficult to endure sound teaching, especially teaching of service and justice. We do not want to hear about poverty, oppression, and global warming. We want to hear about what is convenient or about the latest advances in technology. We choose not only *what* we want to hear or see around us but also *whom* we want to see and hear from. We can easily find teachers who suit our own likings and teachings, shielding us from our dislikes and the challenges of the gospel.

In the presence of God and of Christ Jesus, Paul challenges Timothy as he challenges us today through this reading. He asks him and us to witness to the God of life who brings hope and faith for a new time in history. He asks that we be strong and of good faith, enduring all adversity.

Paul's challenge can become the pillar of our ministry as a relevant answer to God's call: "proclaim...; be persistent...; convince, rebuke, and encourage."

SUGGESTION FOR MEDITATION: **What do you identify as your call to ministry? In your own experience, how do you communicate and answer your call?**

FRIDAY, OCTOBER 19 • Read Luke 18:1-8

One "who neither feared God nor had respect for people" ends up caring for the needs of a widow. A persistent widow moves a hard-hearted judge to grant her justice. The widow in this story has become the exemplary model of endurance and strength in weakness. In her crisis, and from a fragile position, she deals in a very creative and simple way with the authorities of her time.

While we often view this parable as one attesting to the effectiveness of persistent prayer, let us consider it in light of our interrelatedness and social action. The widow, a victim of her society, sets about to address her situation. She identifies her need for the judge to act on her behalf, and she has the wisdom and courage to claim justice. She remains faithful and persistent in her claim. In so doing, she finds grace not only for herself but also for the judge. Her faith, hope, and concrete action impact her life and also that of the judge. He realizes that somehow his well-being is directly linked with her well-being. "Though I have no fear of God and no respect for anyone, yet because this widow keeps bothering me, I will grant her justice, so that she may not wear me out by continually coming."

Our hopes, faith, and expectations for a better future do not find life in isolation. Our courage and commitment to seek justice and claim new life provide others the opportunity to find a new way of being.

PRAYER: **Our God, grant that I seek life and, in so doing, may I help others find you and glimpse a new life. Amen.**

Saturday, October 20 • Read Jeremiah 31:27-34

This passage in Jeremiah helps us understand something about the nature of God: There is always the possibility of a new opportunity. In the midst of failure, God offers the possibility for a new beginning in the relationship between God and humanity.

In a new covenant God provides space for a new way of doing things. Without prejudice toward human nature God invites us again into a new space and relationship where we participate with God in our own redemptive process.

In this new space God reaches out to us human beings even in our tragic state and situation as unfaithful people. As we accept the invitation into a new space, we find ourselves in God, helping create the space and opportunity for God to continue the divine work in a new redemptive process.

As we participate in the redemptive process, we help nurture life and become part of a new people, a faithful people who complement a faithful and forgiving God. As Christians we understand that God accompanies us in our journey as Jesus Christ—a simple and fragile presence among us, exemplifying the power of a God who works with us over and over again.

PRAYER: Precious God, source of life and wisdom, help me understand that your life and presence are not power as I see and understand them. May I experience your life and wisdom as I come to appreciate and respect life in its own fragile nature and power. Amen.

SUNDAY, OCTOBER 21 • Read 2 Timothy 3:14-17

We take many things in life for granted. Frequently our experiences do not allow for full appreciation or use of the gifts we have received as part of our life and formation process.

The scriptures for today point to the treasure of the teachings by our family that are often so much a part of us that we fail to appreciate them. Through scripture God provides education and training, as well as the capacity to serve. God equips us to be in ministry; yet because this provision is so close to us, we often cannot see it.

Many servants and trained religious leaders do not see or appreciate the incredible opportunities for ministry—the ways made for each of us to enjoy life in its fullness. Many times we expect others to serve us because we know or have been given special titles or positions.

It takes someone like Paul to help us realize that we are to serve with the gifts and graces we have received; we possess the knowledge that will instruct us for salvation through Jesus Christ. We have at our disposal the tools for teaching, correction, and training for righteousness. Another's need may remind us of the great gifts God has provided for us. Serving the needs of others can help us contextualize our gifts and come to understand that in serving we will find abundant life.

PRAYER: Creator God, help me accept your invitation to be part of your redemptive work and, in so doing, come to appreciate and value my own gifts and talents. Amen.

The Bounty of the Spirit

October 22–28, 2001 • John O. Gooch*

MONDAY, OCTOBER 22 • Read Joel 2:23-27

The summer of 1999 for much of the United States was a time of drought. Judah must have experienced such an extended period of drought, because the first sign of God's salvation in these verses is that the early and the later rains will be restored. When the rains return, then prosperity will also return. The threshing floors (grain silos for us) will be full; the vats will overflow with wine and oil.

In addition to the drought, plagues of locusts and grasshoppers have eaten whatever remained from the drought. Starvation must have been a reality for many people in those terrible years. But all those circumstances will now be overturned, the prophet says. We will eat of God's bounty and be satisfied. With the basic needs of life cared for, we will again give God praise. It is hard to praise God when we listen to our children cry because they have no food.

In Israel, the people would view a disaster such as drought as a sign of God's judgment, so the words "And my people shall never again be put to shame" would be as welcome as the rains. In our silent shame and quiet desperation, God's grace still comes to us like the refreshing rain. Justification and forgiveness mean that we no longer have to be ashamed of our past. We can worship God in freedom and joy, because God has overcome our past.

PRAYER: Gracious God, thank you for the gift of life in all the ways it comes to me. Thank you that I can be free from shame and live in joy before you. Amen.

---

*Consultant, teacher, and writer in the field of youth ministry; studies and writes about scripture as the expression of a passion for God's word; living in Liberty, Missouri.

TUESDAY, OCTOBER 23 • Read Joel 2:28-32

In God's good time, God will pour out the Spirit on all flesh, much like the pouring of water from a pitcher into the font for a baptism. The spirit of God in the Hebrew Scriptures is a gift of power for a particular service or deed. The fact that all sorts of persons will prophesy signals that the day of the Lord is near. The gift of the Spirit here is not for a task but for a relationship. Every one of God's people will have a direct and powerful line of communication with God.

There will be signs of the day of the Lord, both on the earth and in the cosmos. The darkening of the sun and moon serve as supernatural signs of warning. There will be judgment and destruction beyond anything the creators of apocalypse movies can imagine. Even Bruce Willis and Arnold Schwarzenegger would shrink in terror at the wrath of God.

Peter quotes this passage in his sermon on the Day of Pentecost, and we read his sermon in Joel's light. The promise of salvation is fulfilled for us in Jesus Christ. We believe that he is Lord and that God has raised him from the dead. That faith, Peter says, will allow us to live in the power of the kingdom of God, here in this world. This invitation excludes no one—it is extended to "whoever calls."

Finally, calling on the name of the Lord means telling others what God has done, telling them that they too are offered the bounty of the Spirit in salvation on the day of the Lord.

PRAYER: O God, give me your salvation and pour out your Spirit on me. Strengthen me to tell others of your saving love. Amen.

WEDNESDAY, OCTOBER 24 • Read Psalm 65

What immediately catches our attention in this psalm is the bounty of the harvest. Rain showers soften the earth and cause the crops to grow. Wagons cannot hold the rich harvest, and grain fills the ruts. Pastures, rich with grass, encourage flocks and herds to multiply. All of nature sings for joy.

Thanksgiving is important. We need to remember, however, that the main thrust of the psalm is not the bounty of the harvest. Bounty is only a result of God's awesome power and love. Praise is due to God in Zion and in every city and town where this psalm is read. God who established the mountains and set limits to the seas causes the earth to be bountiful. Thanksgiving comes as a "thank you, God," rather than the kind of self-congratulation that often accompanies a rich harvest, or a productive year in business and manufacturing, or a year when the stock market has done well and our portfolio bulges.

The key to the psalm, then, is what God does. God answers prayer, forgives sins, calls people to live in God's courts. God controls nature and brings the rain. God makes "the gateways of the morning and the evening shout for joy."

And what about us? What is our role in all this joyous bounty? Our role is to give praise and "perform vows"—to fill our days and nights with moments of praise and thanksgiving for all God has given us. A "vow" was a thanksgiving offering, usually a communal meal in the Temple, to which the poor were invited. In this case, the people received literal satisfaction.

PRAYER: Help me give thanks to you, O God, and to recognize you as the source of all that I am and have. Amen.

THURSDAY, OCTOBER 25 • Read 2 Timothy 4:6-8

How would you sum up your life? If you were nearing the point of death, what would you say about yourself and the way you have lived? Here's what Paul said: Paul is confident that his life is being poured out as a libation, or consecrated drink offering, for God. Paul sees his death as an offering to God, one that will consecrate his followers.

Departure, of course, is a euphemism for death. It literally means release. In Greek, the word was used to describe loosing the moorings so a ship could leave the dock or to describe an army's folding up the tents and breaking camp. Probably Paul sees his death as both a release from this life and a departure for a better life with God.

And the metaphors keep coming. Verse 7 offers several images from the world of sports. The fight would be either wrestling or boxing, both popular at the time. The good fight would be the way the writer has lived as a Christian minister. The race is a long-distance one with obstacles thrown in. But Paul has finished it. He has completed his work and done what God intended that he do. Keeping the faith means he has played by the rules but also kept the faith in Christ intact.

So Paul has his reward: the crown of righteousness. Like the laurel wreath awaiting the athlete, Paul's crown is laid up for him in heaven. As he waits for that crown, confident of his future, he acknowledges the Lord as a righteous judge. And the bounty he expects to receive, we can all expect! That's the good news!

SUGGESTION FOR MEDITATION: **Think again about the summary of your life. Rejoice that there is a crown of righteousness ready for you.**

FRIDAY, OCTOBER 26 • Read 2 Timothy 4:16-18

When Paul had his first hearing before the Roman judge, no one in the Christian community appeared with him in court. Apparently, they were afraid. Ironically, Paul forgives them in the same language that Stephen used to forgive those who were stoning him! Ironic, because Paul was present at that stoning.

But the Lord stood by Paul. In tough times, he received the greatest gift of all—the strength to keep going. This text may mean that, in the course of the hearing, Paul was able to explain the gospel he was accused of preaching. In any case, he rejoiced in the opportunity to preach to the entire world!

If it is true that Paul was tried in Rome, he may have felt this was the crowning event of his career and rejoiced that the word would filter down from the imperial judges to their families, servants, clerks, and so on. How many times in our lives have we had the opportunity to explain the gospel in the aisle of the grocery store or in the stands at the ball game or somewhere else as we made our way through our busy day? These moments become crowning events for us, as well, when we communicate the faith to others.

Something happened at the trial that at least delayed the judgment. Church tradition from the end of the first century says that Paul died a martyr in Rome under the Emperor Nero. So being "rescued from the lion's mouth" was only a temporary reprieve. Nevertheless, Paul saw this reprieve as a sign that God rescues us from all evil. Oh, we suffer. But no power in heaven or on earth can do us ultimate harm in the world.

SUGGESTION FOR MEDITATION: **Reflect on what it is that can completely destroy you. Give thanks to God for God's victory over evil and death.**

SATURDAY, OCTOBER 27 • Read Luke 18:9-14

We know already what these two people will be like. The Pharisee is a righteous man—literally, and with no sarcasm. When he describes his piety, we understand just how good a person he is. The tax collector, on the other hand, is the prototype of a sinner. And they both go up to the Temple to pray.

The Pharisee reports to God on how his life is going. He expresses gratitude that he is a good man and not like all those sinners (including the tax collector). And he has some impressive credentials: he fasts twice a week; he gives tithes of all his income. Most of us would like to have the Pharisee in our churches, especially when church budget time rolls around!

The tax collector, on the other hand, won't even look up. He strikes himself on the chest as a sign of repentance and remorse and begs God for mercy.

The story ends with a major reversal. The good man simply goes home. The sinner goes home justified, that is, forgiven and restored. God can do nothing for the man who is so sure of his own piety that he needs nothing. But God can do everything for the man who acknowledges his need of everything.

When we pray, how do we come before God? Do we focus on our own goodness or on the brokenness of our relationship with God? Do we cry out to God for help or tell God how to reward us? And in what state do we come away from our prayers?

PRAYER: God of mercy, have mercy on me, particularly when I begin to appreciate my own goodness. Amen.

SUNDAY, OCTOBER 28 • Read Luke 18:9-14

The way we pray leads to the way we treat one another. The Pharisee is a rugged individualist, confident in his own piety and morality. So he stands apart by himself, positioning himself to assure that no one could accidentally contaminate him. He prays as if he and God are on a first-name basis. Now we all know what that means. A person at the office who calls the CEO by his or her first name often tends to act in a superior way toward those who don't have the same privilege. Guess what? That's what happens here. The Pharisee takes no notice of the tax collector except to give thanks that he is not like him.

One of the sins into which we fall so easily is to say, "Well, I've sinned, but at least I'm not like…." So long as there is someone to whom we can feel superior, we can hold onto a sense of confidence and superiority. No matter that God—and at least some of our neighbors—see right through us. "God, I thank you that I am not like other people."

The tax collector, on the other hand, stands way back, away from the altar, because he is well aware of his own sin. Far from "first-naming" God, he won't even look up to heaven. In humility, he confesses his sin and begs for mercy.

The implication is that if the Pharisee had been aware of those around him, he would have been open to their needs and dreams and would have been more open to living with them in community.

PRAYER: God, I thank you that you love me, even when I try to be superior to other people. Help me remember just who is God in our relationship, and that will keep my other relationships in perspective. Amen.

Our Way Versus God's Way

October 29–November 4, 2001 • Carole K. Webb*

Because I am a counselor, people sometimes cry when they talk with me. My profession is split on whether crying is helpful. Some say that it helps purge emotions; others say that it interferes with the cognitive process of change.

I think it depends, for there are different kinds of tears. I have even read that the chemical content of tears differs depending on the type of tear we shed. There are the tears of frustration when we do not get what we want—when we think we have got it made, and someone gets in our way. Like my two-year-old grandson, we cry crocodile tears of frustration. There are also tears of healing, when a wound is so deep that only a cleansing baptism heals it and releases our pain. Women in ancient times carried these tears in a vial, so precious were they to their souls. Paradoxically, these tears come not from defending our wants but from letting them go. We allow the truth of God to enter our souls, and the self-centered defenses crumble.

Here Jesus encourages us to cry tears of release and healing, the exact opposite of tears of self-defense. When we let go of the tears of self, we are restored in the joy of who and whose we are. It is then that we realize God's blessing.

PRAYER: God, help me honor my precious tears, tears of healing that come when I let go of my selfish desire to have my own way. Amen.

---

*Marriage and family therapist, workshop leader, lay member of Belmont United Methodist Church, Nashville, Tennessee.

TUESDAY, OCTOBER 30 • **Read 2 Thessalonians 1:1-4, 11-12**

I think I know how Paul felt about the Christians he wrote to in Thessalonica. I can almost see his smile as he thinks about them standing strong in the faith against their culture. They suffer persecution, and they rise to the occasion. They endure trials, but they thrive! They pass the test by the way they love!

I think I know Paul's feelings because I have witnessed this steadfast faith among Christians I have known. Although these Christians have not encountered the persecution the Thessalonians faced, the ways of our culture bombard them mercilessly. These Christians do not just feed the homeless; they invite the homeless into community. They include a prison inmate in a Bible study group through letters and E-mails via his son; they run a nursery for children affected by AIDS; they pray for mercy for the man on death row. I admire them, and I want to be like them; but sometimes these actions and attitudes run so counter to the culture's values, I can literally feel the pull to justify going with the crowd. How uncomfortable it is to stand against executing a murderer! We want to say, "Come on, Jesus! This just doesn't make good sense!" But we persevere because God's purpose is clear. God's love is a love that extends all the way to the murderer. How radical! How uncomfortable!

And we hear Paul gently encouraging us when he writes, "We constantly pray for you, that our God will count you worthy of his calling, and that by his power he may fulfill every good purpose of yours and every act prompted by your faith" (NIV). By his power, thank God.

PRAYER: God, thank you for the power you provide through grace. If it were left up to me, I could not carry out your unreasonable love! Amen.

WEDNESDAY, OCTOBER 31 • Read Luke 19:1-10

I wonder why Zacchaeus climbed that tree. Was it the excitement of seeing this charismatic man? What did Zacchaeus hope he could gain by going so far out of his "comfort zone" to climb a tree just to lay eyes on Jesus?

This story reminds me of a chance meeting I had as a teenager with President Kennedy. I was on a trip to Boston with a foreign exchange student from Turkey and our faculty advisor Dilek. When our teacher pulled the car away from the crowd of traffic that had jammed an intersection, we realized that the helicopter in the field a few yards from us belonged to the President! Because my teacher's disability made walking difficult, she parked as close as she could. We jumped out of the car, hungry for the chance for just one peek at him. We got much more than we hoped, as we unknowingly put ourselves right where the President's limo stopped. When he heard the excited Dilek babbling in Turkish, he stopped to talk to us. He asked about her experiences in this country and invited her to the White House. We had eagerly set out just for a glimpse but received an invitation!

I imagine it was like this for Zacchaeus. Drawn by the fame of this charismatic Jesus, he goes ahead of the crowds to climb a tree and wait. He sets out to put himself in a position to see Jesus, but he puts himself in a place where Jesus can actually reach him! The glimpse of Jesus that Zacchaeus hopes for pales in comparison with what Jesus willingly offers him, "I must stay at your house today." Zacchaeus had placed himself in a position to receive an offer, and he finds himself transformed.

PRAYER: God, restore in me the hope that pushes me to place myself where you can reach me. Amen.

THURSDAY, NOVEMBER 1 • Read Daniel 7:1-3, 15-18

ALL SAINTS DAY

Do you believe God still speaks to us in our dreams, as God spoke to Daniel? I never thought so until God awakened me early one morning. I had just moved to a new city with my husband. I was feeling uprooted from my friends and profession. I was in a new house, surrounded by boxes and newspaper, when a former neighbor called to tell me that my ex-husband, David, had been killed in a plane crash! Though I had not seen him in many years, the news stung me with the pain of unfinished anger. I wished that I had not neglected the work of forgiving.

Early the next morning I awoke to hear a choir in my living room! I could hear clearly a hymn that I did not know. It continued for several verses and a chorus. "And God will raise you up on eagles' wings...."* I raced downstairs to confirm that everything was indeed still packed—no radios, no neighbors, no explanation. As I dug out the hymnal and found the chorus to the song, I immediately felt release from the haunting anger. I knew what to do. I called my friend, and she agreed to read these words at the funeral.

When she called back the next day, her voice was shaking. "We said the words at the casket and went to the sanctuary for the service. The organ was playing your song! The choir sang all the verses you heard!" I later learned that David's love of flying had led him back to the church. This hymn symbolized the peace that he found there.

Daniel's visions terrify him until he receives their interpretation. What dreams and visions haunt your living? Who has helped you understand their meaning? How have your dreams empowered your living?

PRAYER: God, thank you for speaking to me through my dreams, releasing me from pain and giving me hope. Amen.

---

*"On Eagle's Wings," by Michael Joncas

FRIDAY, NOVEMBER 2 • Read Psalm 119:137-144

When my husband and I first started dating, we put a lot of energy into finding time to see each other. With business travel, his children, and a stressful commute each day, this was not easy. One disastrous day, we missed each other at the airport where I had agreed to meet him after his trip to Chicago. Because he was better at remembering details, I concluded that I had the wrong spot. As I moved to another place, doubting myself, he was doing the same thing! Back and forth we went, baggage area to gate, anxiously trying to connect. We squandered all the time we had for each other. When we finally talked and realized what we had done, we both felt grief for the lost opportunity to be together. We decided to go back to the time-tested rule our mothers had taught us as children: If we do not see each other at the appointed place, stay there and wait. This rule has worked for generations of lost children and their delayed parents.

The psalmist tells us this rule as well. When you are troubled, when things are not working well, go back to God's rule. Don't give up on God's word because your enemies do not follow it! Though bombarded by thousands of alternatives that promise to bring us happiness, we know that God's rule of life is the one that works. Trusting God's statutes keeps us from doubting our way, from racing around looking for a better way to find each other.

PRAYER: Forgive me, Lord, for doubting your rule of life, throwing it off in my anxious search for immediate gratification. Give me the wisdom to stop and trust your word. Amen.

SATURDAY, NOVEMBER 3 • Read Habakkuk 1:1-4; 2:1-4

A few years ago, I cross-stitched a sampler that reads, "God did not promise us an easy life. God promised us help to live it." As I stitched those words, I wondered over and over if I really believed them. Like Habakkuk, I questioned God for allowing violence and injustice to continue in the world. "How long shall I cry for help, and you will not listen?"

While in training to treat people with alcohol addictions, I attended a prayer group each morning. One man said he was not there to thank God but to ask where God had been all his life. Where was God when his father routinely abused him and his siblings? "How long shall I cry for help, and you will not listen?" Another group member responded, "Maybe God did listen. You survived. God got you through it. You are alive and are here now healing with God's help."

The man sought me out the next day to tell me he had been able to thank God for bringing him to that rehab center. God had actually sent just the words this man needed to accept God's promise of presence, rather than a promise to punish the person who had hurt him. This man now, years later, realized that God had been with him all along; he had only to wait to understand how. "Then the Lord answered me.... there is still a vision for the appointed time;...it does not lie. If it seems to tarry, wait for it; it will surely come, it will not delay."

PRAYER: God, give me hope in times of trouble and injustice. Let me know you are true to your promise to be with me always; I simply must wait. Amen.

SUNDAY, NOVEMBER 4 • Read Ephesians 1:11-23

We all hunger to feel that we belong, that we are connected to others in some meaningful way. In our society, we will go to almost comical lengths to brand ourselves as members of groups—designer labels, school insignias, letters after our names, organizations, clubs, even addresses—to underscore our belonging. We jealously protect our membership from others.

Students of social systems believe that this exclusivity contributes to the violence among youth today, as their feelings of exclusion cascade from disappointment to hurt to anger to revenge. The more we feed this frenzy to belong, the less we feel really attached to others. As I read Paul's words to the struggling community in Ephesus, I wondered how they could speak to our struggling communities today.

First, perhaps Paul identifies the hallmark of the true community. Unlike the false labels of pseudocommunity toward which we might gravitate, Paul dramatically pictures the seal of God as the sign of this community. We belong, Paul tells us, to a body of love designed by God!

Second, Paul turns around the membership requirements: We don't have to earn this membership; we belong because we believe! We don't have to buy it, rush for it, manipulate it, study for it. We are elected, adopted, chosen, predestined, and loved into it.

Third, Paul acknowledges our call to share this community since it is a gift for all humankind. God is working out God's purposes in everything and everyone; we do not have to worry about protecting it from others. Inclusiveness, not exclusiveness, makes community!

PRAYER: O God, as I struggle to grasp and hold onto your generous gift of belonging in your community, help me to let go of the culture's false badges. Amen.

Resting on God's Promises

November 5–11, 2001 • Marion A. Jackson*

MONDAY, NOVEMBER 5 • Read Haggai 1:15b–2:4a

"Yet now take courage, O Zerubbabel, says the Lord." Take courage. Sometimes it is difficult to "take courage," to have hope when the eyes see nothing but destruction and hopelessness. Particularly painful are those memories of times past and former glories. Like going back home. Be it a twenty-five room mansion or a small, cold-water apartment in the past—when it was home, it was beautiful. Now the ravages of time and change have left "home" a place of despair, empty and desolate.

Time takes its toll on the heart too. How is your heart today? For some, the heart was once a place of joy and happiness; there used to be glory there. You may remember a time when God was the focus, when spirituality was new or at least untainted, and when the heart burned to know more about the one who quenches thirst and feeds hunger. How do you see it now, this portrait of your soul?

Sometimes things seem so desolate and hopeless that the will to try is no longer there. *There is no hope for us*, we think. But God's word to us is to live not by what we see and feel but by what God promises. God's promises do not fail; we simply fail to recognize them. Despite what our eyes tell us, God says take courage. In the words of Civilla D. Martin in the old gospel hymn "God Will Take Care of You," "Be not dismayed whate'er betide, God will take care of you; beneath his wings of love abide, God will take care of you."

PRAYER: Lord God, thank you for the reminder of your love and care. Renew in me the joy of your salvation. Amen.

---

*District superintendent, Southwest District, Southern New Jersey Conference, The United Methodist Church; living in Woodstown, New Jersey.

Tuesday, November 6 • Read Haggai 2:4*b*-9

"Work, for I am with you, says the Lord of hosts." "God helps those who help themselves," so Benjamin Franklin wrote in 1757. He was quoting Algernon Sidney, not the Bible, but both Mr. Sidney and Mr. Franklin bespoke a biblical truth. God expects us to have an active faith.

Faith goes beyond believing; it acts on that belief. That is the message God sends through Haggai to the people. "Work," says God. God does not say, "Wait and I will miraculously build the temple." Nor does God say, "Wait until there is a change in the power structure, until all of Israel is free, until all obstacles are out of the way, or until there is no risk." Without risk we need no faith. The only thing to wait on is the Holy Spirit.

Work, and I will be with you, says God. We can believe that because God lives up to God's promises, and God is in control. Look closely at the close of this passage. The Lord is powerful enough to shake the very heavens and the earth by God's will alone. This God can fight your battles, for all resources of the earth belong to God. There is nothing you might need that God cannot supply.

Have faith that what you need when you need it will be there if you step out by faith and work. Act as if you have the victory. "'Tis so sweet to trust in Jesus, and to take him at his word; just to rest upon his promise, and to know, 'Thus saith the Lord.'"

Prayer: Lord God, giver of all things, I trust you. Help me step out by faith and work while I wait. Amen.

WEDNESDAY, NOVEMBER 7 • Read Luke 20:27-38

Do you know your place? This question is important to the Sadducees. Peering at Jesus, perhaps with a smirk, they ask a question. In the resurrection, to whom will a childless woman—married seven times—belong? The query relates not only to the matter of belief in resurrection but also addresses the issue of inheritance. For many Israelites, persons lived on after death through descendants and in memory. If a man died without having children, it became the brother's responsibility to take the wife and have children by her to ensure perpetuation of property within the immediate family. It's important that everyone knows his or her place, important to identify accurately the heirs to assets.

Knowing one's place in society is important. It determines where we sit and what we are allowed to do. Not too long ago we could only sit in our designated pew at church. There was a time when people of color could only sit in the back of the bus. That was their place. In some cultures even the very clothes worn determine a person's place in society. Do you know your place?

In society there are lawsuits over wills or lack of them. Who are the true inheritors? Who is in and who is out of place? Jesus says that in the kingdom of God, none of this is important. All are children of God and therefore inheritors in the kingdom. The joy of being a part of the family of God is that we do not have to worry about fitting in or finding our place. It is already prepared for us. In our religious disputes we seek ways to exclude those who differ. At the Lord's table there is a place for each of us. "In Christ there is no east or west, in him no south or north; but one great fellowship of love throughout the whole wide earth."

PRAYER: Lord God, thank you for making a place for me. Amen.

THURSDAY, NOVEMBER 8 • **Read 2 Thessalonians 2:13-17**

In the musical "Fiddler on the Roof," Tevye sings a song about tradition. The musical relates the story of a man's struggle to hold onto tradition in a changing world. He struggles with the realization that some traditions served a good purpose in the past but are no longer useful. In watching that musical we come to understand that some traditions need to die, but others are the very fiber of our being.

We need some familiar things in our lives. We need some unshakable truths that do not change with the seasons. Imagine a world where everything every day is brand new. Each morning, the wheel is reinvented. Each obstacle brings terror because we have no history of overcoming it or tools by which to do so. Each activity requires thought, elicits foreboding, and raises the question: "What will come next?"

Imagine a new order of worship every Sunday: new hymns never sung before, new patterns to figure out. It is in the balance of tradition and novelty that we find joy and creativity—the ebb and flow of the familiar with the unknown.

The Bible is full of remembrances that set traditions. "Do this in remembrance of me" (Luke 22:19, RSV), says Jesus. Make this supper a tradition, a regular occurrence in your life. Paul says that in doing so "you proclaim the Lord's death until he comes" (1 Cor. 11:26). At every service of the Lord's Supper, we remember the mighty acts of God in Jesus Christ. We remember and affirm that we were chosen by God from the beginning, that we are the "first fruits for salvation."

SUGGESTION FOR MEDITATION: **Pray for wisdom about the traditions in your home and in your church, asking God to show you those that may need to change and those that must be maintained as part of the core of your faith.**

FRIDAY, NOVEMBER 9 • Read Psalm 145:1-5, 17-21

"One generation shall laud your works to another." What a responsibility! Telling the story is a major part of the Christian job description and, as the psalmist notes, especially to the next generation, the children. One of the best ways to teach children is through music. I remember learning to sing my *ABC*s as well as other fundamental principles set to music. More important than the alphabet, however, were the songs I learned in Sunday school. "Jesus loves me this I know, for the Bible tells me so" is a song we teach children. The psalmist bids us tell the world of God's greatness; part of the greatness of God is God's unconditional love and kindness.

This is how it is with God and with children who understand how to live in God's reality: When we teach them a song about how Jesus loves them, they believe it with their whole heart. "Jesus loves me, this I know." Adults need to sing this song every now and then as a reminder of what God's love is all about. "Little ones to him belong, they are weak but he is strong....Yes, Jesus loves me." God is near and God watches and hears our cry and saves us (vv. 18-20). The love of God is available for the weak and for those in danger. God's saving love is the foundation to hand on from one generation to the next.

The knowledge of God's love can get us through difficult times, around difficult supervisors, beyond parents and spouses who expect more than we can give, and even past our own inner voices that demand so much. When we feel we're just one more number on somebody's list, the bottom line is that Jesus loves us. This we know.

PRAYER: Thank you, Lord, for loving me. Amen.

SATURDAY, NOVEMBER 10 • **Read 2 Thessalonians 2:1-5**

Remember Chicken Little? She is so sure the sky is falling, and she even has proof. She has heard it, seen it, and felt it. Henny Penny, Ducky Lucky, Goosey Loosey, and Turkey Lurkey believe her. So off they all run to tell the king. Along the way they meet Foxy Loxy, who taking advantage of their fear and confusion, leads them to his den to devour them.

This story came to mind as I read today's passage. I can almost hear the exasperation in Paul's voice as he reminds the Thessalonians of what he has taught them earlier. They are running to and fro, frightened by misinformation and dangerously close to getting into some real faith dilemmas. Paul had given them detailed information, so they would not be so easily deceived; but some Chicken Little either intentionally or unintentionally has gotten them stirred up and afraid.

Just as he would have talked to little children, Paul reminds them that every preacher is not of God and every word is not the gospel. When we forget the basic truths and teaching of the Bible, we can easily be caught up by the fears of Chicken Littles in our midst. False prophets tell us the sky is falling, and off we run into a state of confusion.

We have the tools we need to discern right teachings from wrong. We find them in John Wesley's quadrilateral: scripture, tradition, experience, and reason. Check to see if the teaching is consistent with the Bible, listen to the inner voice, heed the advice of people you know to be of strong faith, and use common sense.

PRAYER: God who grants wisdom, teach me to seek discernment today and so learn to recognize your true prophets. Amen.

Sunday, November 11 • Read Luke 20:27-33

"And they asked him a question." People often came to Jesus asking questions. His disciples asked about prayer and many other things as they tried to understand the ministry Jesus had called them into. The Sadducees were not disciples of Jesus, and often their questions were either intellectual exercise or a means of entrapment. It is easy to become engaged in great debates about things that have little impact on our presence before God. I have a friend who calls this majoring in the minors.

In levirate marriage, to whom does a childless, seven-times married widow belong after death? These intellectual queries in the hands of Jesus become opportunities to delve deeper into the heart of the one asking the question. Jesus knows what to do with even the most arrogant or nonsensical question.

First, Jesus does not ignore those who ask. He may believe the question is irrelevant or simply a means to trap him, but still he does not ignore them. He does not shake his head, turn his back, and move on to someplace else or something else.

Second, Jesus takes the question and uses it to illustrate a deeper truth. Jesus sees beyond the surface and looks deep inside all persons and situations. Some people ask questions that irk us because we think they are just trying to prove their point. Some ask because they are ignorant. Do we allow these situations to bring out the worst in us, or can we use them as teachable moments? Jesus looks into our hearts and minds and addresses our real needs and our real questions.

Prayer: Lord God, give me ears to hear today. Amen.

Words and Wisdom

November 12–18, 2001 • Mel Johnson*

MONDAY, NOVEMBER 12 • Read Psalm 118:1, 19-29

I have a two-year-old great nephew named Connor whose parents are trying very hard to teach him to say "please" and "thank you." My heart warms every time I hear his little voice say either one. The parents' teaching reminds me that gratitude is a learned response.

Psalm 118 reflects thanks given in several ways, both corporately and individually. First as the procession enters the temple the people say, "O give thanks to the Lord, for he is good." If we use our imagination, we can almost hear the voices raised in song as victory is celebrated. Then later the psalmist says, "I thank you that you have answered me." How often do we pause to say "thank you" when God answers our prayers? Remember Jesus' healing of the ten lepers, and only one returned to say "thank you"? Taking time to give thanks should always follow the asking.

Just as gratitude is a learned art, so too are awareness and use of our gifts as we try new possibilities. We learn much from the way we perceive ourselves. Within each of us is the divine image and voice. May you today pay attention to the times you see, feel, sense, hear and know God is answering you, and give thanks. Pray with the psalmist, "You are my God, and I will give thanks to you." Then carry these words with you throughout the week, that God's words and wisdom might be yours.

PRAYER: Holy God, I begin this week longing to be grateful for who you are in my life. Remind me ever so gently that you are God, and I belong to you. Amen.

---

*Adult studies and journaling teacher, retreat leader and writer, member of Community United Methodist Church, Elm Grove, Wisconsin.

TUESDAY, NOVEMBER 13 • Read Luke 21:5-19

Sometimes we have to read a passage a number of times to uncover the gold. These verses might even be some we would choose to avoid. The warnings leap off the page and clamor for our attention. In this apocalyptic look into the future, Jesus once again responds to questions: When? What will be the sign? As Jesus lays out the signs, we may feel that we are in the middle of the end times: false messiahs, false calculators of time, wars, international conflicts, natural disasters. Not only Israel but all nations, not just all nations but the entire cosmos will be affected by God's fulfillment of the divine intention. In today's verses, Luke describes the present as the time for bearing witness.

I am a morning walker. Most days I follow the same route in my neighborhood. Several years ago I watched as changes took place in one of the homes that I pass—first a ramp up to the front door, then a hospital bed inside the front window. Each day I prayed for those unknown people within, until one day I knew I had to act. Hurrying home, and before I lost my courage, I wrote a note offering to help, which I placed in their mailbox. This small act of kindness bore witness that a neighbor cared, gave testimony to God at work in the world.

Beyond the warnings in today's passage, we read words of hope and comfort; beyond the warnings are gospel truths we can hold in our hearts. As you read and pray, hear Jesus' words and wisdom: "Not a hair of your head will perish. By your endurance you will gain your souls." What glorious reassurance that God in Christ through the presence of the Holy Spirit will always be with us. We are called to be signs of this presence in our world with words and acts of compassion, grace, and justice.

PRAYER: **Precious God, help me read the signs of the times and bear witness to your presence through my words and deeds. Amen.**

WEDNESDAY, NOVEMBER 14 • Read Psalm 118:1-25

We live on this side of the New Testament, which makes it hard to read a psalm such as 118 without jumping ahead to see these verses played out in Jesus' life and ministry. We know that Jesus is the cornerstone of our faith. We know Jesus knew the psalms by heart; and for those of us who call ourselves Christian, he is the embodiment of many of the verses. But it is good also to set aside this knowing and simply rest in the psalms, receiving their words, message, and poetry as God's gift, accepting each day as one the Lord has made.

This psalm of thanksgiving, which expresses gratitude for God's enduring love and rescue in distressing circumstances, speaks powerfully to us today, as distressing circumstances continue to abound. The news in the morning papers and media can be invitations to despair or prayer, to hopelessness or compassion. Just for today think what a difference we could make if we prayed through the morning news in the way we pray through the psalms. Our God can use us to be instruments of grace and mercy in response to the events surrounding us. Our God can use us to be revealers of steadfast love.

Our younger daughter, Kristin, is a seventh-grade math teacher in a lower middle-class suburban school. She has just one rule in her classroom: Be kind to each other. She wants her classroom to be a safe place where children may feel free to express ideas, thoughts, and feelings. May we too create safe places in this fast-paced, chaotic, beautiful, precious world, that we might show others who God is.

PRAYER: Loving God, you came into a troubled world. I live in a troubled world. Help me provide safe places for others. Amen.

THURSDAY, NOVEMBER 15 • Read Luke 21:5-19

During my high school years, George Orwell's *1984* was considered important reading. This imaginative and dramatic novel pointed to an unusual future. I remember wondering if the events described by Orwell could really happen, but the year 1984 came and went with little evidence of the truth in this book. No matter what the year, people worry about what the future will hold, yet rarely do we think of it in terms of apocalyptic end times.

The Lukan concerns in today's text are relevant as an umbrella over past, present, and future, serving as a reminder that bad things will happen. Yet nestled within misfortune and tragedy is the confidence that God in Christ is present in the midst of all things. These verses hint at what we may face if we are inattentive to global activity and to our God who lives in eternal time, time that knows no boundaries. We are so accustomed to the rapid pace of world events that not knowing, waiting, and mystery intrude into our desire for order and control. In the midst of this confusion, God dwells not only in our wants and wishes but also beyond them in a world without time.

For centuries and forever, end times will be a subject for debate. Some will perceive the world's current chaos as a foreshadowing of end times. As concerned people, we respond by living mindfully, creatively, thoughtfully, and generously in the midst of these ordinary, meantime years, doing as Christ would do. We are called to be daily revealers and reminders of God's love. God will give us the words and wisdom. We can trust in that.

PRAYER: All-knowing God, I long to live each day as sufficient unto itself, to be blessed by the past and feel confident of the future. By your grace, may it be so. Amen.

FRIDAY, NOVEMBER 16 • Read 2 Thessalonians 3:6-13

Read these verses from this pastoral letter to the people of Thessalonica aloud. Imagine they are written to you. What words, phrases, or sentences speak to you as words and wisdom for your own journey?

Written as a warning against idleness, a lifestyle that had arisen out of a belief that Christ's coming was at hand, these verses challenge us as we see evidence of idleness in many areas of our society. But what lies behind this seeming idleness?

The words "Anyone unwilling to work should not eat" stay with me as I consider our responsibilities in the nation's inner cities. I volunteer with a soup-kitchen ministry in downtown Milwaukee. We want to expand our meal serving into greater wholeness for our guests by offering job-search help, child care, and transportation. In so doing, we discover many reasons people do not choose to work, including lack of skills, inadequate compensation, child care concerns, and an ease with idleness. In being the body of Christ, we are to feed the hungry —not give up on them—and do what we can to take seriously the writer's directive: "Brothers and sisters, do not weary in doing what is right."

God is in all the work we do, from scrubbing the floor to chairing a board meeting, from sorting clothes for those in need to praying at a patient's bedside. A spirit of idleness is incompatible with the many ways God needs us to be in mission and ministry.

I invite you today to take the word *bread* with you as a sign of Jesus' presence in the bread of Communion and as a reminder that you are to be bread for others. Together we can make a difference.

PRAYER: **Bread-giving God, thank you for this simple symbol. Use me today to be bread for another. Amen.**

SATURDAY, NOVEMBER 17 • Read Isaiah 65:17-25

I recently attended a wedding at which the pastor gathered us together with an invitation to be present to what God was about to do—join this couple in holy matrimony. I found myself being really attentive after that. I didn't want to miss a moment of what God was about to do. We are awaiting the birth of our first grandchild. That too is something significant that God is about to do.

The author of Isaiah 65 informs us that God is about to create "new heavens and a new earth." God has created, is creating, and will create. God is always "about to do" something, and often we are the means through which God accomplishes God's purposes. It is affirming, strengthening, and energy-giving to know God's creative presence in our lives, communities, and world. What does God long to create through you?

The writer of these verses presents some new things that God is about to do, an ideal of earthly life, and a goal toward which we should strive. Yet underlying the ideal is the reality that life will go on much as it has. We face ordinary days and ordinary time into which our God of surprises will come again and again to waken us, giving confidence to do a difficult task, comfort to survive grief, brilliant color to call our attention to autumn's glory, the cry of a newborn to remind us of the wonder of life.

Enter this day with a heart open to God's surprises, eyes ready to see the world's beauty, and ears attuned to hear God's creating voice. Then give thanks because God is about to do all manner of things.

PRAYER: **God, I don't want to miss anything that you are about to do. Keep me attentive to the many ways and places your Spirit touches me. Amen.**

SUNDAY, NOVEMBER 18 • Read Isaiah 65:17-25

When I lead a writing session in journal keeping, a few people are always reticent about the process. Perhaps they even wonder why they came. To bring us together, I begin with an easy first topic to help the participants get the ink flowing and their minds out of the writing. I choose something as simple as "Make a joy list—list those things that bring you joy."

Too often we forget to pay attention to those things that bring us joy. In these verses the prophet writes, "For I am about to create Jerusalem as a joy." Take a moment now to recall something you have created that was a joy. Was it a loaf of bread? a beautiful photograph? a poem? a flow chart? Remember the circumstances, feelings, colors, and sounds; give thanks. God uses us to bring joy to this world: to speak words that heal, to build bridges that reconcile, to share love that warms. When we recognize our joy, we—like the inhabitants of the new Jerusalem—rejoice because we too have been blessed by God. Joy is one of God's gifts to us. Joy is one of the fruits of the Spirit (Gal. 5:22).

The passage reveals another gift in the image of the wolf and the lamb feeding together—the gift of peace. This image serves as an invitation to be like the Christ we follow and to make our table a place of harmony and reconciliation; a place where grudges are set aside, disagreements abandoned, and listening happens. To have peace in this world, we must listen to one another. God is always present at our tables. May that Presence be our blessing.

PRAYER: Generous God, thank you for the gift of this day and this week. I pray for your blessing upon me as your peace bearer and kingdom keeper. Amen.

Experience the Joy

November 19–25, 2001 • Ray Waddle*

MONDAY, NOVEMBER 19 • Read Luke 1:68-79

What if God told you to shut up, then struck you dumb for an indefinite time? Imagine how Zechariah felt, forced on one of religion's first "silent retreats"—a forced march into a terrifying, awesome silence. A good man, full of piety, he fell short in his reaction to angelic news. He'd forgotten his scriptural antecedents, those personalities in Jewish past who had received similar news of amazing births. He knew the smell of incense but not the presence of God. Maybe Zechariah was out of practice—maybe God had not spoken in years, perhaps centuries.

So Zechariah was struck dumb for doubting the divine prerogative. Luke doesn't tell us how Zechariah spent his silence. We can imagine it clarified his mind, gave him something whopping to think about, even as the child grew inside his wife, Elizabeth. Zechariah got his speech back when the newborn baby was properly circumcised and named—John, not little Zechariah. That must have been hard, not having your first and only son named after you after so many childless decades. By now, though, the rules had changed for Zechariah, and soon enough for the whole world too. When he got his voice back, he broke into prayer and prophecy.

We can imagine he had pondered his words a long time during his enforced silence, perhaps berating himself, making himself sick with regret. Now he offered a clear public word about John's destiny. No one recorded any doubts this time. Certainly not Zechariah.

SUGGESTION FOR MEDITATION: If God shut you up for an indefinite time, forced you to sit still and ponder God's latest miracle, what words would come when you got your wits back again?

---

*Religion editor, *The Tennessean* newspaper, Nashville, Tennessee.

TUESDAY, NOVEMBER 20 • Read Luke 23:33-43

This is the most famous and poignant execution scene in history. Amazing things are said despite the agony and noise and injustice of the moment. Yet one word stands out like a message written across the sky—*Today*: "Today you will be with me in Paradise."

It's not the first time Luke records Jesus' using the word. In Luke 4:21, Jesus reads prophecy from Isaiah in the synagogue and says, "Today this scripture has been fulfilled in your hearing." In both cases, the use of the word *today* gives rise to violence. In Luke 4, the crowd wants to kill him for his presumption. And now on the cross, of course, Jesus sags under the weight of state violence and rejection of his message. Resistance to the idea of *today* is always extreme. Taking today seriously means toppling the bullying of past and future. It dethrones our plans and ambitions, including our ambitious worries. Today is real, carrying responsibility to act. Tomorrow is an abstraction, though we might spend considerable time imagining the heavenly kingdom of the future. Yesterday, especially the distant nostalgic yesteryear, has its own mythology.

Either way, today gets passed over. This matter of tasting the kingdom today can be perplexing. Paul, in Second Corinthians, contends against another way of embracing paradise today—by ecstatic experience, as embraced by some of his brethren. Even that's a rejection of present reality, if it means saying: To touch present paradise, I prefer the self-drama of ecstasy to these boring materials of the everyday. But Jesus didn't suggest that. His here and now—reading from a text or bleeding from a wooden rail—was his laboratory for creating new life and inviting us to share in its making. Today.

PRAYER: God, you've brought me to this moment. After all that's happened, in the long span of history and in my little life, this is my time and our time together. May it transform me in gratitude to your service. Amen.

WEDNESDAY, NOVEMBER 21 • Read Colossians 1:11-20

By one estimate, we're assaulted by 7,000 images a day—mail-order catalogues, slogans, billboards, visual seductions of the good life. The sheer volume of images can overwhelm. It shatters the world into fragments and rival cheering sections, without unity. Religious ideas are filtered this way too. They come at us in bits—self-help snippets, Bible quotes, eastern mystical sayings, astrology columns, fundamentalisms, the rustlings of angel wings. With such materials, Americans like to build their own faith statements, garage-style, on the run, from available parts and phrases and notions that seem so easily pulled down from the air, the media, the Internet.

Today's passage is a rebuke to that tendency and that despair—the tendency to cook up a gumbo of belief that might taste zesty but feels mushy and goes stale fast, and the despair of concluding the world is too fragmented to hope for unity or a First Principle that undergirds it.

Paul tells us in sweeping, challenging words that Jesus is the beginning and the end, the one who casts a shadow over all the ranks of angels and arguments. Believers don't need, therefore, to fiddle with other powers or sorcerers, as the Colossae church is reportedly doing. They distract, draining energy and shifting focus. Acknowledging the power of Jesus—the power of God who filled his life, work, death, and resurrection—frees us from the mesmerizing, glamorous emptiness of esoteric doctrine and mind control. Christ built his kingdom on the graveyard of discredited powers in the Roman Empire that were too feeble to back up their claims and on practices that were finally a waste of time because of the smallness of their vision of life's possibilities.

PRAYER: Jesus, I stand in awe and gratitude of your spirit, which meets me in a walk through the woods and in the sickbed and the library and in music and the hospital nursery. May I hear the whole creation sing its fanfare to its king. Amen.

THURSDAY, NOVEMBER 22 • Read Deuteronomy 26:1-11

THANKSGIVING DAY, USA

If you follow the religious news, Thanksgiving always brings a refreshing change of climate. Religious partisanship, the jostling for attention, gives way to something else—the vocabulary of thanks and common ground, the generosity of a meal shared together, suspension of debate on culture wars and doctrinal differences.

But the big meal on this big day raises other issues that grow more urgent every year, as the passage in Deuteronomy reminds us. It's harder and harder for us to connect with agricultural life. At Thanksgiving, most of us stare in wonder at the piles of hot food we enjoy with fierce abandon. How easy it is these days to feel cut off from the land, indifferent to the world of farming and "first fruits," the awesome outdoor dramas of raising crops and finding God's touch in the details of soil and sweat and uncertain weather. In an information society, we're removed from the information of the natural world. We soak in the digital, the sound of clicking keyboards, the flashy performances of an Internet screen.

Reading this passage, encountering the bounteous food and the holiday's slowed-down pace on a key work day, we might ponder the cost of alienating ourselves from the rhythms and fruits of the natural world. Today's a good day to acknowledge our humble dependence on nature and its Creator. Virtual reality isn't the real thing.

SUGGESTION FOR MEDITATION: **Are you mindful of the needs of farmers in your prayers? Does your church have a "farm policy," a feel for the problems of farming, an outreach to farmers? Is the church raising its voice for public action that respects farm families and God's creation?**

FRIDAY, NOVEMBER 23 • **Read Jeremiah 23:1-6; Psalm 100**

An angry wind blows through Jeremiah, the anger of God at the political and spiritual behavior of God's sponsored nations. Special venom and threat are saved for Judah and its rulers. They have forgotten their commitments to the one God. What's jarring is Jeremiah's vivid insistence that God cares about politics and public morality and treats even God's most beloved nations as dispensable. Judah's decline took hundreds of years, and it ended badly—crushed by a foreign power. Things come to such despair that God, exasperated, declares it's better to toss away the old branch and start again. Suddenly surfacing is the idea of a messianic figure from the house of David. A familiar Christian expectation momentarily finds daylight.

We worry a lot about leadership these days. We debate about which values should guide us in a democracy. Some of us invoke God; others do not. Some twenty-six hundred years ago, Jeremiah listed the values of right political life—wisdom, justice, righteousness. Indeed, today some claim the banner of righteousness, others justice or wisdom. It's rare to hear any leader talk about all three or to be praised for embodying any of them. Would we recognize righteousness, justice, or wisdom in public life if we saw it? Are we sure we'd want to? Could we live with the sacrifice it required? If there is a lack of leaders today, one solution is to start with the quality of our own prayers, our own vision of national life or city or neighborhood. And that starts with the words we utter to the Eternal Spirit in the quiet places inside us, where a fire glows for all good things—justice, righteousness, wisdom.

PRAYER: God above and within, you've given me the power of prayer and speech to seek and say your name and to cry out for the values you have for this life. Help me be about the business of the welfare of your world. Amen.

SATURDAY, NOVEMBER 24 • Read Philippians 4:4-9

At first, Paul's words seem to mock us at every turn.

- Rejoice, he says. Yet the world's violence is random and close.
- Be gentle, he says. Yet it's not the favored style just now for getting ahead or even for driving to work.
- The Lord is near, he says. Yet we secretly look for a sign, doubting.
- Don't worry about anything, he says. Yet we consult the horoscope and take loads of pills and lose sleep over what the boss is thinking.
- God will guard us, he says. Yet gun sales and gated communities are hot consumption trends.

One of my most gratifying encounters as a writer has been with John McQuiston II, a layman from Memphis, who wrote a little book on faith and simplicity called *Always We Begin Again*. He was a Christian of unfocused spirituality until his father died and a clergy friend told him about the ancient Rule of Benedict, those practical guidelines that have governed monastic life for fourteen hundred years or so. McQuiston decided to write a paraphrase of it for himself and others.

By stripping away anxiety-ridden routines and focusing on a few faith principles of humility and discipline, it's possible to find something unexpected—a capacity to rejoice, a sense of trust in the world God has made, an open road of well-being.

Paul's words embody the same discovery. Our daily map shows two roads: one of joy, one of worry. Both lead to the same place, the place called the end of the day. On one of those roads, joy reveals itself, seemingly out of nowhere. It's present oriented, offering no ironclad guarantees about the future but drenched in present possibility. And Paul's vision of rejoicing then looks plausible, compelling, the necessary next thing.

SUGGESTION FOR MEDITATION: **Take a walk and give thanks for the blessings of your life. See where the feeling leads.**

Sunday, November 25 • Read John 6:25-35

There are some nice bread shops in town, but the closest one is nearly three miles away. That means getting in the car and driving ten minutes every week just for a decent loaf of bread. This is vaguely distressing. I feel like I'm in the middle of an accusatory parable every time I run the errand. It's a parable about the pampered times we live in: A person gets into his or her car and wastes gasoline just to go to a specialty shop to get bread and nothing else. Others are in line at the shop too, of course, triumphantly doing the same thing. And there are many breads — too many—to choose from. It takes leisure to go to this sort of trouble for bread, passing up other neighborhood stores. It also declares one's own ignorance of the art of breadmaking.

People who make and bake their own bread always seemed to me to be culinary mystics, keepers of precious but esoteric knowledge, toiling with patience, filling the house with joyous aromas, keeping a tradition that's as old as scripture. In biblical days, bread was synonymous with survival itself. Bread made its first appearance as early as Genesis 3 and was at the center of Israel's experience of Exodus and the wilderness. Every day was a day for baking, as the *Oxford Companion to the Bible* declares. Now, as then, breadmaking makes for a messy kitchen and time spent and mistakes made and occasionally running off to get more ingredients. That sounds like a parable too: The struggle to feed ourselves and find sustenance never ends in the kitchens of this world. This wearing fact of life makes the passage from John always fresh and startling: The bread Jesus offers is everlasting life, leavening the world with hope.

PRAYER: Lord God, I pray that I never neglect to give thanks for my daily bread and all the more for the everlasting bread of Jesus' presence. Amen.

The Coming

November 26–December 2, 2001 • *Jo Carr**

MONDAY, NOVEMBER 26 • Read Isaiah 2:1-5

The season is Advent. It's just now upon us, so maybe we aren't quite used to it yet, we being the sort of folks who don't really take to the idea of a season of waiting.

Maybe we're getting ready to sing that wonderful old Advent hymn, "O Come, O Come, Emmanuel." Perhaps the tune is ringing in our heads. May our hearts catch up with the melody so we can say, "Yes, Lord God! *Come*, Emmanuel! That's what we are waiting for in this waiting season! Come, be with us. Come."

Then, as though on top of all that, Isaiah says to us, "Come! *you* come. Let us go to the house of the Lord. Get up off the couch and come. Let's go together to the house of the Lord, so God can teach us how to be people of God, here where we are."

So the movements are two: (1) Come, Lord, come to us! and (2) Come, all of you. Come to God. Come to the house of God. Come be the people of God.

Do you suppose that this Advent, what with God's coming toward us and our coming toward God, we might *meet* on God's holy mountain? It is toward this meeting that we move and for this meeting that we wait.

SUGGESTION FOR MEDITATION: **Sing softly to yourself as a prayer "O Come, All Ye Faithful," reflecting on the words. Think of two or three things you can do today that will be a part of your "coming." Close with an expression of gratitude.**

---

*Retired United Methodist clergy; former missionary to Zimbabwe; mother of five, grandmother of six; now a gardener in local food bank garden living in Lubbock, Texas.

TUESDAY, NOVEMBER 27 • Read Psalm 122

The word *advent* means "to come to." The early church fore-bears, in their wisdom, set it aside as a season of "coming to," of "getting ready for," knowing that we need the approach time in order to prepare room in our hearts for the one who, in turn, will fill our hearts to overflowing with the blessing of his presence. (We also find ourselves unprepared for Easter, unready to jump into the joy suddenly. We need "the snows of Lent" to prepare him room.)

So let us then approach. Let us come to the house of the Lord. Some of us may need to make that our seasonal vow: to be at corporate worship each week. Some need to remind ourselves to come to the time and place of our daily meditations, because that too is a coming to a holy place, to a house of God. Let us come gladly, eagerly, to each day's appointed time and place to offer our praise and our gratitude,

The house of God where I worship on Sundays is plainly marked. A sign out front tells folks that it is a special place, built to be God's place. We know, of course, that it is not the only "house" where God dwells—that God does not even require a house but can be worshiped anywhere, that God is, in fact, everywhere. Yet my heart quickens a beat when I go into the church. My pulse stills when I sit in the pew and responds distinctly to the rhythms of hymn and ritual. I am often graced in this place. I am *glad* to go to this house of God.

Now, though, it is Advent, and the house of God that I want to approach is a stable in old Bethlehem. How am I to come, when I am two millennia and ten thousand miles away? Perhaps only by keeping the mind and heart open to the possibility, open to the grace, open to the promised blessing.

PRAYER: O God, who came as the child of Bethlehem, let me seek you now, remembering that simple stable. Amen.

WEDNESDAY, NOVEMBER 28 • Read Psalm 122

To be fair, we must recognize that the "house of God" to which the psalmist refers is not in old Bethlehem but in old Jerusalem. Moreover, the same psalmist said Jerusalem is where our feet have been standing all along. It is where we are planted and where our tradition grounds us: That is home.

Hmmm. The house of God is *home* to us. (Saint Augustine said it another way: "I find no rest until I rest in Thee.") The house of God is the place where I can find rest within.

I have read this psalm a number of times through the years, but it seems that only now have I paid much attention to the last two verses. Apparently what I am supposed to *do* there in the dwelling place of the Lord is to offer signs of peace to my brothers, sisters, and companions (that is, those with whom I break bread).

Could it be that my willingness to pass the peace is part of what makes *any* place the house of God? Because the psalmist insists on my doing that and seeking the good of others—not for their sakes (though it is bound to do them good) and not for my sake (though it is bound to do me good), but for God's sake (as though it is bound to do *God* good.)

Well, then, this Advent season, let me go about seeking good for all the folks I meet: tired clerks and postal personnel, overspent parents and kids, the lonely ones and the uninvolved, the crochety and the belligerent, the impoverished and the "different"—all, *all*—for the sake of the God who loves us all.

SUGGESTION FOR MEDITATION: Ask God for that *spirit* of peace-passing, of desiring good for others, as you go through the dailiness of this pre-Christmas season. Ask it in the name of the triune God: Father who loved us enough to send, Son who loved us enough to come, and Spirit who holds us in that love.

THURSDAY, NOVEMBER 29 • **Read Matthew 24:36-44**

Actually, the season of Advent is the waiting time not just for the first coming of Christ but for the second coming as well. The first time he came so unobtrusively that except for Mary and Joseph and a few shepherds, nobody much noticed. He says he will come again but points out that nobody knows or is going to know when that will be—never mind trying to "crack the codes" in Revelation in order to predict the date. *No one* knows the day or the hour. Just be ready, that's all.

Be ready? Like, how? Ready as some folks prepared for Y2K, just last year? I doubt it. Salting away extra provisions doesn't sound like the right answer—though *giving away* part of our possessions very well might be part of it.

Maybe Jesus is telling us just to live ready by anticipating the presence of God, passing the peace to all the folks we know, and working for the good of the ones we don't know. Good advice for Advent, isn't it? To live anticipating the presence of God would enable us to put the trappings of Christmas into divine perspective. It would put the season's focus on the first and greatest gift, Emmanuel! Emmanuel means "God with us": the presence of God sneaking into our consciousness at some moment when we hear a certain scripture, when we read a few words written with love on a Christmas card, when we remember a line from a hymn or from the children's Christmas play; when we see a star, feel the touch of a friend, or share or sing or pray or say a word in the house of God. The very presence of God sneaks right into our lives, blessing the socks off us...again, this year!

PRAYER: God, bless us every one! Amen.

FRIDAY, NOVEMBER 30 • Read Romans 13:11-14

This segment from Paul's letter to the Romans almost sounds like a P. S. to yesterday's text from Matthew. We may not know the day or be able to predict the hour of the Second Coming, but we do know this: It is closer than it was last week. So wake up!

Paul gives us four pieces of advice: (1) Wake up! (2) Cast off darkness. (3) Conduct yourselves becomingly (which my mother used to say to me). (4) Put on Christ. So what would it be like if we were to apply these pieces of advice to our lives today? to the rest of this week? or even to all the remaining days of Advent?

(1) Wake up! It would be too bad to sleep right through the days of preparation, sleepwalking through the getting ready for Christmas without spending any time at all getting ready for Christ. Let's wake up to all the things we will see and hear today that might remind us of the coming of Jesus.

(2) Cast off darkness! There is no need for mullygrubbing about too much traffic or a too-long "gotta do today" list. It ill behooves us to be touchy or ill-humored or mean during this blessed season.

(3) Conduct ourselves becomingly. (My mother was right!) After all, we who have been so wondrously blessed might look for ways of bringing (or being) small blessings to others.

(4) Put on Christ. Put on Christ! Clothe ourselves in the garments of love, justice, peace, caring concern, and spiritual beatitude that we recognize in Christ. After all, that is why he came that first Christmas, to show us God's way of living. Let us wake up then, and live it.

PRAYER: **Come into my heart, Lord Jesus. Stir up in me your spirit. Wake me up to the needs around me, and equip me for service. Amen.**

Saturday, December 1 • Read Isaiah 2:1-5

O house of Jacob, come, let us walk in the way of the Lord! O followers of Christ, O all of us, come, let us walk in the way of the Lord. Let us, this very day, this Advent season, lay aside the weapons we use to attack, browbeat, belittle, or take from one another. Instead, may we use the plain old, raw materials from which those weapons were made (like words and money and time) and fashion from them tools that we will give to one another, nourishing and building one another up.

Isaiah's prophecy gets a little personal when we think of it in those terms, doesn't it? I can read over Isaiah's words, *sword and shield, plowshares and pruning hooks*, without even flinching, because I do not own a single one of those items. But I do own money and time. I do use words. And yes, I guess I do use them to build up or tear down, often without even thinking about it.

Perhaps I should think about how I use my money and time and words. Isaiah may be challenging me to think about it repeatedly today. I do have choices about how I will use my money, my time, and my words today—whether as weapons or as tools of nurture.

Suggestion for meditation: Come. Think about it. Pray about it until the actions follow the insight. Amen! which means "May it be so."

SUNDAY, DECEMBER 2 • Read Romans 13:11-14

FIRST SUNDAY OF ADVENT

We read again Paul's four helpings of advice, and I find my mind halting on the third one: "Let us conduct ourselves becomingly" (RSV). It's not a statement I thought came from the Bible. Miss Manners might have said it or the Emily Post of another era or our mothers. But it seems unlike Paul.

Yet in parables the lesson so often lies in the "unlikely" parts: in the hyperbole itself or in some strange twist or juxtaposition. Keeping that in mind, let's look into this oddity. I go to the dictionary. *Webster's* defines *becoming* as having to do with "propriety." The dictionary gets a little closer to Paul with "befitting" and only later mentions "coming into being." For this meaning *Webster's* gives an example, a quotation from G. B. Shaw: "Life is a constant becoming."

So the word in English can speak to us on three levels. First, I think Paul tells us it is appropriate to act without guile, to be people who have nothing to hide ("Do no wrong"). Second, it is befitting to conduct ourselves according to Jesus' instructions ("Do good"). The *Interpreter's Bible* suggests "a certain congruity" between the way we live our lives and the way we ought to live them.

Third, may we come into being godly people: putting on Christ, walking with God, constantly coming toward and becoming the persons God created us to be.

PRAYER: O Holy One, in this season of approach, we come to you over and over again. Help us in that coming; keep us aware of your presence with us. Amen.

A World Transformed

December 3–9, 2001 • Dan R. Dick*

MONDAY, DECEMBER 3 • Read Isaiah 11:1-5

Righteous judgment

A doctor received a poor family into his home. The father, recently paroled from prison, had been unable to find work. The mother struggled with multiple addictions. Both children were ill and showed signs of abuse. All were undernourished and dirty. Penniless, they sought help from a community hospital that turned them away. Colleagues criticized the doctor's judgment, warning him of the dangers inherent in opening his home to strangers, especially in light of the family's history.

We tend to close our doors to the needy because of the dangers and inconvenience they may pose. The naïve hope is that these problem people will go away if we simply ignore them. But to ignore them requires that first we pass judgment on them. Our fear, ignorance, and prejudice cause us to deem other people threats or problems. These self same people God judges to be the meek, the lowly, the lost—those most needing grace, kindness, and love.

Often, taking care of the unloved and unlovable defies wisdom and good common sense. But believing in Jesus Christ also appears foolish to most people. True wisdom requires that we see the world, especially the people of this world, with the eyes of God—eyes of compassion, eyes of faith, eyes of justice.

PRAYER: God, grant me eyes of kindness and compassion with which to view all people. Give me eyes of faith and hope to envision a better world. Give me eyes for justice and truth that will empower me to do right in every situation. Lord, grant me your eyes with which to see. Amen.

---

*Director of Quest and FaithQuest resourcing for The General Board of Discipleship, The United Methodist Church, Nashville, Tennessee.

TUESDAY, DECEMBER 4 • Read Isaiah 11:6-10

Creating peace

Most people learn the fundamental lessons of peace and justice at home. In homes where families value fair play, courtesy, consideration, and honesty, people gain a sense of how to live harmoniously in the world. Conversely, in homes that foster discord, competition, selfishness, and even violence, people receive the message that the world is a hostile and dangerous laboratory in which to test the survival of the fittest.

Regardless of experience, many people hold in their hearts a vision of what their world could be if all were peaceful and just. An East St. Louis gang member says that he uses violence as a way to make himself and his family safe. If he is strong enough, no one will bother him. He sees no other way to establish peace in his life. Entire nations have adopted the same philosophy. So many people miss the obvious contradiction in trying to create peace out of violence.

The promise of God to usher in a paradise of justice and peace depends on an earth that is "full of the knowledge of the Lord." This knowledge allows us to live lives of tolerance and love, kindness and forgiveness, mercy and justice. It is not enough to wait for peace to come upon the earth. Peace is a decision. We choose to be just. We choose to be kind. We choose to turn the other cheek. We choose whether to live in peace or in conflict. Together we fashion a reality based on the vision of the peaceable kingdom from Isaiah. For many of us, this decision begins at home.

SUGGESTION FOR MEDITATION: **Reflect on all the occasions this past week where you have been faced with a choice to be kind, just, merciful, tolerant, or considerate. What choices did you make?**

WEDNESDAY, DECEMBER 5 • Read Psalm 72:1-7, 18-19

The wisdom to live in peace

What do you want more than anything in the world? Think about this question for a few minutes. Now consider what you are doing currently that will help you realize your deepest desire. Most people desire security, love, a safe world for themselves and their children, for peace and good health. Many people dream of a different kind of future, but they do virtually nothing to turn their dream into a reality.

Christian discipleship is not a passive exercise. Many Christians wait for God to establish peace, justice, equity, forgiveness, and harmony on the earth. But the call to follow Jesus Christ invites us into partnership with God. We become the cocreators of peace, justice, equity, forgiveness, and harmony. We experience the promises of God by living the promises of God. The Holy Spirit empowers us to realize God's promises. We model for the world a different way of living.

John Wesley strongly believed that Christian people could live in God's kingdom here on earth. Faithful practice of the means of grace equips God's people to counter the human cultural practices of greed, selfishness, prejudice, dishonesty, and intolerance. Prayer, the study of scripture, regular worship, and accountable Christian conversation lead to acts of mercy and service. Our orientation shifts from our own needs to the needs of our community and world. Our desire to see the world transformed into a place of love and peace will only happen through our commitment to live as faithful disciples.

PRAYER: **Gracious God, help me do more than just believe in a world of peace and justice. Help me live a life of peace, work for justice, and spread the love of God wherever I go throughout the day. Amen.**

THURSDAY, DECEMBER 6 • Read Matthew 3:1-12

Behaving only when watched

A psychology experiment placed two different groups of children in a playroom; a bowl of candy sat on a low table. In one group, no instructions were given. In the other, children were told that they could not have any of the candy. Both groups played peacefully while adults were in the room. Then the adults left. In the room where the group received no instructions, the children played on peacefully. In the other group, however, attention shifted from toys to candy. When the children felt sure that no one was watching, they sneaked pieces of candy.

How often do we live our lives of Christian discipleship as children who behave beautifully while watched, but who give in to their urges and desires behind closed doors? For many, Christian behavior is a matter of expediency rather than a foundation for living. Our culture reinforces the notion that the only time you are truly guilty is when you get caught, not when you commit the offense.

The scathing words of John the Baptist remind us that consistency and commitment are the hallmarks of true Christian discipleship. It is easy to remain faithful and obedient when we feel we are being watched. It is much more difficult to behave in complete obedience when we think no one is watching. Ultimately, we fool ourselves any time we think that God does not observe our every move, thought, and comment. Our faith is not measured by outward behavior alone. Much more it is measured by our intentions and the desires of our hearts.

SUGGESTION FOR MEDITATION: **How often do I act differently when I think others can see me? What kinds of changes would I need to make in my life to live the same way behind closed doors as I do out in the open?**

Friday, December 7 • Read Romans 15:4-6

The ground of our hope

What is God's desire for our lives? One desire is that we learn to live in harmony with one another so that we might "with one voice glorify the God and Father of our Lord Jesus Christ." Paul writes that our entire tradition—the scriptures and our church—is given that we might find unity. But look at what so often happens. People use scripture to judge and separate rather than to heal and connect. The church becomes a clique of righteousness and rules, not a place of harmonious welcome. Rather than let faith give us the confidence to welcome the stranger into our midst, we clutch our faith as a talisman to ward off all who are different. What's gone wrong?

Doubt is not the opposite of faith. Fear is faith's opposite. When characterized by fear, the fruits of the Christian faith are intolerance, judgment, condemnation, prejudice, and anger. Only when faith prevails over fear do we find acceptance, tolerance, hospitality, joy, and true fellowship.

One clear indicator of fear's rule over faith is our focus on what people are doing wrong instead of all that God is doing right. As we enter the healing, loving work of God, we quickly find that we no longer have the time or energy to condemn people who disagree with us or who differ from us. The world looks brighter, and we experience harmony and peace. Let our goal be to lift one voice together to honor and glorify the love of God in Christ Jesus.

Prayer: **This day, O Lord, fill my heart with love so that fear might find no place in me. Where fear appears, give me the strength and courage to deny it, embracing instead your grace and power. Amen.**

SATURDAY, DECEMBER 8 • Read Matthew 3:1-12

Justice known by its fruits

I have two good friends who occupy the same body. In church, my friend is a saint. He will do anything for anyone; he is kind; he is generous; and he never speaks a harmful word. In the world, however, he is harsh and aggressive. No one takes advantage of my friend, and no one gets the better of him. He is a competitive driver, an impatient customer. He is intolerant of the poor, the uneducated, and the unemployed. Somehow, he has compartmentalized his life of faith from the rest of his life, and he sees absolutely no contradiction.

John the Baptist exposes this same behavior in the lives of the religious leaders of the first century. From the outset, Matthew's Gospel reminds us that actions speak louder than words. Being a person of God requires more than pietistic posturing. The fruits of our faith are the behaviors we engage in day to day. Love, justice, kindness, and forgiveness are not feelings or abstract concepts—they are the driving forces behind our living.

Christian disciples commit themselves to creating a more loving, just, kind, and merciful world by all that they think, say, and do. When we fail to be part of the solution to the world's ills, we become part of the problem. The call of John, and later of Jesus, is a call to a life of integrity—where what we say we believe is borne out in the way we live each and every day.

SUGGESTION FOR MEDITATION: **What does it mean to live a life of integrity? Think of three fundamental teachings about Christian behavior from the scriptures that you believe God wants you to practice and employ each day. How will you improve these behaviors today?**

SUNDAY, DECEMBER 9 • Read Romans 15:4-13

SECOND SUNDAY OF ADVENT

Justice for all

Who doesn't belong in the church? Whom doesn't God love? Who has done something so terrible that they do not deserve forgiveness and grace? Who decides whom we are to care for and who must care for themselves? What standards do we use to determine someone's acceptability?

Sometimes we forget that the scripture does not read, "For God so loved the church," but "God so loved the world." We tend—as good Christian believers—to use our faith and our Bible as a bludgeon to teach those people a lesson who dare to differ from us or disagree with us. Why? In what way do we think that judging and condemning others will make our world a better place?

Paul and the authors of the Gospels teach that all of us are broken, sinful, selfish, stuck, and stupid. God loves us anyway. We do not receive love, tolerance, acceptance, justice, and grace because we deserve them. They are given because they are needed. Look around you and find anyone who has earned the right to be part of Christ's church. You won't find anyone. We don't deserve it. But thank God we're not the ones in charge. Our church is God's church, and God makes the rules.

We honor God most when we hurt others least. Our place in the church is to make a place for others. Regardless of what they believe, say, do, or think, God calls us to love them, care for them, forgive them, and treat them with respect. God does it for us. Can we do any less?

PRAYER: O Lord, give me your mind to think with, your grace to forgive with, your patience to respond with, and your heart to love with. Amen.

A New Song

December 10–16, 2001 • Vance P. Ross*

My eldest daughter found herself in trouble. It was of such import that she was exiled to her bedroom for several hours. She tramped off, elementary rage seething through her four-year-old body. I walked by her room later to hear her singing a peculiar song, one I was certain I had not heard before.

> *Oh Jesus! Won't you come down*
> *and save me from these people!*
>
> *Oh Jesus! Won't you come down*
> *and save me from these people!*

As she sang, I was quite amused that she felt so put upon. I stepped inside and asked, "Kristina, do you think Jesus is going to come and get your mother and me?"

"Daddy," Kristina declared, "Jesus is stronger than (the cartoon hero) He Man! He can come and save me—and he will!" Again she sang with exuberance. "Oh Jesus! Won't you come down and save me from these people!"

That is what Isaiah is saying to us—the God we serve can save us from any issue. This God will accomplish the rescue of a world and a people from all oppression. God almighty can turn the world right side up, and God will! Have faith and believe—God will save us!

PRAYER: Awesome God, as you promise deliverance through the holy scriptures, give us the audacity to believe the promise. Fill us with hope in Jesus' name. Amen.

---

*Senior pastor, First United Methodist Church, Hyattsville, Maryland; husband, father, pastor by training and trade; preacher by calling.

Tuesday, December 11 • Read Psalm 146:5-10

"O God, our help in ages past, our hope for years to come, our shelter from the stormy blast, and our eternal home!"

The hymn writer describes the one who is blessed, according to the psalmist. This one has tasted God's benefits and knows God as a source of help and assurance in any situation. No trouble, trial, situation, or circumstance perplexes or discourages the Almighty. The hymn writer places hope, trust, and assurance in the One who knows everything. Faith and hope reside in the precept that the source of all assistance, every accomplishment, every good and perfect gift is God. But there is more!

God takes sides. God is predisposed to those who are downtrodden. God has a unique disposition, a peculiar fondness for those who despair. When in the center of injustice and strife, maltreated and persecuted, we discover that God's personality is predisposed toward us. This is a blessing for followers of Jesus. Many a home that once was a battlefield has found renewal in this fact. Many a life has been redeemed by God's taking up the cause of distress and bringing relief. Many a Christian leaps today in declared witness that God almighty fought his or her battle, and the battle was gloriously won! God is not merely for those who seem favored. God is for those who are scorned!

Christians today need to ask the question: In what do we place our hope? We can easily exchange faith for the trappings of the world. We can overlook morality, integrity, ethics and character when times get hard. But we need not. We ought not. The God of our eternal salvation is also a saving God in the now! We need to know and believe that God saves, rescues, and delivers in the now! Face your trials with this assurance: God takes your side. You are not abandoned, nor are you alone. Be blessed by this certainty now and always.

Prayer: God of the oppressed, as storm clouds hover, help me experience your favor. Give me surety now and always. Amen.

WEDNESDAY, DECEMBER 12 • Read Luke 1:47-55

William Matson, a member of the congregation where I am privileged to serve, was moved by God to compose a hymn for the congregation. The hymn speaks to what God has done in his life, what God is doing in our congregation, and what God in Jesus means to our world. It is God's song for us, sung first through Mr. Matson.

Luke tells us that God gave Mary a song. Hers is a song of great joy and adoration. It is a song that praises God for God's work in her life and that remembers God's work in her ancestors' lives. It is a song that connects Mary to a faith-filled past, exalts in God's glorious future, and rejoices in her wondrous present. It is God's song for us through Mary.

What is your song? "Amazing Grace"? "Blessed Assurance"? "Spirit Song"? Or has God blessed you with an original, a new song, a song filled with the glory of your present experience with God?

No one can sing your song as you can. The words may be the same as someone else's; the tune may be in the exact meter of another. Still, no one can sing your song in the same manner that you can. No one can bless others with the song the way you can. One hymn writer described the uniqueness of each person's song this way: "God gave me a song that the angels cannot sing. I've been washed in the blood, in the blood of the Lamb."

Today sing your song. Lift it with all the praise and glory you can muster. Remember that God gave it to you and through you. Through your song God will bless you and those around you.

PRAYER: Thank you, Lord, for the special song you gave me. Let me sing it for your glory and in Jesus' name. Amen.

THURSDAY, DECEMBER 13 • Read James 5:7-10

I'm so glad trouble don't last always,
I'm so glad trouble don't last always.
O my Lord, O my Lord, what shall I do?

This song, composed by my ancestors during the enslavement, remarkably speaks to perseverance in misery and affliction. The Africans who were ripped from their native land, deprived of their culture, and robbed of their religion appropriated the Christian faith in amazing ways.

How did they do it? They embraced the word of God as spoken through the prophets. Holy scriptures were living documents in their faith. When the Bible says, "I believe that I shall see the goodness of the Lord / in the land of the living" (Ps. 27:13) and "those who wait for the Lord shall renew their strength" (Isa. 40:31), these sisters and brothers heard more than metaphor. They heard God.

Those enslaved could resonate with the message from today's lection. They, like the farmer, waited patiently, strengthening their hearts. They, like the farmer, acknowledged that their present experience was one of waiting for "the precious crop from the earth"; what they most desired and the song their hearts sang was not yet a reality.

As you sing this day, sing despite the struggle. In due season, your spiritual landscape will usher forth a bounteous crop. Look for and listen for God in your song—you will find divine liberation there.

PRAYER: **God of responsible freedom, help me see and hear your liberation from slavery. In my suffering, give me again the joy of your promised salvation, now and in the world to come, in Jesus' name. Amen.**

Friday, December 14 • Read James 5:7-10

What are you willing to wait for? Can you wait for the goodness, holiness, and righteousness of the Lord to be revealed in your life? Can you wait on the Lord in these days and times?

James tell us to think about the farmers who wait patiently for the spring and summer rains to make their crops grow. The farmer awaits rain, but the farmer never leaves the soil unattended. She watches over the fields with great care. Her patience resides in an active waiting, a perseverance that ministers to the ground until God sends the rain.

God has sent great rains upon our society. As this devotion is recorded, our nation is in the midst of unparalleled economic growth. The Internet age has altered almost all understandings of space and time. In God's own time God has sent wonderful rains to water our commonwealth. The society of techies and computer competence has produced a bumper crop.

Yet oppression reigns in many places. There are still homes where God's gift of potential is snuffed out by struggling parents. There are still children who have no hope of eating tonight. There are people living in the shadows of our worship centers who have no share in the bounty and treasure that signifies the American landscape. Some men and women in our culture have amassed more wealth than entire nations. How long will such abominations continue? How much oppression will our brothers and sisters, sons and daughters endure while we watch?

Waiting on God does not necessarily mean sitting. The God we claim to trust and upon whom we wait still looks for laborers, workers who will be agents of God's grace. Are you willing to be such an agent today? What is your call?

Hear God calling you to wait, but to wait in a kingdom-building fashion!

PRAYER: God, bless and help me to live as a kingdom builder this day. I pray in the name of your son and our Savior. Amen.

SATURDAY, DECEMBER 15 • Read Matthew 11:2-11

I'm on the battlefield for my Lord.
I'm on the battlefield for my Lord.
And I promised him that I would serve him 'til I die.
I'm on the battlefield for my Lord.

What makes for greatness? Where does Matthew's message validate the songwriter's remarks? The answer is simply this: service. All people, especially Christians, can and should be great. Greatness is our call from God because all of us can serve.

Service implies that we have a divine call and mission. We acknowledge our responsiveness to God almighty through our deeds and creeds. Service is obedience, without apology and only with praise, to the specific way God commands.

John's service caused Jesus to exalt him before others. His witness provided important service to the kingdom. Called forth as a herald of the good message, John told the story with a boldness and daring that made some suspect his sanity but made Jesus exalt his value: John was as important a man as ever was born. His importance did not rest on his credentials, his schooling, or the news media. What made him important was his service.

How are you serving God today? No, you cannot do what the angels in heaven do; you cannot have their greatness now, but you can be great among earth dwellers. Would you be renowned? Serve, dear friend. It is still the way to go!

PRAYER: Bless me, God, to serve as much as I seek service, so that your name will be praised in Jesus' name. Amen.

SUNDAY, DECEMBER 16 • Read Isaiah 35:1-10

THIRD SUNDAY OF ADVENT

In whom do you place your trust? Especially when turbulence attacks your life and your soul, when ominous clouds of ill will surround your spirit, on whom do you rely? A favorite song of the African American Christian tradition posits trust where it ought always be, saying:

I will trust in the Lord,
I will trust in the Lord,
I will trust in the Lord,
'Til I die.

Trust is difficult when we have been unfairly accused or unjustly encumbered. It is hard to believe in justice when injustice surrounds us. When the right seems long gone and the wicked seem to prosper, even the idea of trust becomes cloudy.

The prophet speaks in such a way that many in the African American church and other oppressed peoples have heard a marvelous chance for hope. Isaiah taught them and teaches us that tempests do indeed have a master. When oppression pounds us, when we are at a point of surrender, we can rely on another reality in the universe. Our Lord will vanquish oppression. Unfair oppression does have an enemy, one who is accomplished in bringing justice and establishing righteousness.

Know today that the One in whom Isaiah places his trust is faithful and true. This God will take care of you. Give yourself, no matter the circumstance, to God's love, power, and grace. You shall overcome when you trust in the Lord.

PRAYER: God, you are worthy of my trust. Empower me to have faith in you whatever the circumstance. I pray this in the name of Jesus. Amen.

Emmanuel: God with Us Now

December 17–23, 2001 • Kent Ira Groff*

MONDAY, DECEMBER 17 • Read Isaiah 7:10-16

In reading brief lectionary selections or in praying with short texts of scripture, we can easily overlook reading a text in its context. Isaiah 6 is the great chapter that contains Isaiah's call: "Here am I, send me!" Then comes chapter 7, where the prophet tests out his call by telling King Ahaz of Judah to trust that a remnant of the faithful will be restored—despite violent opposition from two competing kings.

In the context of Ahaz's fears and prior to reading 7:10-16, we need to hear Isaiah's prophecy in 7:4: "Take heed, be quiet, do not fear, and do not let your heart be faint because of these two smoldering stumps." Here the prophet calls Ahaz to contemplation, which can sustain action. He then gives the famous promise in 7:9: "If you do not stand firm in faith, / you shall not stand at all." Or to recapture the original Hebrew poetry, we might paraphrase it: "If you are not assured, you will not be secured."

Isaiah put forward a postmodern way of understanding faith that has shaped great theologians like Anselm of Canterbury. Simply put, believing creates a new way of seeing. Only then does Isaiah say to ask for a sign—one that is quite ordinary: "Look, the young woman is with child and shall bear a son, and shall name him Immanuel," meaning "God is with us." Yet finding assurance that God is with us *now* begins with contemplation.

SUGGESTION FOR PRAYER: Try repeating the words of 7:4: "Take heed, be quiet, do not fear, and do not let your heart be faint because of…" (allow various concerns to come to mind).

---

*Author; founder and director of Oasis Ministries for Spiritual Development, Camp Hill, Pennsylvania; adjunct professor at Lancaster Theological Seminary.

TUESDAY, DECEMBER 18 • Read Psalm 80:1-7, 17-19

Since the psalms are already real prayers, writing about a psalm seems once-removed from a devotional reading. Maybe the best we can do is to "re-psalm" the psalms; that is, find a way to make them our own prayers in this time, in this place— Emmanuel: God with us *now*. Psalm 80 expresses a real experience of all humankind: the feeling that God does not seem to hear our prayers, that often when we pray we get not blessings but tears, that faithfulness to God seems to be rewarded not with success but the scorn of neighbors and the laughter of enemies:

> *O Lord God of hosts,*
> *how long will you be angry with your people's prayers?*
> *You have fed them with the bread of tears,*
> *and given them tears to drink in full measure.*
> *You make us the scorn of our neighbors;*
> *our enemies laugh among themselves.*

Reflect on some experience of suffering, injustice, or grief. Then imagine that your tears are your prayers. What are (or were) your tears saying? Or if you can't (or couldn't) cry, what would your tears say if you were able to cry? The ancient Romans used a powerful Latin phrase: *lacrimae rerum*—literally, "the tears of things," or "things have tears." Psalm-like praying invites us to offer the real tears of real experience as an offering of prayer.

SUGGESTION FOR MEDITATION: **Allow your mind to go to a place, a building, a room, or an object that recalls difficult memories. Write your own psalm, gathering up feelings of hypocrisy and cynicism often unexpressed. Then find a way to offer these to God. Try writing, "This is what my tears are saying or would say:...." End your psalm-prayer with gratitude that God is present in negative and positive life experiences.**

WEDNESDAY, DECEMBER 19 • Read Psalm 80:3, 7, 19

For many people, the Advent-Christmas season reverberate in stark contrast to their own experience. All about us we see gaily decorated surroundings and hear lively music, while inwardly we experience the absence of a loved one no longer living, the sadness of a broken relationship, the pain of world hunger and suffering, the charade of being caught up in consumerism rather than giving and receiving love. The contrast makes us question our own purpose in life, and how, or if, we can ever break this cycle of cynicism to find the true meaning of Emmanuel: God is with us *now*.

SUGGESTION FOR MEDITATION: Do not wait for tomorrow. Today try this way of re-psalming your experience: Start with the refrain that's repeated three times in Psalm 80:3 (7 and 19):

> *Restore us, O God;*
> *let your face shine,*
> *that we may be saved.*

Allow your mind to ponder for several minutes the events of the world and of your life, meditating on some of the distractions of Christmas one by one while repeating the above refrain in your mind after each one.

Now see if a simple refrain of your own emerges, a single line that expresses your yearning beneath the glitter of the world's version of Christmas. Sit quietly, breathe deeply, and listen attentively to your heart. See if a phrase or a few words come to mind....If so, jot them down. In the next few minutes, begin to repeat the words or phrase—or just be in silence. (Be attentive if a simple musical tune emerges in your heart along with the words.)

Now go back to the concerns you prayed earlier in this meditation. Begin again, silently, to allow concerns to emerge in your heart, this time offering each one to God by repeating your own refrain or verse.

THURSDAY, DECEMBER 20 • Read Romans 1:1-4

The real celebration of Christmas is to allow the Word to become flesh in us. Emmanuel: God with us revealed in us *now*. In the familiar carol "O Little Town of Bethlehem" we sing, "Be born in us today."

The real celebration of Christmas is a movement through the Jesus of history to the Christ of experience. Paul lays out these twin themes in Romans 1:3-4: "The gospel concerning [God's] son, who was descended from David according to the flesh and designated Son of God in power according to the Spirit of holiness by his resurrection from the dead, Jesus Christ our Lord" (RSV).

Jesus, born "according to the flesh," through resurrection is God's declared unique offspring. So each of us is born of human parents; yet we, baptized and raised with Christ, become a unique son or daughter of God!

For the Word to become flesh in us, we need to pay attention to our biological selves. Only through one's own particular combination of genetics and life experiences can one become the unique child of God that each can be in Christ. Yet only through meditating on our own spiritual experiences can we realize our unique divine potential.

SUGGESTION FOR MEDITATION: **Set aside a block of time for prayer. Use a journal or notebook to meditate on your two genealogies: human and divine. Take out a family Bible or another list of your own relatives and converse with family members about your ethnic traditions and family stories. Now chart your personal biological timeline: date of birth, a few significant human life events (painful or joyful) up to the present. Then alongside these, note your spiritual experiences: times of awakening, confusion, or renewal that have given meaning and "resurrection" to your life events. In Christ, you too are descended from human lineage yet blessed with a divine heritage!**

FRIDAY, DECEMBER 21 • **Read Romans 1:5-7**

One of the positive aspects of Christmas traditions is the pattern of receiving and giving. Paul proclaims "Jesus Christ our Lord, through whom we have received grace and apostleship." For us to experience God with us *now*, God revealed in us *now*, we need to receive grace and give in response. The process of Christ's being reborn in us continues in this rhythm.

The problem comes when we reverse the order: We try to give love without first receiving love. In ever so few words, Paul expresses the full gospel: "To all God's beloved in Rome [fill in your address], who are called to be saints: Grace to you and peace from God our Father and the Lord Jesus Christ."

Meditate silently for a few minutes on the word *beloved*. Hear it as if spoken directly to you, over and over. Yet Paul uses this word in the plural; for each of us to realize our unique belovedness, we need to be in a healthy spiritual community. Only then can we realize our calling "to be saints." One can never be a saint alone.

Grace: We cannot earn or manufacture it like the toys of Christmas; it is something we can only receive. *Peace*: Here is something we are called to fill up, to complete; it is our response to grace, something we experience by giving it away.

We are called to be active contemplatives. To be peacemakers we continually need to offer ourselves as grace-receivers.

PRAYER: O God, let me be a grace-receiver, to hear at the beginning of each new day the word spoken in my baptism: "You are my beloved child." Then help me live out that call: "Blessed are the peacemakers, for they will be called children of God." Amen.

Saturday, December 22 • Read Matthew 1:18-25

Two ways of praying scripture especially open us to allow the Word to become flesh in us today. One is to meditate on a short phrase of the text that lures you or disturbs you (as with Psalm 80:3 on Wednesday). The second is to visualize a scene, creating your own little Hollywood video. Some personality types find it more natural to create a "back then" scene with sights, smells, colors, gestures, conversations, and all. Other personality types may find it easier to picture a "here and now" setting, with events and characters from life today.

In today's meditation I invite you to create a "back then" scene. Reread Matthew 1:18-25. Picture Mary and Joseph, newly engaged, and then Mary's telling Joseph she is pregnant by the Holy Spirit, not Joseph. Picture Joseph's reaction in your mind's eye: first planning to call the whole thing off and Mary's response to his plan. Then imagine Joseph's dream in which an angel says, "Joseph, son of David, do not be afraid to take Mary as your wife...." Picture Joseph's face as he awakens. Imagine his feelings as he ponders an apprentice carpenter's reaction or townsfolk who will not believe the story that "the child conceived in her is from the Holy Spirit." Visualize the couple deciding to go ahead with the wedding, recalling the verse from Isaiah, "Look, the virgin shall conceive and bear a son, and they shall name him Emmanuel." Picture them being comforted and saying together, "God is with us."

Suggestion for meditation: Begin to repeat "Emmanuel: God is with us now, revealed in me now." Continue this for several minutes. Close by singing a verse of the hymn "O Come, O Come, Emmanuel."

SUNDAY, DECEMBER 23 • Read Matthew 1:18-25

FOURTH SUNDAY OF ADVENT

Yesterday I invited you to visualize a "back then" scene of Mary and Joseph's engagement, the sights, smells, colors, gestures, conversations, and all. This way of praying with scripture—this inner drama—allows us to get in touch with parts of ourselves and our world in the presence of God. Some personality types consider it more natural to create a little Hollywood video in the present day.

So today I invite you to picture a "here and now" setting with events and characters from contemporary life. This visualization may also prove difficult because your mind may want to censor your video! So dedicate this experience to God, praying that God will speak to you. Think today about a troubled couple. It could be yourself and a loved one or another couple, known or unknown to you, married or single, living together or living separately. (Or allow a story to emerge from reading or TV.) Imagine the two arguing over an issue that threatens their trust in each other. See what conversations may occur in your imagination. Then picture an angel entering the scene, a heavenly or earthly messenger—someone who comes in a moment of crisis—to speak to one or both of them. What does the angel say?

Visualize the couple recalling the verse from Isaiah, "Look, the virgin shall conceive and bear a son, and they shall name him Emmanuel." Picture some new life coming out of this situation. Picture the couple being comforted and saying together, "God is with us."

PRAYER: O God, with whom darkness is as light, let me see your joy in all of life. Amen.

God's Reconciling Ways

December 24–30, 2001 • *Carol Carruth Johnson**

Righteous reign

On this day, with fresh expectation, we await Jesus' coming again to begin a royal reign upon which all history hangs. No ordinary baby, this. Fully human and fully divine, he is also fully available to us forever in personal relationship.

In Jesus Christ, the righteous ruler, all authority resides. But he will administer authority in boundless peace, justice, and righteousness. On the shoulders of this mighty one we may cast all the weight of our humanity. The promise inherent in the advent of the Prince of Peace is that he brings peace to the deepest places within us.

SPIRITUAL EXERCISE: **Still yourself before God. Fold your hands, then slowly open them as a symbol of opening the deepest part of your being to Jesus Christ, welcoming him as the coming righteous ruler, Mighty God, and Prince of Peace of your life. Extend your open hands to encompass the space around your body, and pray the following prayer.**

PRAYER: **O Jesus, I fling wide the portals of my heart to receive the coming again of your reign of righteousness and peace in my life. I do not know how to do this apart from your empowering, but I offer you my willing "yes." Amen.**

---

*Assistant Professor of Pastoral Care and Spiritual Formation, Oral Roberts University, Tulsa, Oklahoma; licensed marriage and family therapist and Episcopal layperson.

Tuesday, December 25 • Read Psalm 98:1-4

CHRISTMAS DAY

A song of God's remembering

The psalmist points worshipers to God's merciful act in remembering Israel's need for a redeemer. The birth of Jesus Christ demonstrates that on a particular day in time and space God remembered to keep the promise to redeem creation, sending that promise enfleshed into the world.

Today, the day of Christ's coming, we ponder God's loving patience in bearing with humanity over the events of history and then acting at just the right moment for Jesus to be born.

We often forget our Creator; but in the birth of Jesus, God faithfully remembers us. This is the mystery—that God should love us so much and desire so passionately to forgive us when we confess and seek forgiveness.

SPIRITUAL EXERCISE: **Write a journal page, reflecting on your thoughts and feelings when others keep or forget to keep their word to you. How has others' trustworthiness or lack of it impacted your sense of being loved, cared about, connected with another? Relate these reflections to your sense of connectedness to God as one who has remembered you.**

PRAYER: **O God, thank you for remembering me in Jesus Christ. I beseech you on behalf of those who have forgotten that you remembered them—and for those who have never known it. This Christmas Day, I remember your faithfulness—and rejoice! Amen.**

WEDNESDAY, DECEMBER 26 • **Read Hebrews 2:10-18**

Relationship

This passage tells us that as believers we all are part of a particular family, brothers and sisters intimately united in our relationship in Jesus Christ. Jesus came, not as one outside that family, but as one deeply and centrally within the family.

Jesus understood this family relationship and challenges the faith family to discover what this kind of familial relationship means and how we participate with God in our sanctification. Sanctification, being made holy, is a lifetime process and an often frustrating one. The good news is that God, the sanctifier, is not an absentee, home-on-weekends Creator but a deeply interested and involved parent.

For some people the experience of family life does not stimulate a desire to be a part of any family. This passage, however, confirms that God offers us healing at this very point. In the context of the family of believers, something holy happens. The sanctifying action of the Holy Spirit transforms us into the image of our family center, Jesus. How will we receive this sanctification and claim our relationship?

SPIRITUAL EXERCISE: **Draw pictures of symbols that represent the holy to you. How is the Holy Spirit forming you into these holy things by God's sanctifying processes in your life? What family resemblances—marks of sanctification—do the members of God's family bear in common?**

PRAYER: **As you offer me relationship, O God, show me how to receive it, how to be awake to and aware of the sanctifying processes you are working out in my life. Amen.**

THURSDAY, DECEMBER 27 • Read Matthew 2:13-23

Remaining

In this story of Joseph's faithfulness in listening for God's direction, the simplicity of Joseph's obedience astounds us. He walks forward, stands still, and remains in accordance with God's instructions.

Joseph cares for his family by obeying God. He does not return to his homeland until all things are safely in place. Joseph's choice to obey God and, like the wise men, to go home another way, preserves the life of Joseph's holy charge, God's son Jesus. It also fulfills prophecy spoken long before Jesus' birth. God's direction and Joseph's obedience have eternal purpose.

We may find ourselves in Egypt as we obey God in journeying to and remaining in unfamiliar, unhomelike deserts— waiting for medical reports, dealing with chronic illness, standing by as loved ones suffer the consequences of their own hurtful choices. Are you in a place of desert waiting where God has called you to remain? How does this story give you hope?

SPIRITUAL EXERCISE: Share with a spiritual friend or director the desert obediences you have faced or may be enduring now. Talk about what it means to obey, how it feels, how it challenges your faith in God and God's ultimate plans for your life. How can sharing these feelings with another strengthen your own resolve and focus your faith?

PRAYER: O God, I sometimes wait in places of obedience that I do not enjoy or understand. Your faithfulness to Joseph and his family encourages me to wait obediently and to expect your purposes to be revealed in my life. As I walk by faith, give me the grace to wait by faith as well. Amen.

Friday, December 28 • Read Matthew 2:13-23

The power of obedience

The story of Joseph's remaining in Egypt is full of power. It reminds us of the importance of doing what God tells us even when we do not fully understand or see the path far ahead. In our obedience we act out loving trust in Omnipotent Wisdom. In our obedient remaining we do God's will and participate in God's ultimate plans.

Pattern and plan in our lives may only emerge as we, in the fullness of time, take a backward look at the path we have walked. Then we may see the picture of God's purposes as we obeyed God by faith, often without sight. Likewise, the Gospels state God's ultimate design in directing Joseph, thereby revealing the power released through Joseph's obedience.

Henri Nouwen, in his book *Reaching Out: the Three Movements of the Spiritual Life*, asks, "What if our history does not prove to be a blind, impersonal sequence of events over which we have no control, but rather reveals to us a guiding hand pointing to a personal encounter in which all our hopes and aspirations will reach their fulfillment?"

SPIRITUAL EXERCISE: **On a journal page draw a time line representing your spiritual journey in the past year. On this line mark high and low points. At which points did you remain until God directed you to move on? Be aware of your feelings during those waiting times. What outcomes followed your waiting times? How did these outcomes spiritually form you this year?**

PRAYER: **O Lord, give me the grace to go in obedience to places where you have called me and there to remain, as did the wise and faithful Joseph, until you direct my next steps. Thank you for your pattern and plan unfolding in my life. Amen.**

SATURDAY, DECEMBER 29 • Read Isaiah 63:7-9

Recounting and releasing

Isaiah recounts the loving-kindness of the Lord in redeeming, lifting up, and carrying Israel. Prayer recounts, tells again, the story of God's faithful lifting up. This recounting confirms our history with God.

Yet while a part of prayer recounts, another part intentionally releases and moves us into the future with God. As Michael Casey says in *Toward God*, "Prayer is intended to keep us moving, which means constantly saying good-bye to the past.... Prayer is chiefly about the present and the future."

What then is the purpose of recounting? It continues our relationship with God in reminders that keep us going, keep us flowing, give us forward momentum. Recounting affirms our faith in the God of the past and in the God of now. Recounting releases us into experiencing the God of the future.

SPIRITUAL EXERCISE: Recount in writing specific examples of God's activity in your life. Identify what God has done for you today since your day began. Write down a specific date in the future on which you will return to this writing and remember the actions of God. In silence, release yourself and life into God's care for the future.

PRAYER: O Jesus, the same yesterday, today, and forever, your truth is beyond my full comprehension. Yet may I recount your love and faithfulness in the past, release myself to know you here and now, and look with confidence to future companionship with you. Amen.

Sing out the old, sing in the new

Just as the ancient carol summons heaven and nature to sing at the coming of Christ, so the psalmist in these verses echoes the praises of God in the context of awareness of all things in heaven and in earth. This psalm gloriously summarizes the vast expanse of God's creation and its continual reflecting back to the Creator the glory and praise due to the living God.

Continual wonder emerges as each verse articulates the specific things God commanded into existence and then established forever. God's way is to make something out of nothing and to make it beautiful, real, and permanent.

What transformations has God wrought in you? What boundaries has God established in your life that create order and safety, giving you direction? How does the experience of joining with all created things in heaven and earth energize your entry into the new year?

SPIRITUAL EXERCISE: Write your own psalm of praise to God as you end one year, soon to begin another. Using Psalm 148 as a guide, write specific memories of time, place, and circumstance in which God specifically has been present to you in the past twelve months. Sing your psalm, chant it, dance to it.

PRAYER: Receive, O Lord, the praise that I, your creation, offer you for your love and goodness to me. I praise you that your name is Love. In that love I have lived, moved, and had my being in this past year. With confidence I joyously go forward with you into the year ahead. Amen.

God's Gifts and Divine Presence

December 31, 2001 • Jan Sprague*

MONDAY, DECEMBER 31 • Read Psalm 72:1-7

Do you remember in days gone by, hopeful anticipation (your own as a child or that of a child you knew) when the Christmas catalogs would arrive? Wonder, magic, hope intertwined; reality, even for a moment, could be set aside.

Is your Christmas tree still up? Do candles flicker in your windows? The last vestiges of the long-heralded holiday wrestle with the reality of today, tonight, tomorrow. Our souls call us to reflect, ponder, question, pray. We stand on the threshold of another year; a clean slate, a new beginning with abiding, tenacious hope that will not give up.

Today still begs for deepest faith and the wonder of a child. The psalmist prays for deliverance and justice, voice cadenced with certainty, looking to God for the promised, anticipated gift of hope.

The aftermath of Christmas wish lists, holiday hubbub, and decorations are once more winnowed out by this day's realization, new again, that material gifts don't fill the aching of our souls. With the psalmist, we cry. In our hearts we know what is important, what will satisfy, even this very day and especially tonight and for the tomorrows.

Our souls cry out for our deliverance, shared peace, God's justice, and the presence of the only gift that satisfies.

SUGGESTION FOR PRAYER: **Pray that you might recognize and share the gift of certainty, wonder, and hope this new year.**

---

*Pastor of Birmingham United Methodist Church, Birmingham, Ohio.

The Revised Common Lectionary* for 2001
Year C – Advent / Christmas Year A
(Disciplines Edition)

January 1–7
BAPTISM OF THE LORD
Isaiah 43:1-7
Psalm 29
Acts 8:14-17
Luke 3:15-17, 21-22

> **NEW YEAR'S DAY**
> Ecclesiastes 3:1-13
> Psalm 8
> Revelation 21:1-6*a*
> Matthew 25:31-46

> **EPIPHANY, JANUARY 6**
> *(These readings may be used Sunday, Jan. 7.)*
> Isaiah 60:1-6
> Psalm 72:1-7, 10-14
> Ephesians 3:1-12
> Matthew 2:1-12

January 8–14
Isaiah 62:1-5
Psalm 36:5-10
1 Corinthians 12:1-11
John 2:1-11

January 15–21
Nehemiah 8:1-3, 5-6, 8-10
Psalm 19
1 Corinthians 12:12-31*a*
Luke 4:14-21

*Copyright © 1992 by the Consultation on Common Texts (CCT). All rights reserved. Reprinted by permission.

January 22–28
Jeremiah 1:4-10
Psalm 71:1-6
1 Corinthians 13:1-13
Luke 4:21-30

January 29–February 4
Isaiah 6:1-13
Psalm 138
1 Corinthians 15:1-11
Luke 5:1-11

February 5–11
Jeremiah 17:5-10
Psalm 1
1 Corinthians 15:12-20
Luke 6:17-26

February 12–18
Genesis 45:3-11, 15
Psalm 37:1-11, 39-40
1 Corinthians 15:35-38, 42-50
Luke 6:27-38

February 19–25
THE TRANSFIGURATION
Exodus 34:29-35
Psalm 99
2 Corinthians 3:12–4:2
Luke 9:28-43

February 26–March 4
FIRST SUNDAY IN LENT
Deuteronomy 26:1-11
Psalm 91:1-2, 9-16
Romans 10:8*b*-13
Luke 4:1-13

February 28
ASH WEDNESDAY
Joel 2:1-2, 12-17
 (*or* Isaiah 58:1-12)
Psalm 51:1-17
2 Corinthians 5:20*b*–6:10
Matthew 6:1-6, 16-21

March 5–11
SECOND SUNDAY IN LENT
Genesis 15:1-12, 17-18
Psalm 27
Philippians 3:17–4:1
Luke 13:31-35 (*or* Luke 9:28-36)

March 12–18
THIRD SUNDAY IN LENT
Isaiah 55:1-9
Psalm 63:1-8
1 Corinthians 10:1-13
Luke 13:1-9

March 19–25
FOURTH SUNDAY IN LENT
Joshua 5:9-12
Psalm 32
2 Corinthians 5:16-21
Luke 15:1-3, 11*b*-32

March 26–April 1
FIFTH SUNDAY IN LENT
Isaiah 43:16-21
Psalm 126
Philippians 3:4*b*-14
John 12:1-8

April 2–8
PALM/PASSION SUNDAY

 Liturgy of the Palms
 Luke 19:28-40
 Psalm 118:1-2, 19-29

 Liturgy of the Passion
 Isaiah 50:4-9*a*
 Psalm 31:9-16
 Philippians 2:5-11
 Luke 22:14–23:56
  (*or* Luke 23:1-49)

April 9–15
HOLY WEEK

 Monday
 Isaiah 42:1-9
 Psalm 36:5-11
 Hebrews 9:11-15
 John 12:1-11

 Tuesday
 Isaiah 49:1-7
 Psalm 71:1-14
 1 Corinthians 1:18-31
 John 12:20-36

 Wednesday
 Isaiah 50:4-9*a*
 Psalm 70
 Hebrews 12:1-3
 John 13:21-32

 MAUNDY THURSDAY
 Exodus 12:1-14
 Psalm 116:1-2, 12-19
 1 Corinthians 11:23-26
 John 13:1-17, 31*b*-35

 GOOD FRIDAY
 Isaiah 52:13–53:12
 Psalm 22
 Hebrews 10:16-25
 John 18:1–19:42

 HOLY SATURDAY
 Exodus 14
 Isaiah 55:1-11
 Psalm 42
 Romans 6:3-11
 Matthew 27:57-66

April 15
EASTER SUNDAY
Acts 10:34-43
   (*or* Isaiah 65:17-25)
Psalm 118:1-2, 14-24
1 Corinthians 15:19-26
John 20:1-18
   (*or* Luke 24:1-12)

April 16–22
Acts 5:27-32
Psalm 150
Revelation 1:4-8
John 20:19-31

April 23–29
Acts 9:1-20
Psalm 30
Revelation 5:11-14
John 21:1-19

April 30–May 6
Acts 9:36-43
Psalm 23
Revelation 7:9-17
John 10:22-30

May 7–13
Acts 11:1-18
Psalm 148
Revelation 21:1-6
John 13:31-35

May 14–20
Acts 16:9-15
Psalm 67
Revelation 21:10, 22–22:5
John 14:23-29
   (*or* John 5:1-9)

May 21–27
Acts 16:16-34
Psalm 97
Revelation 22:12-14, 16-17, 20-21
John 17:20-26

   ASCENSION DAY, **May 24**
   *(These readings may be used
   Sunday, May 27.)*
   Acts 1:1-11
   Psalm 47 (*or* Psalm 110)
   Ephesians 1:15-23
   Luke 24:44-53

May 28–June 3
PENTECOST
Acts 2:1-21
Psalm 104:24-34, 35*b*
Romans 8:14-17
John 14:8-17, (25-27)

June 4–10
TRINITY SUNDAY
Proverbs 8:1-4, 22-31
Psalm 8
Romans 5:1-5
John 16:12-15

June 11–17
1 Kings 21:1-21*a*
Psalm 5:1-8
Galatians 2:15-21
Luke 7:36–8:3

June 18–24
1 Kings 19:1-15*a*
Psalm 42
Galatians 3:23-29
Luke 8:26-39

June 25–July 1
2 Kings 2:1-2, 6-14
Psalm 77:1-2, 11-20
Galatians 5:1, 13-25
Luke 9:51-62

July 2–8
2 Kings 5:1-14
Psalm 30
Galatians 6:1-16
Luke 10:1-11, 16-20

July 9–15
Amos 7:7-17
Psalm 82
Colossians 1:1-14
Luke 10:25-37

July 16–22
Amos 8:1-12
Psalm 52
Colossians 1:15-28
Luke 10:38-42

July 23–29
Hosea 1:2-10
Psalm 85
Colossians 2:6-19
Luke 11:1-13

July 30–August 5
Hosea 11:1-11
Psalm 107:1-9, 43
Colossians 3:1-11
Luke 12:13-21

August 6–12
Isaiah 1:1, 10-20
Psalm 50:1-8, 22-23
Hebrews 11:1-3, 8-16
Luke 12:32-40

August 13–19
Isaiah 5:1-7
Psalm 80:1-2, 8-19
Hebrews 11:29–12:2
Luke 12:49-56

August 20–26
Jeremiah 1:4-10
Psalm 71:1-6
Hebrews 12:18-29
Luke 13:10-17

August 27–September 2
Jeremiah 2:4-13
Psalm 81:1, 10-16
Hebrews 13:1-8, 15-16
Luke 14:1, 7-14

September 3–9
Jeremiah 18:1-11
Psalm 139:1-6, 13-18
Philemon 1-21
Luke 14:25-33

September 10–16
Jeremiah 4:11-12, 22-28
Psalm 14
1 Timothy 1:12-17
Luke 15:1-10

September 17–23
Jeremiah 8:18–9:1
Psalm 79:1-9
1 Timothy 2:1-7
Luke 16:1-13

September 24–30
Jeremiah 32:1-3*a*, 6-15
Psalm 91:1-6, 14-16
1 Timothy 6:6-19
Luke 16:19-31

October 1–7
Lamentations 1:1-6
Psalm 137
2 Timothy 1:1-14
Luke 17:5-10

October 8–14
Jeremiah 29:1, 4-7
Psalm 66:1-12
2 Timothy 2:8-15
Luke 17:11-19

October 11
THANKSGIVING DAY, CANADA
Deuteronomy 26:1-11
Psalm 100
Philippians 4:4-9
John 6:25-35

October 15–21
Jeremiah 31:27-34
Psalm 119:97-104
2 Timothy 3:14–4:5
Luke 18:1-8

October 22–28
Joel 2:23-32
Psalm 65
2 Timothy 4:6-8, 16-18
Luke 18:9-14

October 29–November 4
Habakkuk 1:1-4; 2:1-4
Psalm 119:137-144
2 Thessalonians 1:1-4,
   11-12
Luke 19:1-10

November 1
ALL SAINTS DAY
(May be used Sunday, Nov. 4.)
Daniel 7:1-3, 15-18
Psalm 149 (*or* Psalm 150)
Ephesians 1:11-23
Luke 6:20-31

November 5–11
Haggai 1:15*b*–2:9
Psalm 145:1-5, 17-21
2 Thessalonians 2:1-5, 13-17
Luke 20:27-38

November 12–18
Isaiah 65:17-25
Isaiah 12 (*or* Psalm 118)
2 Thessalonians 3:6-13
Luke 21:5-19

November 19–25
REIGN OF CHRIST
Jeremiah 23:1-6
Luke 1:68-79
Colossians 1:11-20
Luke 23:33-43

November 22
THANKSGIVING DAY (USA)
Deuteronomy 26:1-11
Psalm 100
Philippians 4:4-9
John 6:25-35

November 26–December 2
FIRST SUNDAY OF ADVENT
Isaiah 2:1-5
Psalm 122
Romans 13:11-14
Matthew 24:36-44

December 3–9
SECOND SUNDAY OF ADVENT
Isaiah 11:1-10
Psalm 72:1-7, 18-19
Romans 15:4-13
Matthew 3:1-12

December 10–16
THIRD SUNDAY OF ADVENT
Isaiah 35:1-10
Psalm 146:5-10
  (*or* Luke 1:47-55)
James 5:7-10
Matthew 11:2-11

December 17–23
FOURTH SUNDAY OF ADVENT
Isaiah 7:10-16
Psalm 80:1-7, 17-19
Romans 1:1-7
Matthew 1:18-25

December 24–30
FIRST SUNDAY AFTER
CHRISTMAS DAY
Isaiah 63:7-9
Psalm 148
Hebrews 2:10-18
Matthew 2:13-23

December 24
CHRISTMAS EVE
Isaiah 9:2-7
Psalm 96
Titus 2:11-14
Luke 2:1-20

December 25
CHRISTMAS DAY
Isaiah 52:7-10
Psalm 98
Hebrews 1:1-12
John 1:1-14

December 31–January 6
Isaiah 60:1-6
Psalm 72:1-7, 10-14
Ephesians 3:1-12
Matthew 2:1-12